Introduction to Structured COBOL

Data Processing Training Series
Ruth Ashley and Judi Fernandez, *Series Editors*

INTRODUCTION TO COMPUTER PROGRAMMING, by J. Fernandez and R. Ashley

STRUCTURED COBOL, by R. Ashley and J. Fernandez
INTRODUCTION TO STRUCTURED COBOL, COBOL 1
USING STRUCTURED COBOL, COBOL 2
TAPE AND DISK FILES, COBOL 3
ADVANCED STRUCTURED COBOL, COBOL 4

IBM SYSTEM/370 ARCHITECTURE, by J. Leben and J. Arnold (The Arben Group)
IBM CPU AND STORAGE ARCHITECTURE System/370, 4300, 3030, and 3080 Processors
IBM VIRTUAL STORAGE AND I/O ARCHITECTURE System/370, 4300, 3030, and 3080 Processors

IBM OS ASSEMBLER LANGUAGE, by D. Tabler, R. Ashley, and J. Fernandez
IBM OS ASSEMBLER LANGUAGE: LANGUAGE BASICS

Introduction to Structured COBOL

COBOL Book 1

Ruth Ashley

Judi N. Fernandez

DuoTech, Inc.

Data Processing Training Series

John Wiley & Sons, Inc.

New York • Chichester • Brisbane • Toronto • Singapore

Copyright © 1984 by John Wiley & Sons, Inc.

All rights reserved. Published simultaneously in Canada.

Reproduction or translation of any part of this work beyond that
permitted by Section 107 or 108 of the 1976 United States
Copyright Act without the permission of the copyright owner is un-
lawful. Requests for permission or further information should be
addressed to the Permissions Department, John Wiley & Sons, Inc.

Library of Congress Cataloging in Publication Data

Ashley, Ruth.
    Introduction to structured COBOL.

    (Data processing training series)
    Includes index.
    1. COBOL (Computer program language) 2. Structured
programming. I. Fernandez, Judi N.
II. Title. III. Series.
QA76.73.C25A836   1984   001.64'24   83-21591
ISBN 0-471-87025-0

Printed in the United States of America

84 85 10 9 8 7 6 5 4 3 2 1

Introduction

COBOL . . . . It's the universal computer language of industry. You're about to learn a language that will let you communicate with and control almost any computer in existence today.

If you're seeking a new career or trying to upgrade your skills, you've chosen the right language. Most medium to gigantic businesses have at least one computer, and most of those computers speak COBOL. Almost all government installations have COBOL-speaking computers. If you can learn only one computer language, make it COBOL.

Learning COBOL is like learning a spoken language such as French. COBOL has a vocabulary; each word in the vocabulary has a specific meaning. The words are combined into statements. If you give the computer a statement, it should respond by doing what you command. But if you have used the wrong words or the wrong structure for the statement, the computer won't be able to understand you, any more than French-speaking people will be able to understand you if you misuse their language.

Just as sentences are combined into paragraphs in a spoken language, COBOL statements are combined into paragraphs. COBOL paragraphs accomplish complete functions; they might also be called routines.

As you study this book, keep in mind that you are studying a language. Learn its vocabulary and its syntax and you won't have too many problems.

This is the first of four books on the COBOL language. This book gets you started in writing COBOL programs. You'll learn how to develop, compile, test, and debug relatively simple programs. The remaining books in the series teach you how to handle increasingly complex programs. When you finish all our books, you'll be a very accomplished COBOL programmer.

This book is divided into four sections. The first section discusses the nature of the language. You'll learn a bit about where COBOL came from, then see how a complete program is put together. You'll learn the structure of a COBOL statement and the rules for coding individual lines.

The second section teaches you how to write the most basic kind of programs—those that use no files for input or output. By the end of that section you'll be able to code a complete but very short program.

The third section shows you how to compile, test, and debug COBOL programs. By the end of the section, you'll be able to run the programs you wrote in Section Two.

The final section then teaches you how to use the most basic type of files (unit record files) in a program. This is equivalent to using cards for input and print for output. By the end of that section, you'll be able to write a complete program using files. That program will involve sequence, decision, and repetition structures.

You will actually be able to write many useful programs using the techniques you learn in this book. The remaining books in this COBOL series add to and refine the skills you learn here.

We are interested in your feedback to this book and encourage you to fill out the last page of the book and mail it to us.

Prerequisites We expect you to know a bit about computers and computer programming before you start reading this book. We will not be defining basic concepts (such as *record* and *file*). We will assume that you can solve basic problems in programming logic and are familiar with sequence, decision, and repetition structures. Another book in this series, *Introduction to Computer Programming* by Fernandez and Ashley, covers the necessary material. If you have completed that book, or if you have studied basic programming concepts elsewhere, then you are ready for this book.

How to Use this Book This is a self-study book. The chapters are composed of lessons. Each lesson involves an introduction, objectives, rationale, a few pages of reading material, and some questions. The objectives tell you what you're supposed to get out of the lesson. The rationale tells you why the information in the lesson is important in COBOL. The quesitons help you practice what you have studied. Use them to make sure you didn't miss or misinterpret anything. Feel free to look back in the lesson if you can't remember an answer; this is how you learn to remember it the next time. The questions are important to your successfully completing this course.

Each chapter ends with chapter review questions, drawing together the material presented in that chapter. They are also an important step in your learning process.

Most of the sections end with section exercises. These require you to actually compile, test, and debug the programs you have written. You will need a computer system and a COBOL compiler to do this. DON'T SKIP THESE SECTION EXERCISES. The system is your COBOL tutor. You won't really begin to understand COBOL until the compiler has slapped your hand a few times, then finally your program does what it's supposed to. All told, this course includes three section exercises, so you will need access to the computer on three separate occasions.

Trainer's Guide If you are a trainer preparing to administer a COBOL course, you will find helpful suggestions and extra exercises (for homework and testing) in the Trainer's Guide for this book. For a copy of the Trainer's Guide, the Training Sales Department, John Wiley and Sons, 605 Third Ave., New York, NY 10158.

Acknowledgments Our thanks go to the many people who have acted as technical reviewers, student reviewers, typists, editors, and artists on this project. These are more than we can mention here, but we'd like to particularly acknowledge the technical expertise of Donna Tabler and Russ Miller. Our editor at John Wiley and Sons, Maria Colligan, also deserves a hearty round of applause.

COBOL Acknowledgment The following acknowledgment is reprinted from *American National Standard Programming Language COBOL*, X3.23-1974, published by the American National Standards Institute, Inc.

Any organization interested in reproducing the COBOL standard and specifications in whole or in part, using ideas from this document as the basis for an instruction manual or for any other purpose, is free to do so. However, all such organizations are requested to reproduce the following acknowledgment paragraphs in their entirety as part of the preface to any such publication (any organization using a short passage from this document, such as in a book review, is requested to mention "COBOL" in acknowledgment of the source, but need not quote the acknowledgment):

COBOL is an industry language and is not the property of any company or group of companies, or of any organization or group of organizations.

No Warranty, expressed or implied, is made by any contributor or by the CODASYL Programming Language Committee as to the accuracy and functioning of the programming system and language. Moreover, no responsibility is assumed by any contributor, or by the committee in connection therewith.

The authors and copyright holders of the copyrighted material used herein

> FLOW-MATIC (trademark of Sperry Rand Corporation), Programming for the UNIVAC I and II, Data Automation Systems copyrighted 1958, 1959, by Sperry Rand Corporation; IBM commercial Translator Form No. F28-8013, copyrighted 1959 by IBM; FACT, DSI 27A5260-2760, copyrighted 1960 by Minneapolis-Honeywell

have specifically authorized the use of this material in whole or in part, in the COBOL specifications. Such authorization extends to the reproduction and use of COBOL specifications in programming manuals or similar publications.

Contents

Introduction
  How to Use This Book

The COBOL Language

Chapter 1

The Language Itself

COBOL is a programming language used by industries all over the world for their business applications. First and foremost, COBOL is a language; it is used to communicate, through a translator, with a computer. This chapter will focus on the scope and structure of the COBOL language.

This chapter consists of two lessons:

Lesson 1.1: What Is COBOL?
Lesson 1.2: Structure of a COBOL Program

What Is COBOL?

You already know something about COBOL from your previous study. You know it is a high-level programming language that uses English-like statements. You know it is used primarily for business applications and is found in the vast majority of American business computer installations. You probably wouldn't be reading this if COBOL weren't used at your installation.

In this lesson you'll learn a bit more about the history and uses of COBOL.

Objectives   When you finish this lesson, you'll know how COBOL developed and what it can do for you.

Rationale   If you know how COBOL was developed and what problems it was designed to solve, you'll be in a better position to take advantage of it, as well as being more tolerant of its shortcomings.

Where Did COBOL Come From?

In ancient times (before 1960), almost every computer manufacturer developed its own language and translator to take advantage of specific features of its machine. As a result there were many different computer languages, each of them incompatible with the others. A program written for one computer would not run on a different manufacturer's computer without extensive revisions. By the late 1950's it became apparent that this was inefficient, so business and the government got together and established the **CO**nference on **DA**ta **SY**stems Languages (CODASYL).

CODASYL decided to create a language that was not machine-specific and that would use English-like statements that could be translated into each machine's language by programs called compilers. The language would be designed to solve business problems. CODASYL called this new language the **CO**mmon (because it could be used with many machines) **B**usiness **O**riented (because it was designed to solve business problems) **L**anguage; in other words, COBOL.

In 1960 CODASYL released COBOL-60, a set of minimum standards for COBOL compilers, to help ensure that COBOL programs could be compiled on any machine. The standards defined the COBOL language. If they were followed, changes would have to be made only in certain minor machine-dependent sections of a program when it was transferred from one machine to another.

This worked fine for a while, but manufacturers kept adding extensions and enhancements to their compilers to simplify certain coding tasks and perform more functions. In 1968 the American National Standards Institute consolidated many of the most useful and popular nonstandard features and released a new set of standards, which became ANS COBOL. ANS COBOL was updated in 1974 and again in 1983.

This series is primarily concerned with COBOL as defined by the current ANS document. It covers the minimum language requirements (what ANS calls level 1) and those ANS extensions that most compilers incorporate (level 2). Every once in a while, you will be warned about a feature your compiler may not have. However, if you stick to the features covered in this course, your programs should be compatible with most major compilers. Even though most compilers have additional extensions of their own, what you learn here can be translated by most systems.

Why Learn COBOL?

The primary reason you are learning COBOL is so you can write and run programs using your company's COBOL compiler. Your company has selected COBOL as its language for business application programs. But why did it do that?

Compatibility One major advantage of COBOL is that COBOL compilers are available for virtually every type and model of computer that might be used in a business installation, and most of those compilers are compatible with the ANS standard. The vast majority of business computer installations use COBOL for their application programming.

Personnel problems are reduced if a company uses COBOL. Programmers who have experience in using other COBOL compilers can quickly learn the few machine-specific entries for a new computer. Software packages that run with COBOL can be acquired and used, lessening the need to develop new programs for many common applications.

Businesses may have several different models of computers, and they may upgrade their computers as their needs change. COBOL allows programs to be run on a variety of computers with very minor revisions, or none.

Self-Documenting Ability Historically, a problem in programming departments has been a lack of technical documentation to explain programs to maintenance programmers and others. COBOL has the advantage of being largely self-documenting. The statements do what they look like they do. For example, a MOVE statement moves data; an ADD statement adds values. COBOL uses names up to 30 characters long; this allows specific names for files and data items such as MASTER-PERSONNEL-FILE and EMPLOYEE-HOME-PHONE.

Many companies impose standards beyond the COBOL requirements to require their programmers to use COBOL's documentation features. Complete and meaningful names such as QUANTITY-ON-HAND help readers to understand what the statements are accomplishing and what data is affected. Comments can also be included in COBOL programs to allow extra explanation when the code isn't clear.

A structured approach to program design goes a long way toward making the result clear to human readers as well as effective in operation. COBOL makes it fairly easy to structure programs. You'll find that pseudocode can almost always be translated directly into COBOL statements. We'll be using the pseudocode approach throughout the COBOL programming series. Be aware, however, that it is ultimately up to the programmer to produce a well-documented program. The features are available, but they aren't automatic.

Ease of Learning As you know, COBOL uses English-like commands, which makes COBOL fairly easy for English-speaking people to learn. For example, the READ statement reads data, the WRITE statement writes data, and the MOVE statement moves data.

While individual statement formats may be puzzling, the overall concepts are not. When you want to add two values, for example, you use a statement such as ADD THIS-VALUE, THAT-VALUE GIVING NEW-VALUE. The COBOL compiler handles the details, such as putting the values into the proper formats, aligning decimal points, and using the correct signs. You don't have to be concerned with *how* such things are done; you just use the COBOL statement to perform the entire operation.

Business Problems

COBOL is especially suited to most business applications. It is set up to handle input and output of large amounts of data. Inventory maintenance, production scheduling, shipping records maintenance, personnel records maintenance, and payroll operations all can be handled with COBOL programs. These are the types of problems that application programmers are most often called upon to solve. COBOL would not be as easy to use for mathematical programs to calculate ballistic missile curves, for example, or for writing system programs, but installations that do these things seldom code them in COBOL.

Program Categories   Many business problems fall into four general categories: update, summary, report, and edit problems. Most problems are combinations of the four.

Update problems involve changing or modifying master sets of data. For example, most large companies maintain master files or data bases of their inventories. Every time a new shipment of goods is received, the items must be added to the master inventory file. Every time a new employee is hired or an old one terminated, a change must be made in the master employee file. Every new customer requires a change in the master customer file. Every time an invoice is sent, the accounts receivable master file must be changed. All of these are update problems.

Summary problems use the master files to calculate totals in various categories. For example, you might need to calculate the total cost of goods on hand using the inventory master file. This requires going through the file, calculating the cost for all pieces of each item, and finding the total; this is a summary problem.

Report problems require that specific data be printed from a file. For example, you might have to list all items from the master inventory file for which the total cost is less than $1000, or you might have to list all parts that are sold to Chevrolet dealers.

Sometimes a problem involves verifying input data in preparation for its use by another program. This is called an **edit** problem; you need to edit, or verify, the input to make sure it is acceptable. An edit routine does not correct errors. Instead, it generally tells the user what corrections are needed.

Figure 1.1 Typical Application

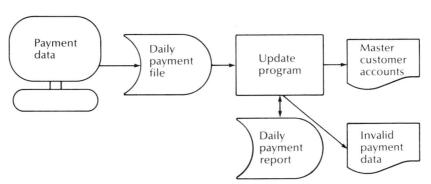

Example   Consider a department store that has a large file of customer account records. Every day the accounting department receives several hundred payments by mail. A data entry clerk works at a terminal to put the payment data into the system, where it will be used as input to what is basically an update program (see Figure 1.1). The major component of the program, the update component, records each payment in the appropriate customer account record. This will result in updated records for the customers who paid their bills. Before updating, however, the data must be edited by the program's edit component, which verifies that the data entered by the clerk is in the correct format and that the account numbers and monetary amounts are within the valid range. One report component then creates a list of any erroneous data, which must be corrected and reentered. A second report component creates a report of all payments received and indicates whether any customers overpaid or underpaid their accounts. At the bottom of the report is a summary of how much was received that day and the current total of money still owed (accounts receivable).

The preceding example, like many you will code as a programmer, includes elements of all four types of program.

As you continue in this series, you'll discover that COBOL can be used to solve most everyday business problems like this one, as well as many not-so-common problems.

Summary   In this lesson you have learned a bit about the history of COBOL. You reviewed some advantages of COBOL that may influence an installation's decision to use COBOL for its application programming. You also saw the four categories of problems that might be solved using COBOL: update, summary, report, and edit. Most programs contain elements of more than one of these.

Review Questions

1. Which of the following is the standard form of COBOL?

a. COBOL-60
b. CODASYL
c. ANS COBOL

2. COBOL has three major features that have made it the most widely used computer language. What are they?

a. It allows compatibility between different machines.
b. Its execution is highly efficient.
c. Control is completely the programmer's responsibility.
d. English-like commands make it easy to learn.
e. Documentation is produced automatically.
f. It can be self-documenting if used properly.

3. True or false? Pseudocode seldom can be translated directly into COBOL.

4. Identify the category of each problem below. *More than one may be correct.*

_____ A. Records must be checked to ensure that the part number is in the correct format.

_____ B. You need a count of the number of parts with X83 as the last three characters in the part number.

_____ C. You need a formatted listing of all parts that are currently out of stock.

_____ D. You need to increase selling prices by 10%.

_____ E. You need a listing showing the number of parts in each division and their total cost.

a. Update
b. Summary
c. Report
d. Edit

5. What year was the current COBOL standard released? _____

6. What release does your installation use? _____

7. Suppose a COBOL program written to ANS standards runs on your computer. Your installation is considering acquiring a second computer produced by a different reputable manufacturer. Which of the following is true?

a. There is little chance of converting the program.
b. The COBOL source program may need minor changes, then it can be compiled on the second computer.
c. The COBOL source program will need major changes before it will compile on the second computer.
d. The second computer is not likely to have a COBOL compiler available.

8. Which of the following are features of COBOL that help it to be self-documenting? *More than one may be correct.*

   a. Names can be long enough to be easy to read.
   b. You can code statements in pure English, just as you speak.
   c. You can use pseudocode as COBOL statements.
   d. You can include comments as needed.

9. Identify the category of problem described in each example below. You may need from one to four categories for each problem.

   a. You need to verify that each employee's time record was reported in the proper format and calculate the total of hours worked for all employees.

   _____

   b. You need to calculate pay and modify the year-to-date payroll file to keep track of the total payroll and tax withholding.

   _____

   c. You need to print paychecks.

   _____

Answers

1. c 2. a, d, f 3. False 4. A - d; B - b; C - c; D - a; E - b, c 5. 1983 6. Depends on your system 7. b 8. a, d 9. a. Edit, summary b. Update c. Report

Structure of a COBOL Program

Now let's get right into COBOL, beginning with how a COBOL program is structured. Like any language, COBOL has its own grammar, syntax, and requirements. You'll start to learn them in this lesson.

Objectives   By the end of this lesson you'll know the four divisions included in COBOL programs and what type of information is supplied in each division.

Rationale   Before you can begin learning to code COBOL programs, you need to know what a program looks like and how it is put together. This lesson will get you started.

A COBOL Program

Figure 1.2 shows a complete COBOL program. Notice the braces we have added on the left; they mark four separate parts or divisions of the program. Each part begins with an entry that names the division.

Figure 1.2 Sample COBOL Program

```
IDENTIFICATION DIVISION.
PROGRAM-ID.  SAMPLE1.
AUTHOR.  LESLIE LEVINE.
*
*        THIS PROGRAM LISTS ALL THE RECORDS IN
*            THE MEMBERSHIP FILE IN ORDER
*
ENVIRONMENT DIVISION.

CONFIGURATION SECTION.
SOURCE-COMPUTER ...
OBJECT-COMPUTER ...

INPUT-OUTPUT SECTION.
FILE-CONTROL.
    SELECT MEMBERSHIP-FILE
        ASSIGN TO ...
    SELECT LISTING-OF-MEMBERS
        ASSIGN TO ...

DATA DIVISION.

FILE SECTION.
FD  MEMBERSHIP-FILE
    LABEL RECORDS ARE OMITTED.
01  MEMBERSHIP-DATA            PIC X(80).
FD  LISTING-OF-MEMBERS
    LABEL RECORDS ARE OMITTED.
01  MEMBER-LINE.
    05  FILLER                 PIC X(10).
    05  MEMBER-OUT             PIC X(80).

WORKING-STORAGE SECTION.
01  MEMBERSHIP-EOF             PIC X        VALUE "N".

PROCEDURE DIVISION.
CONTROL-ROUTINE.
    OPEN INPUT MEMBERSHIP-FILE
        OUTPUT LISTING-OF-MEMBERS.
    PERFORM READ-ONE-RECORD.
    PERFORM LIST-RECORDS
        UNTIL MEMBERSHIP-EOF = "Y".
    DISPLAY "ALL RECORDS LISTED".
    CLOSE MEMBERSHIP-FILE LISTING-OF-MEMBERS.
    STOP RUN.
LIST-RECORDS.
    MOVE MEMBERSHIP-DATA TO MEMBER-OUT.
    WRITE MEMBER-LINE.
    PERFORM READ-ONE-RECORD.
READ-ONE-RECORD.
    READ MEMBERSHIP-FILE
        AT END MOVE "Y" TO MEMBERSHIP-EOF.
```

Don't worry about the statements and details in this program. You'll learn to handle all these before the end of this course.

Every COBOL program consists of these four divisions, in the sequence you see in the figure. The information you supply in these divisions provides the computer with all it needs to solve your problem.

Identification Division

The **Identification Division** comes first in every COBOL program. The first line of every COBOL program looks just like the first line in the sample program in Figure 1.2. The next entry in the Identification Division identifies the program by stating its name. Other information such as the author's name, the date the program was coded, and narrative explanations can also be included as part of the Identification Division.

Environment Division

The second division in Figure 1.2 is the **Environment Division.**

The Environment Division provides information about the computer environment, such as what computer to use and what files are needed. The Environment Division includes a Configuration Section, which describes the environment of the computer system itself, and an Input-Output Section, which describes the file structure and processing environment of the program. You can see the section names in Figure 1.2.

The entries in the Environment Division are often machine-specific; we have left the SOURCE-COMPUTER and OBJECT-COMPUTER entries blank because you'd probably have to change them to make your program work on another compiler. Most COBOL programs, however, spend their entire life on one computer. For this reason, some COBOL compilers, in keeping with the 1983 ANS standard, have made the Configuration Section optional. In all compilers, however, the Environment Division is required if the program uses any file input or output.

Data Division

The third COBOL division is the **Data Division**, as you can see in Figure 1.2. The Data Division provides information on the data used by the program; it reserves space in memory for the data and tells the program how to refer to the data. All the fields that make up a record and every piece of data used in the program must be defined in the Data Division. The records related to each file must be defined and associated with that file in the Data Division.

The Data Division can have several sections. Two of them are shown in Figure 1.2. The File Section defines any input and output files and the records and data affiliated with each. We've left the ASSIGN clauses blank because they depend on your compiler. The Working-Storage Section defines all other data that needs storage space reserved for use by the program. Other Data Division sections are defined by ANS, but they are optional. Most programs do not include them.

Procedure Division

The last COBOL division is called the **Procedure Division**. The Procedure Division of a COBOL program contains the "programming" part of the program. The code derived from pseudocode makes up the Procedure Division.

The Procedure Division contains the logic of your program, but it will not solve any problem without the support of the other divisions. Data-names that you use in the Procedure Division must have been defined in the Data Division. Every file referenced in the Procedure Division must have been identified in the Environment Divison and further defined in the Data Division. The required entries in the first three divisions are as critical to the success of a COBOL program as is the coding in the Procedure Division.

The Components of a COBOL Program

Now you know the broad framework of a COBOL program—the four divisions. The divisions form the second level of the COBOL program hierarchy, as shown in Figure 1.3.

The divisions in a COBOL program may contain sections, paragraphs, entries or statements, and clauses. Sections are not included in all divisions, nor are paragraphs. When both are included, the section is at a higher level than the paragraph. A section may include several paragraphs. The details of a COBOL program are coded in entries or statements. The Procedure Division includes statements, while the first three divisions include entries. Either statements or entries may include clauses that change or add to their effect.

Figure 1.3 shows the hierarchy in which all the components of a COBOL program are arranged. You can see which divisions include sections and which contain paragraphs. As you learn to code COBOL programs, you'll learn about all of these components in detail.

Summary   Four divisions form the framework of any COBOL program. The Identification Division gives the program a name and may provide other identification data. The Environment Division describes the hardware and software environment for the program. The Data Division defines all data used by the program. The Procedure Division contains the actual processing statements.

Figure 1.3 COBOL Program Structure

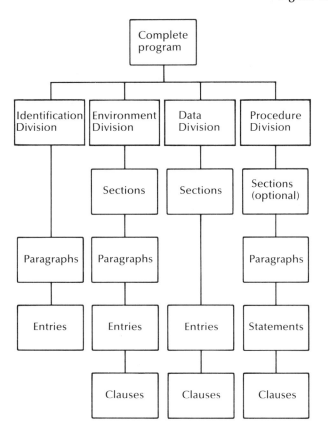

Review Questions

1. List the four divisions of a COBOL program, in sequence.

_____   _____

_____   _____

2. Name the division(s) indicated by each item below.

a. Contains the programming logic

_____

b. Provides the program-name

_____

c. Specifies the hardware configuration

_____

d. Defines all fields referred to in the program

_____

e. Identifies the file requirements of the program

_____

3. What two divisions of a COBOL program are used to provide information about input and output files?

_____

_____

4. Data items are defined in the Data Division. In what division are these data items used?

_____

5. Name one kind of information you could supply in the Identification Division.

_____

6. What division may be omitted with some compilers if a program doesn't use any files?

_____

7. The Identification Division contains paragraphs and entries. Which is a higher level in the COBOL hierarchy?

_____

8. The Environment Division contains paragraphs and sections. Which is a higher level in the COBOL hierarchy?

_____

9. Complete the chart below, referring to Figure 1.3. Use these codes:

R = required
O = optional
N = not allowed

	Sections	Paragraphs	Entries	Statements
Identification				
Environment				
Data				
Procedure				

Answers

1. Identification, Environment, Data, Procedure   **2.** a. Procedure b. Identification c. Environment d. Data e. Environment and Data   **3.** Environment, Data **4.** Procedure   **5.** Program-name, author, date-written, and so on. **6.** Environment   **7.** Paragraph (the paragraph includes entries)   **8.** Section (the section includes paragraphs)

9.	Sections	Paragraphs	Entries	Statements
Identification	N	R	R	N
Environment	R	R	R	N
Data	R	N	R	N
Procedure	O	R	N	R

Chapter Review Questions

1. Which of the following represents standard COBOL?

    a. CODASYL COBOL
    b. IBM OS COBOL
    c. ANS COBOL

2. A program is needed to verify input values and make changes to an employee master file. What type of problem is this? *Choose all that apply.*

    a. Edit
    b. Report
    c. Summary
    d. Update

3. Which division of a COBOL program is indicated by each of the following?

    a. Appears first in each program

    _____

    b. Specifies the hardware configuration

    _____

    c. Contains coding to solve a problem

    _____

    d. Defines any data used by the program

    _____

4. The Environment Division contains paragraphs, sections, entries, and clauses.

    a. Which is the highest level in the COBOL hierarchy?

    _____

    b. Which is the lowest level in the COBOL hierarchy?

    _____

Answers

    1. c   **2.** a, d   **3.** a. Identification b. Environment c. Procedure d. Data
4. a. Sections   b. Clauses

Chapter 2

COBOL Syntax

The COBOL language has structure and grammar rules just like any other language. These rules are called its syntax. This chapter presents the general COBOL coding rules and the layout of lines in a COBOL program.

You'll see a variety of sample lines and learn the meaning of several symbols you can use in coding. You will be prepared to begin coding in COBOL in the next chapter.

This chapter consists of three lessons:

Lesson 2.1: COBOL Coding Format
Lesson 2.2: Rules for Coding
Lesson 2.3: Format Notation

COBOL Coding Format

COBOL programs must be coded with a fairly specific format. In this lesson you'll learn the overall layout of lines in a COBOL program and the features common to all lines and all programs.

Objectives By the end of this lesson you'll know the general format of any COBOL line.

Rationale Before you can code a complete COBOL program, you must be able to code a single line. How that line is coded depends on the basic COBOL syntax that you'll learn in this lesson.

Starting to Code

A COBOL program is coded in lines. The lines all have the same general format. Most COBOL compilers use an 80-character line, a tradition left from the days when 80-column punch cards were the most widely used input medium. Some compilers may allow a different line length. Lines are limited to 80 characters in this course.

At one time most COBOL programs were punched into 80-column cards. Then machines were developed that allowed people to key a

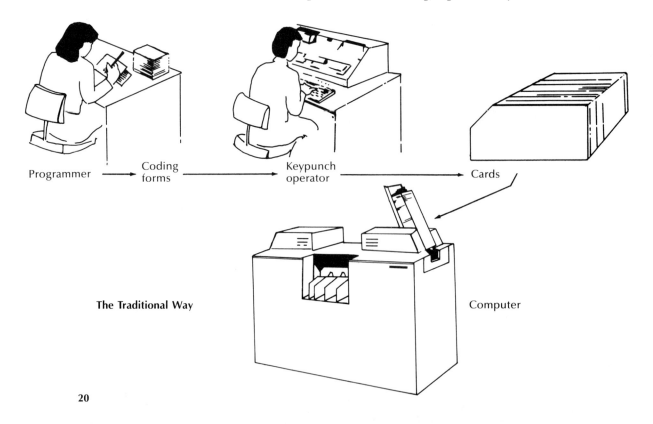

Programmer ⟶ Coding forms ⟶ Keypunch operator ⟶ Cards

The Traditional Way

Computer

program directly onto a magnetic tape or disk. Nowadays many computers are equipped with video terminals through which source programs can be entered directly into the system.

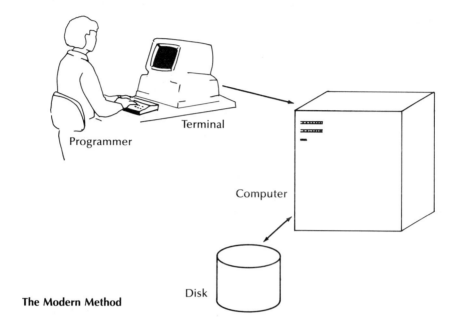

Programmer

Terminal

Computer

Disk

The Modern Method

Even though they aren't actually on cards, we call source programs **card-image** files because they look like card files to the computer. Many of the messages you'll see in compiling and running programs refer to "cards," even though the installation may never have had a card reader. When used this way, a "card" is equivalent to a program line. A listing of a source program is often called an 80-80 listing because it lists 80 characters of input at 80 characters per line output.

Even with a video terminal, programmers do not just sit down and type out a program. First they design the program, perhaps using pseudocode, as was discussed in *Introduction to Computer Programming*. When their pseudocode (which may contain many COBOL or near-COBOL statements) is detailed enough, they go to the terminal and begin to code the program.

The Layout of a Line

Figure 2.1 shows a reduced copy of a COBOL coding form. These forms are available in computer and office supply stores everywhere. We will use this form to demonstrate the correct layout of a COBOL line, whether it's being coded on a form, on plain paper, or at the terminal.

The information at the top of the form helps to label the form but does not become part of the program. The program is written on the lines that are marked off into columns.

Sequence Numbers   The first six positions on each line are reserved for an optional line number. On this coding form the line number is broken down into two parts, the page number and the line number; thus, the first line on the first page might be 001001. However, you

Figure 2.1. COBOL Coding Form

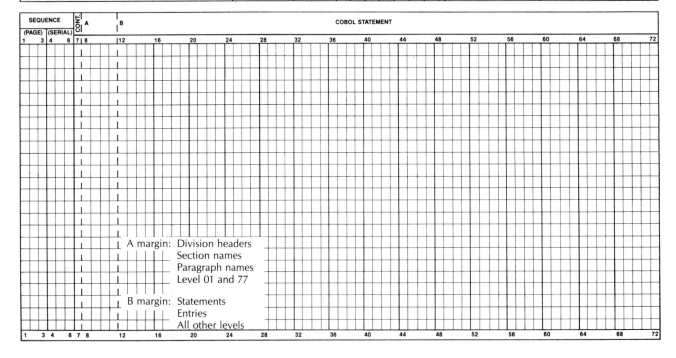

can number pages and lines any way you like, or not at all. Many programmers prefer to number the lines sequentially, without using page numbers, as in 000001, 000002, and so on. Increments of 10 or 100 are often used instead of 1. For example, the numbers on the first three lines might be:

```
010010
010020          if you use page and line numbers with
010030          increments of 10
```
or
```
000100
000200          if you use straight sequential numbers
000300          with an increment of 100
```

This way of numbering makes it easier to insert lines later, something that programmers often do. If you're using an online editor, you probably don't have to number the lines yourself. Many online editors can be set up to assign the line numbers in the first six positions automatically and even to renumber the lines in even increments if you add, rearrange, or remove lines.

Column 7   Column 7 is called the indicator area because it is used to indicate that a line has an unusual function, such as acting as a comment line.

You can code an asterisk (*) in column 7 to indicate a comment line. Comments help other people who read your program understand what it is doing. Comments can be used to explain how a section of code works, for example, or to explain where data comes from and how it will be used. Whatever else you code on a line coded with an asterisk will be ignored by the compiler, but it will be included in any listing of the source program, including printed listings. You can include as many comments as you like; just place an * in column 7 of each comment line. (With many compilers, however, you can't use comments before the first program line or after the last program line.) Be wary, by the way, of comments in existing code. They may be misleading. Often programs are modified but comments aren't brought up to date.

Some compilers allow you to use a slash (/) in column 7 instead of an *. This causes the listing to start a new page. The slashed line, with any comment, is printed at the top of the next page. Other compilers use the slash as another comment indicator; you'll have to check its effect on your compiler.

Some programmers like to make their comments really stand out by putting them in "flower boxes" like this:

```
*   *   *   *   *   *   *   *   *   *   *   *   *   *   *   *   *   *   *   *
*                                                                          *
*   This program runs the quarterly tax report.                           *
*   It should be used only after the last payroll                         *
*   for the quarter has been completed and the                            *
*   employee pay file is up to date.                                      *
*                                                                          *
*   *   *   *   *   *   *   *   *   *   *   *   *   *   *   *   *   *   *   *
```

The asterisks in column 7 identify the lines as comments. The other asterisks are for decoration, to catch the reader's eye. Using lowercase letters (if your system has them) also helps to set off the comments, because most compilers require all capital letters for code that is to be translated. Your installation may have requirements about where and how to code comments.

Figure 2.2 shows a coding example. The first eleven lines will appear on the first page of the listing. The last five lines will appear on the second page. A comment could be included on the / line; it would be printed at the top of page 2.

A hyphen (-) in column 7 indicates that the current line is a continuation of the previous line. However, most modern COBOL compilers allow you to continue a line at any space without putting the hyphen in column 7, so you won't see or use that hyphen unless you are breaking a long constant value.

Margins   As you can see on the coding form, column 8 is labeled "A." This column is called the **A margin**. Columns 8 through 11 make up **area A**; column 8 is its leftmost margin. Only certain components of a COBOL program, such as division headers, can begin in area A. Columns 8 through 11 are always blank on continuation lines.

Column 12 is labeled "B"; it is called the **B margin**. Columns 12 through 72 make up **area B**; column 12 is its leftmost margin. The bulk of a COBOL program is coded in area B.

Whether you code on a coding form, on plain paper, or at a terminal, you need to be aware of the columns. Remember that column 8 is the A margin; it marks the beginning of area A. Column 12 is the B margin; it marks the beginning of area B. Column 72 is the last valid position for a COBOL statement in most older compilers. The current COBOL standard, however, allows compilers to use a wider or narrower B area. Most compilers use column 72 as the right margin in order to be compatible with all the existing COBOL source programs.

Figure 2.2 Coding Example

SEQUENCE			CONT.	A	B								COBOL STATEMENT			
(PAGE)	(SERIAL)															
1	3	4 6	7 8	12	16	20	24	28	32	36	40	44				

```
ØØØ1ØØ   IDENTIFICATION DIVISION.
ØØØ2ØØ   PROGRAM-ID.
ØØØ3ØØ        LISTDATA.
ØØØ4ØØ   ENVIRONMENT DIVISION.
ØØØ5ØØ   INPUT-OUTPUT SECTION.
ØØØ6ØØ*     INPUT FILE AND OUTPUT FILE ENTRIES
ØØØ7ØØ   FILE-CONTROL.
ØØØ8ØØ        SELECT PERSONNEL-FILE
ØØØ9ØØ            ASSIGN TO DISK.
ØØ1ØØØ        SELECT LISTING-FILE
ØØ11ØØ            ASSIGN TO PRINTER.
ØØ12ØØ/
ØØ13ØØ   DATA DIVISION.
ØØ14ØØ   FILE SECTION.
ØØ15ØØ   FD   PERSONNEL-FILE
ØØ16ØØ        LABEL RECORDS ARE STANDARD.
```

Identification   The last eight positions on a COBOL program line, columns 73 through 80, were reserved for identification purposes (the program's name) in many early compilers. The older compilers took away 14 characters from every line for sequence numbers and identification because of the problems that occurred when someone dropped a box of punched cards and scattered six source programs on the floor. Line numbers in columns 1–6 and program names in columns 73–80 of every card helped all the king's men (and an automatic sorting machine) put the programs back together again.

Programmers who use online editors generally do not use the last eight positions of the line. There is no way a line or group of lines in their programs can get separated from the rest, unlike the situation with a card deck. Also, some online editors do not display 80 full columns. It is simply a great deal less bother to enter just 72 columns. Some installations prefer that the official program identification be inserted in the last eight positions of each line, however.

Legible Coding

If someone else will have to enter your program, either at a terminal or a key punch machine, it is essential that your hand-written coding be legible. Use all capital letters, one for each block on the form. Use a standard way of differentiating between similar characters. Many COBOL installations recommend these marks:

$\mathcal{I}$	letter I	$/$	number 1
O	letter O	$\emptyset$	number 0
$\mathcal{S}$	letter S	5	number 5
$\not{Z}$	letter Z	2	number 2

We'll use these marks in any hand-coded material you see in this book.

Summary Most compilers use 80-column lines for coding COBOL programs. Columns 1–6 are for optional sequence numbers. Column 7 is the indicator column. An * in this column indicates a comment; a / indicates a new page (with or without a comment); and a — indicates a continuation line. Columns 8–72 are used for the COBOL code. Column 8 is called the A margin; columns 8–11 are called the A area. Column 12 is called the B margin; columns 12–72 are called the B area. Columns 73–80 may be used for identification purposes.

No matter where or how you code a COBOL program, it must be laid out to conform to the structure of a COBOL coding form. The COBOL compiler expects this and will generate error messages galore if you ignore the columns. In the next lesson you'll learn what sort of entries you code in each area.

Appendix A of this book contains a full-size copy of a COBOL coding form. You can reproduce this and use it as you work through this book. You will become very familiar with the column and area requirements of COBOL, and you'll be able to use plain paper or the terminal in your work.

Comprehension Questions

1. What columns on a COBOL code line are used for each of the following?

_____ a. Sequence numbers

_____ b. Indicator

_____ c. Area A

_____ d. Area B

2. How many columns are represented by a standard line of COBOL code?

3. What column represents the A margin?

4. What column represents the B margin?

5. In what area would you indicate a comment?

6. What is the effect of these lines in a source program listing?

7	8		12		16		20		24		28		32		36		40
/					PROBLEM		SOLUTION										
PROCEDURE		DIVISION.															

1. a. 1 through 6 b. 7 c. 8 through 11 d. 12 through 72 (or through whatever your compiler specifies)   2. 80 (a card-image record)   3. Column 8 is the leftmost margin of Area A.   4. Column 12 is the leftmost margin of Area B.   5. Indicator area (column 7)   6. Start a new page, print PROBLEM SOLUTION at top, then print PROCEDURE DIVISION on the next line.

Application Questions

1. Suppose a COBOL line is coded like this:

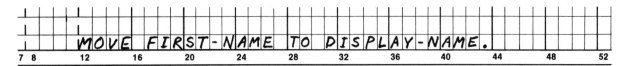

In what area is it coded?_____

2.

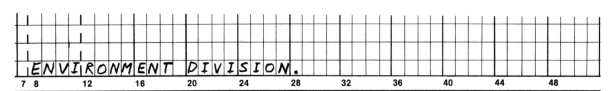

In what area does this coding begin? _____

3.

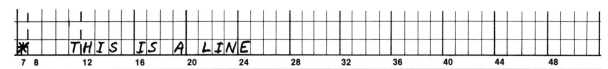

In what area is the asterisk coded? _____

4. Code these lines beginning in area B of the form section below.

```
ADD 12000 TO INPUT-COURSE
    GIVING PRIZE-MONEY.
```

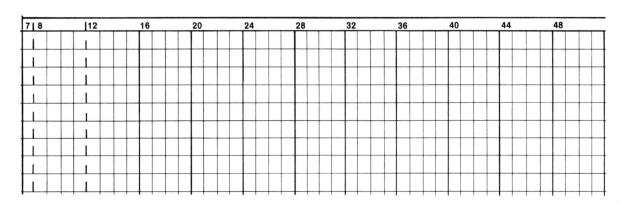

5. On the form below, code the first five sequence numbers in a sequence that starts with 6000 and uses an increment of 100.

SEQUENCE		CONT.	A	B	COBOL STATEMENT
(PAGE)	(SERIAL)				
1 3	4 6	7 8	12	16 20 24 28 32 36 40 44	

6. On the form below, code the comment "Start a new page" to appear at the top of a new page in the listing.

SEQUENCE		CONT.	A	B	COBOL STATEMENT
(PAGE)	(SERIAL)				
1 3	4 6	7 8	12	16 20 24 28 32 36 40 44	

7. On the form below, code the comment "This is a practice program."

SEQUENCE		CONT.	A	B	COBOL STATEMENT
(PAGE)	(SERIAL)				
1 3	4 6	7 8	12	16 20 24 28 32 36 40 44	

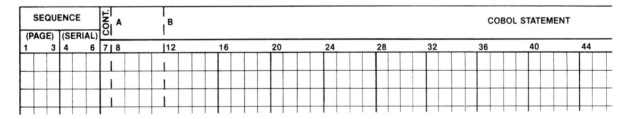

Continued

Answers

1. B **2.** A **3.** Indicator

4.

7	8		12	16	20	24	28	32	36	40	44	48
	ADD 12ØØØ TO INPUT-COURSE											
	GIVING PRIZE-MONEY.											

Your indentation may be different.

5.

SEQUENCE		CONT.	A	B						COBOL STATEMENT		
(PAGE)	(SERIAL)											
1 3	4 6	7 8		12	16	20	24	28	32	36	40	44
ØØ6ØØØ												
ØØ61ØØ												
ØØ62ØØ												
ØØ63ØØ												
ØØ64ØØ												

6.

(PAGE)	(SERIAL)										
1 3	4 6	7 8		12	16	20	24	28	32	36	40	44
		/		START A NEW PAGE							

You could start the comment in any column.

7.

(PAGE)	(SERIAL)										
1 3	4 6	7 8		12	16	20	24	28	32	36	40	44
		*		THIS IS A PRACTICE PROGRAM.							

You could start the comment in any column.

Rules for Coding

The basic coding of COBOL statements takes place in area A and area B. Only certain components of a program may be coded in area A. The rest of the program is coded in area B.

Objectives You will be able to place various COBOL headers and entries in their proper positions.

Rationale If a COBOL component is not coded in the proper position, the compiler can't read it and will reject it with a message such as AREA A VIOLATION. You must use the correct placement or you'll never get a program to compile.

Coding Placement

Figure 2.2 is repeated below. Notice that the division-names, section-names, and paragraph-names begin in area A, as do FD, 01, and 77 entries. Other components are entirely within area B.

SEQUENCE (PAGE) (SERIAL)	CONT.	A	B	COBOL STATEMENT
000100		IDENTIFICATION DIVISION.		
000200		PROGRAM-ID.		
000300		LIST DATA.		
000400		ENVIRONMENT DIVISION.		
000500		INPUT-OUTPUT SECTION.		
000600	*	INPUT FILE AND OUTPUT FILE ENTRIES		
000700		FILE-CONTROL.		
000800		SELECT PERSONNEL-FILE		
000900		ASSIGN TO DISK.		
001000		SELECT LISTING-FILE		
001100		ASSIGN TO PRINTER.		
001200	/			
001300		DATA DIVISION.		
001400		FILE SECTION.		
001500		FD PERSONNEL-FILE		
001600		LABEL RECORDS ARE STANDARD.		

Identification Division   In the preceding figure the first line is a division header, which names the first division; it begins in area A. The second line is a paragraph-name, PROGRAM-ID. It also begins in area A. The third line you see is an entry within the PROGRAM-ID paragraph; it begins in area B.

Area A and area B entries can begin anywhere in the area. For example, the second and third lines in the above figure could be combined as shown here:

```
PROGRAM-ID.  LISTDATA.
```

The paragraph-name starts in column 8, which is the A margin. (Most programmers invariably start area A components at the A margin.) The entry starts in column 21, which is well within the B area; it does not have to start at the B margin.

Environment Division   The Environment Division header and Input-Output Section header begin in area A, as does the FILE-CONTROL paragraph-name. The SELECT entries are coded entirely within area B, since they are part of a paragraph. The indentation of the ASSIGN clause is a convention (not a rule) to make the entry more readable. As long as the entire entry stays within area B, the compiler doesn't care where you put it.

Data Division   In the Data Division, some additional entries can be made in area A. Figure 2.3 shows part of a Data Division. Notice that letters and numbers are used to introduce some lines. The FD (file description) code always appears in area A. The clauses that follow FD are always in area B; if you start FD at the A margin, you must skip at least two spaces to get into the B area. The numeric codes indicate data item descriptions. The 01 and 77 codes you see in the figure must appear in area A. All other codes and entries in the Data Division, with the exception of section headers, may be coded in either area; some compilers restrict these entries to area B.

Procedure Division   The division header, any section headers, and all paragraph-names in the Procedure Division begin in area A. All statements must be completely within area B. You can begin state-

Figure 2.3 Sample Coding of Data Division

```
FD   LISTING-FILE
     LABEL RECORDS ARE OMITTED.
//   LISTING-LINE                 PICTURE X(90).
WORKING-STORAGE SECTION.
77   PERSONNEL-END-OF-FILE        PICTURE X
                                  VALUE    "N".
77   VALID-RECORD-FLAG            PICTURE X.
//   WORK-RECORD.
     05  PERSONNEL-CODE           PICTURE 9(9).
```

ments at any point in area B. We'll begin the statements in the main sequence at the B margin, column 12. Indentation is totally up to the programmer; it doesn't affect how the COBOL compiler interprets the program. You can use indentation to show a continued line, the flow of control, or whatever you wish. Use indentation to make the structure of a program or routine easily apparent, as you do in pseudocode.

Spacing Considerations

You can make COBOL program listings more readable by separating divisions, sections, and paragraphs with blank lines. Blank lines generally have no effect on the compiler or the executable program, although some compilers object to blank lines within a paragraph.

When an entry begins in area A, it can begin anywhere in that area. We'll use the A margin in this course, but you can begin in any of columns 8, 9, 10, and 11. Most entries that begin in area A extend into area B.

When an entry begins in area B, it must be entirely contained in that area. If you continue a line, the continuation must also begin somewhere in area B.

Indentation also helps to make a program more readable. We'll use a regular indentation of four spaces, but the amount you use is up to you. Four is a good number since the required indentation from the A margin to the B margin is four spaces.

Separating Words

Each word in a COBOL line is separated from the next by at least one space. This "separation" space can be replaced by many spaces. This means that you can break a COBOL line between any two words and continue the entry on the next line, anywhere in area B. It also means that you can code several statements or clauses per line, using as little as a single space after each word.

In structured COBOL, code one statement or major chunk of a statement per line; this makes the program much more readable. Here are two ways you could code the same statement:

```
READ PERSONNEL-FILE AT END MOVE "Y" TO PERSONNEL-EOF.

READ PERSONNEL-FILE
    AT END MOVE "Y" TO PERSONNEL-EOF.
```

While both are valid, the second way has advantages in addition to readability. Errors detected during compilation will be listed with a line number indicating where each error was detected. If each clause is on a separate line, you will know what part of the statement caused the problem.

These two sets of COBOL entries are also technically identical:

```
ADD 7 TO BALANCE.  MOVE BALANCE TO OUT-BALANCE.  DISPLAY
OUT-BALANCE.

ADD 7 TO BALANCE.
MOVE BALANCE TO OUT-BALANCE.
DISPLAY OUT-BALANCE.
```

Again, any error generated by one of these statements would provide a more useful line number if you code in accordance with the second example.

Additionally, it is easier to locate lines, modify them, and insert new ones as needed if you code one statement or clause per line.

Summary In this lesson you've seen how code is placed on lines in a COBOL program. Division and section headers and paragraph names must start in area A. In the Data Division, the codes FD, 01, and 77 must start in area A. Other entries and statements must start and be contained in area B. Some compilers allow other Data Division entries to start in area A.

Blank lines and indentation may be used to make source programs more readable. They do not affect the compilation. Separate clauses and statements should be coded on separate lines for readability and to make debugging easier.

Comprehension Questions

1. Which of the following must begin in area A?

    a. Division header
    b. Section header
    c. Paragraph-name
    d. Statement

2. Which of the following must begin in area B?

    a. Division header
    b. Section header
    c. Paragraph-name
    d. Statement

3. A COBOL entry reads:

    ```
    LABEL RECORDS ARE STANDARD.
    ```

    Which of the following is/are a valid way to code this entry?

    ```
    a. LABEL RECORDS ARESTANDARD.
    b. LABEL R ECORDS ARE STANDARD.
    c. LABEL RECORDS ARE STANDARD.
    ```

4. A valid COBOL entry reads:

    ```
    ADD BONUS-AMOUNT TO GROSS-PAY.
    ```

    Which of the following is/are a valid way to code this entry?

    ```
    a. ADDBONUS-AMOUNT TO GROSS-PAY.
    b. ADD BONUS-AMOUNT      TO      GROSS-PAY.
    c. ADD BONUS-AMOUNT
         TO GROSS-PAY.
    ```

5. Which of the following is true?

    a. Division headers must begin in column 8.
    b. Division headers may begin anywhere in columns 8–11.
    c. Division headers may begin anywhere in columns 8–72.

6. Which of the following is true?

    a. You may insert blank lines anywhere you want in a COBOL program.
    b. You must code blank lines between divisions in a COBOL program.
    c. There must be no blank lines in a COBOL program.

7. Which of the following is true?

    a. You must code only one clause or statement per line in COBOL.
    b. You may code several clauses or statements per line in COBOL.

8. Which of the following is true?

    a. The compiler ignores indentation in the B area.
    b. The compiler uses indentation to determine the flow of control.

9. Which is better from the standpoint of readability and debugging?

    a. Code one clause or statement per line.

    b. Code as many clauses and statements per line as possible.

Answers

    1. a, b, c **2.** d **3.** c **4.** b, c **5.** b **6.** a **7.** b **8.** a **9.** a

Application Questions

On the coding form below, code the following:

1. An "environment division" header
2. An "input-output section" header
3. A "file-control" paragraph-name
4. An entry that reads "SELECT IN-FILE ASSIGN TO DISK"
5. A "procedure division" header
6. A "main-logic" paragraph name
7. A statement that reads "OPEN INPUT IN-FILE OUTPUT OUT-FILE"

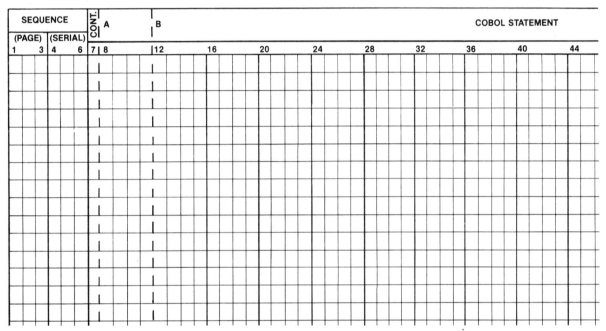

Answers

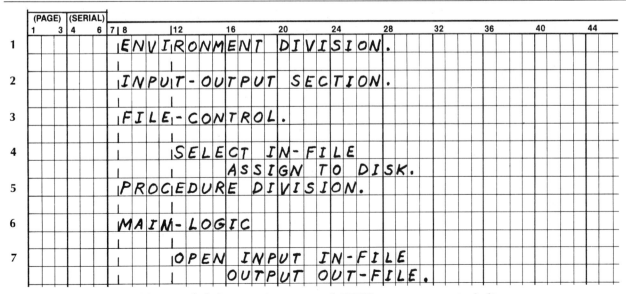

You could have coded the SELECT entry and OPEN statement on single lines.

Format Notation

You are now familiar with the general format of a COBOL program, and you know what type of information is coded in each area. Each COBOL entry and statement also has a specific format. For example, to increment LINE-COUNTER you can say ADD 1 TO LINE-COUNTER, but you can't say ADD LINE-COUNTER + 1. Special notation is used in most books and manuals to show the formats of the COBOL entries and statements. You'll learn to interpret the format notation in this lesson. Then you'll be ready to learn the entries and statements themselves.

Objectives When you have completed this lesson, you'll be able to interpret formats for most types of COBOL statements and entries.

Rationale You need to be able to read and interpret COBOL format notation for several reasons. This COBOL course (all four books) uses the format notation to introduce and explain each COBOL entry and statement. It is the same notation the CODASYL manual employs, so you'll be able to read that manual too (if it's available to you). Also, your installation's COBOL manuals will use the same notation, or one that's very similar.

Using Format Statements

A format statement is *not* COBOL. Instead, it shows you the format of a COBOL entry or statement. Here is a sample format statement, showing exactly how to code the WRITE Statement.

```
WRITE record-name
     [FROM data-name-1]

    [{BEFORE}  ADVANCING  {data-name-2 LINES }]
    [{AFTER }             {integer LINES    }]
                          {mnemonic-name    }
```

This lesson will explain why some words are capitalized, some are in lowercase, some are underlined, some are in brackets ([ ]), and some are in braces ({ }).

Every COBOL entry and statement includes a number of elements, separated by spaces. These elements are usually words, but they may be punctuation or other characters. The format statement tells you what part of the statement is required and what is optional, along with what information the programmer must supply. This lesson covers the most common features of format statements. The elements must be included in a COBOL entry or statement in exactly the same sequence that you'll see in the format statement.

Words

A format statement may contain uppercase words and lowercase words.

Uppercase Words   Any uppercase underlined word in a COBOL format statement is a required key word. This means you must include the word *exactly as it is shown* in the format statement. Here is a sample COBOL format statement:

```
IDENTIFICATION DIVISION.
```

Each word that appears in underlined uppercase letters is required in the COBOL entry. When a period appears in a format statement, it is also required. This COBOL entry (it's a division header) must be coded exactly as you see here.

Uppercase words that aren't underlined are optional; you can omit them if you like. Here's an example:

```
BLANK WHEN ZERO
```

Here the words BLANK and ZERO are required key words. WHEN is not required, but you can use it if you wish. Thus, you could code this particular clause as BLANK ZERO or BLANK WHEN ZERO. It's a good idea to use optional words, especially when, as here, they help indicate the function of the entry. If you use optional words, be sure you spell them correctly.

Lowercase Words   Lowercase words indicate something the programmer must supply. In RECORD CONTAINS integer CHARACTERS, you need to supply an integer (whole number) to specify how many characters each record contains. All of the following are valid ways to specify that a record is 120 characters long:

```
RECORD 120
RECORD CONTAINS 120
RECORD CONTAINS 120 CHARACTERS
RECORD 120 CHARACTERS
```

Here's another example:

```
PROGRAM-ID.   program-name.
```

Here the word PROGRAM-ID, followed by a period, is required. The programmer supplies a valid program-name, which is followed by another required period.

The lowercase word always indicates the sort of entry you need to supply. Notes with the format statement will provide additional explanations if needed. In the example above, you supply the name of the program.

Some other words you'll have to supply are called literals, data-names, and procedure-names. Literals are constants, such as 73.2, −1, or "ABACUS". Numeric literals are numeric quantities, while nonnumeric literals may be any characters enclosed in quotation marks. Some format statements are even more specific; if an integer is required, the format may specify integer rather than literal. Data-names are names defined in the program. These are referred to in various statements. Sometimes a format will include data-name-1 and data-name-2; this means you can use two different data-names. Procedure-names are generally paragraph-names in the Procedure Division. You use these in some statements. You'll learn more about all these terms later.

A COBOL statement may also include other statements. The format may specify the type of statement to be included. As you learn each new format, we'll explain the meaning of any unfamiliar words or statements.

Brackets ([ ])

Brackets in a format statement indicate that the bracketed portion is optional or used only under certain conditions. Here's an example:

```
[RECORD CONTAINS integer CHARACTERS]
```

This indicates that the entire RECORD clause is optional. Here's another example:

```
READ file-name RECORD [INTO data-name]

      AT END imperative-statement
```

The brackets show that one clause in the READ statement is optional. However, that does not mean you can include or exclude this clause without changing the meaning of the entry, as you can with RECORD and AT. Optional clauses have specific effects; include them only when you want those effects. When you learn to use a statement, you'll learn under what circumstances you'd want to use any optional clauses.

Braces ({ })

Braces indicate a choice. Several items are stacked in the braces. You must select one of them for inclusion in the statement, unless a default is provided. (A default is an option that is assumed if you don't specify differently.) Here's one format of the ADD statement:

```
ADD { data-name-1 } TO data-name-2
    { literal-1   }
```

Here you must supply either a data-name or a literal after the word ADD. These are both valid COBOL statements that use the preceding format:

```
ADD OVERTIME TO GROSS-PAY.

ADD 25.00 TO GROSS-PAY.
```

Of course, OVERTIME and GROSS-PAY must be defined correctly in the program.

Ellipsis (. . .)

An ellipsis is sometimes used in a format statement to indicate that a section of the format may be repeated. Here's an example:

```
MOVE { data-name-1 } TO {data-name-2}...
     { literal-1   }
```

Notice that an extra set of braces encloses data-name-2. This defines the effect of the ellipsis. The effect is that you can specify several data-name-2 names; all will be treated as separate objects of

TO. For example, MOVE SPACES TO HEADING-LINE assigns the value SPACES to the data item HEADING-LINE. MOVE SPACES TO HEADING-LINE DETAIL-LINE assigns the value to both fields.

Here's another format statement example:

$$\underline{\text{ADD}} \quad \left\{ \begin{array}{l} \texttt{data-name-1} \\ \texttt{literal-1} \end{array} \right\} \dots \underline{\text{TO}} \ \texttt{data-name-2}$$

This format statement indicates that you can list several data-names or literals to be added to the last data-name, but you can't put more than one data-name after the word TO. You can use ADD 6 BONUS-AMOUNT TO GROSS-PAY, but not ADD 6 TO BONUS-AMOUNT GROSS-PAY.

Format Figures

When we introduce the format of a statement to you for the first time, we'll include a figure laid out as in Figure 2.4. The format notation will be at the top, followed by examples. A very simple format might include only one example, while a more complex one might include several. The notes in the lower part of the figure explain any values or words you have to supply. They might also explain rules for using the entry and its options. The text material that accompanies the figure will have more details explaining the format and how the statement is used.

Figure 2.4 Sample Format Figure

Format:
```
MOVE  { literal      }  TO {data-name-2}...
      { data-name-1  }
```

Examples:
```
MOVE "1982" TO YEAR-FIELD.
MOVE CURRENT-YEAR TO YEAR-FIELD.
MOVE SPACES TO MESSAGE-1 MESSAGE-2.
```

Notes:
1. Any form of literal may be used as sending field.
2. Sending field is unchanged.
3. Receiving field is completely overlaid.
4. Can use multiple receiving fields.

Summary You've seen the basic elements of format notation. Here's another example to summarize them.

$$\underline{\text{DIVIDE}} \left\{ \begin{array}{l} \text{data-name-1} \\ \text{literal-1} \end{array} \right\} \underline{\text{INTO}} \ \{\text{data-name-2} \quad [\underline{\text{ROUNDED}}]\}\dots$$

$$[\underline{\text{ON}} \ \underline{\text{SIZE}} \ \underline{\text{ERROR}} \ \text{imperative-statement}]$$

This format of the DIVIDE statement always requires the words DIVIDE and INTO. You must supply either data-name-1 or literal-1, along with data-name-2. You can repeat the {data-name-2 [ROUNDED]} phrase, as indicated by the ellipsis; this allows you to perform several division operations with one statement. The ROUNDED clause is optional, but if it is used, it must be used as is. The ON SIZE ERROR clause can be omitted; when it is used, the word ON may be omitted, but you must include SIZE ERROR and an imperative statement. (You'll learn details of all this later.) Figure 2.5 summarizes COBOL format notation.

Figure 2.5 Format Notation Summary

CAPITALIZED	COBOL key word Must be spelled exactly as shown
UNDERLINED	Must be used if clause is used
NOT UNDERLINED	May always be omitted
lowercase	Must be supplied if clause is used
{ }	Braces—choose one of enclosed items
[ ]	Brackets—optional; use if function needed
. . .	May repeat preceding clause in braces or brackets

Comprehension Questions

1. An uppercase underlined word in a format statement means that word:

   a. is optional.
   b. is required.
   c. represents a word supplied by the programmer.

2. An uppercase word that is not underlined in a format statement means that word:

   a. is optional.
   b. is required.
   c. represents a word supplied by the programmer.

3. A lowercase word in a format statement means that word:

   a. is optional.
   b. is required.
   c. represents a word supplied by the programmer.

4. Brackets ([ ]) in a format statement mean that the enclosed entry:

   a. is required.
   b. is optional.
   c. represents a set from which you must select one.
   d. may be repeated.

5. Braces ({ }) in a format statement mean that the enclosed item:

   a. is required.
   b. is optional.
   c. represents a set from which you must select one.
   d. may be repeated.

6. An ellipsis (...) in a format statement means that the unit preceding the ellipsis:

   a. is required.
   b. is optional.
   c. represents a set from which you must select one.
   d. may be repeated.

Answers

1. b   2. a   3. c   4. b   5. c   6. d

Application Questions

1. Here's a sample format statement:

```
DIVIDE  {data-name-1}  INTO {data-name-2 [ROUNDED]}...
        {literal-1   }
     [ON SIZE ERROR imperative-statement]
```

   Which of the following statements adhere to the format?

   a. DIVIDE 6 INTO 12
   b. DIVIDE 12 INTO TOTAL-BALANCE
   c. DIVIDE 12 INTO TOTAL-BALANCE
          ON SIZE ERROR PERFORM PROBLEM-DIVIDE
   d. DIVIDE 12 INTO TOTAL-BALANCE ROUNDED ON SIZE
          ERROR

2. What is wrong with each invalid statement above?

   a. _____

   b. _____

   c. _____

   d. _____

3. Here is another format statement:

```
PERFORM procedure-name-1 [ {THROUGH} procedure-name-2]
                          {THRU   }
```

   Which of the following statements adhere to the format?

   _____ a. PERFORM THRU CALCULATE-PAYROLL.

   _____ b. PERFORM CALCULATE-PAYROLL.

   _____ c. PERFORM CALCULATE-PAYROLL THROUGH.

   _____ d. PERFORM CALCULATE-PAYROLL THRU CALCULATE-EXIT.

4. What is wrong with each invalid statement above?

   a. _____

   b. _____

   c. _____

   d. _____

Answers

1. b, c 2. a. 12 is a literal, not a data-name. d. If you use SIZE ERROR, you must use an imperative statement. 3. b, d 4. a. No procedure-name follows PERFORM. c. No procedure-name follows THROUGH.

Chapter Review Questions

The coding below is used in this review:

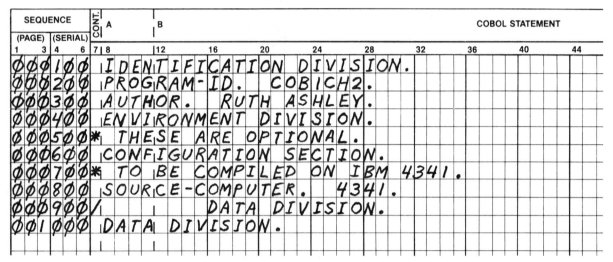

1. What lines contain comments? _____

2. Which division header(s) begin(s) in the correct area? _____

3. In what column would you begin a line that contains

   WORKING-STORAGE SECTION? _____

4. Recode line 000200 so that it takes up two lines (don't worry about the
   sequence numbers).

   _____

   _____

5. Can you add a blank line before ENVIRONMENT DIVISION? _____

6. ADD $\begin{Bmatrix} \text{literal-1} \\ \text{data-name-1} \end{Bmatrix}$ ... TO $\begin{Bmatrix} \text{literal-2} \\ \text{data-name-2} \end{Bmatrix}$

   ```
   GIVING {data-name-3 [ROUNDED]}...
   [ON SIZE ERROR imperative-statement]
   ```

   Which of the following statements adhere to the format?

   a. ADD VALUE-1 VALUE-2 ROUNDED.
   b. ADD VALUE-1 VALUE-2 GIVING ROUNDED.
   c. ADD VALUE-1 VALUE-2 GIVING NEW-AMOUNT.
   d. ADD VALUE-1 VALUE-2 GIVING VALUE-3
         ON SIZE ERROR PERFORM NEXT-PART.

Answers

1. 500, 700, 900   2. all of them   3. 8, 9, 10, 11   4. PROGRAM-ID.
                                                         COB1CH2.

5. yes   6. c, d. Here's what's wrong with the others: a - The GIVING option is
needed if ROUNDED is specified. b - No data-name is specified following GIVING.

Programs Without Files

Chapter 3

The First Three Divisions

This chapter focuses on coding the basic entries needed in the first three divisions of a COBOL program. The compiler uses the information you supply in these divisions to solve the problem addressed by the logic, which is reflected in the fourth division.

This chapter consists of three lessons:

Lesson 3.1:   The Identification Division
Lesson 3.2:   The Environment Division
Lesson 3.3:   The Data Division

The Identification Division

The Identification Division is required in every COBOL program. It identifies the program for the system and for human readers.

Objectives   By the time you have finished studying this lesson, you will be able to code all the possible entries in the Identification Division of a COBOL program.

Rationale   The Identification Division occurs in every COBOL program. Most entries in this division are optional, but they are all very easy to code and help to provide full documentation for your programs, so you will want to use them often.

Required Identification Division Entries

Every COBOL program begins with an Identification Division that names the program and supplies other, optional information. Figure 3.1 shows the format of the required Identification Division entries.

Figure 3.1 Required Identification Division Entries

Format:
```
IDENTIFICATION DIVISION.
PROGRAM-ID.  program-name.
```

Examples:
```
IDENTIFICATION DIVISION.
PROGRAM-NAME.  PERSONNEL-UPDATE.

IDENTIFICATION DIVISION.
PROGRAM-NAME.
     INVENTORY-CONTROL.
```

Notes:
1. Program-name may be up to 30 characters long. Some compilers limit the name to six or eight characters, however.
2. Program-name can include letters, numbers, and hyphens.
3. The first eight characters of the program-name must be unique.
4. Some compilers require the first character of the program name to be alphabetic.
5. Some compilers convert hyphens to zeros.

Division Header   The division header for the Identification Division is the first line in a COBOL program. (Comments cannot precede this line.) Every division header begins in area A and occupies a separate line. It is terminated with a period, as you can see in Figure 3.1. This header can be shortened to ID DIVISION in most compilers.

Required Paragraph   Only one paragraph is required in the Identification Division. The PROGRAM-ID paragraph must be used to provide the program-name that will be used internally. Figure 3.1 shows two examples. Notice that the paragraph-name begins in area A in both examples, while the program-name entry begins in area B. The program-name is terminated by a period, followed by at least one space. Paragraph-names need not be on a separate line. They, too, always end with a period.

The program-name must adhere to a few rules:

- The name can have up to 30 characters.
- Any letters or digits or hyphens may be used. But some compilers will replace hyphens with zeros.
- The first eight characters (six in some systems) must be unique among program-names in the same system.
- The first character must be a letter in some compilers.
- A hyphen may not be the first or last character.

These are all valid COBOL program-names: PAY7, PREPARA-TION, TAX1982. Some systems will use the first eight characters (or even six) of your program-name as the official stored name, which is why these characters must be unique. With such systems you couldn't name two programs PERSONNEL-UPDATE and PERSONNEL-TAXES in their PROGRAM-ID paragraphs, for example.

The system won't warn you about program-name duplication. If such duplication occurs, however, the second program you compile will overlay the first. For this reason, many installations have standards for naming programs.

The program-name you provide in the PROGRAM-ID paragraph is used internally for your program. You can store your program in a source file under a different name. The PROGRAM- ID name is used by the system to locate an executable program, while the source file-name is used only for the source code.

Optional Paragraphs

You can use any or all of several optional Identification Division paragraphs in a COBOL program. Figure 3.2 shows the format for all standard Identification Division entries. Any that you use must be in the sequence shown here, following the PROGRAM-ID paragraph. Each paragraph-name must end with a period followed by a space, as must the associated entry.

Figure 3.2 All Identification Division Entries

Format:
```
IDENTIFICATION DIVISION.
PROGRAM-ID.  program-name.
[AUTHOR.  comment-entry.]
[INSTALLATION.  comment-entry.]
[DATE-WRITTEN.  comment-entry.]
[DATE-COMPILED.  comment-entry.]
[SECURITY.  comment-entry.]
```

Example:
```
IDENTIFICATION DIVISION.
PROGRAM-ID.  CHAP3L1.
AUTHOR.  MACASHLEY.
DATE-COMPILED.  March 17, 1989.
SECURITY.
    THIS PROGRAM IS RESTRICTED TO THOSE
    WHO HAVE THE PROPER AUTHORIZATION.  THE
    DATA FILES PROCESSED ARE PROTECTED.
    CALL EXTENSION 386 FOR INFORMATION.
```

Notes:
1. Any or all of the optional paragraphs may be included.
2. Comment-entries may contain anything. They aren't checked for syntax.
3. Optional paragraphs must be in the order shown.
4. Some compilers insert the current date in the DATE-COMPILED paragraph of a source listing.

The entries you make for any of these optional paragraphs are treated as comments; that is, the compiler will ignore them, but they'll be printed in any listing of the source program. You can enter anything at all, in any format. You can use as many lines as you like. Everything you enter, up to the next entry in area A, is considered part of the previously named paragraph. Just remember to end the last word with a period. Other periods won't cause any trouble.

A REMARKS paragraph can also be used with many compilers, although it is not part of the current COBOL standard. REMARKS provides a specific location in the program for explaining the program's purpose.

Many installations require several optional paragraphs for documentation, for example, to tell the human readers of the program who wrote the program and when. Other installations prefer that you use comments (asterisks in column 7) for this sort of information. You'll use your installation's particular conventions. Meanwhile, let's look briefly at each optional paragraph.

AUTHOR The AUTHOR paragraph is generally used to provide the programmer's name. Since the format isn't checked by the compiler, you can include the author's department, phone number, or anything else you wish to make available to human readers of the program. Here's an example:

```
AUTHOR.   DAVID REED      EXT. 397
          PREPARED FOR INVENTORY STUDY.
```

Notice that an extra period is used in the phone number. This won't be a problem because the next line doesn't begin in area A.

INSTALLATION The INSTALLATION paragraph, as the name implies, is used to document where the program was developed. If your company has several sites, or if your programs are widely distributed, you might want to use this entry.

DATE-WRITTEN This paragraph, like the others, can contain data in any format. Ideally, you'd include the date the program was written. Depending on your installation's standards, you might update this comment entry any time you modify the program.

DATE-COMPILED Some compilers place the date of compilation as a comment entry in this paragraph for you. This doesn't affect the source program, but that date will appear in any listing resulting from the compilation. If your compiler doesn't have this feature, you may want to code the date here yourself. However, most compiler listings include the current date on each page.

SECURITY   The paragraph doesn't have any effect on the security of the program or its data, but you can use it to provide an explanation to human readers if any security problems exist.

Examples

The example in Figure 3.2 shows a typical Identification Division. The division header is on a line by itself. Each paragraph-name begins in area A; we use column 8, the A margin. The program-name and each comment-entry are entirely within area B. The SECURITY comment-entry shows that entries can be continued on the following lines. Each new line of the comment-entry begins in area B.

You can include comments and blank lines at any point following the division header. Here's an example:

SEQUENCE		CONT.	A	B	COBOL STATEMENT
(PAGE)	(SERIAL)				

```
IDENTIFICATION DIVISION.

*THIS IS A SAMPLE DIVISION
 PROGRAM-ID.   CH3LES1.

 AUTHOR.       RUTH ASHLEY
               SAN DIEGO.

 DATE-COMPILED.   DATE-HERE.
```

Summary   The Identification Division header and the PROGRAM-ID paragraph are required in every program. You can include the AUTHOR and/or the INSTALLATION paragraph to document the source of the program. You can use the DATE-WRITTEN and/or DATE-COMPILED paragraph to document when the program was prepared. Finally, you can use the SECURITY paragraph to provide a narrative explanation of any security considerations that affect the program. Only the PROGRAM-ID paragraph is meaningful to the compiler; all other Identification Division paragraphs are ignored. Comments and blank lines may be used anywhere after the division header.

Comprehension Questions

1. Which of the following are Identification Division paragraph names?

    a. PROGRAM-NAME

    b. AUTHOR

    c. COMMENTS

    d. DATE

    e. INSTALLATION

    f. ENVIRONMENT

    g. SECURITY

2. Name the required paragraph in the Identification Division.

_____

3. Which of the following are correctly coded?

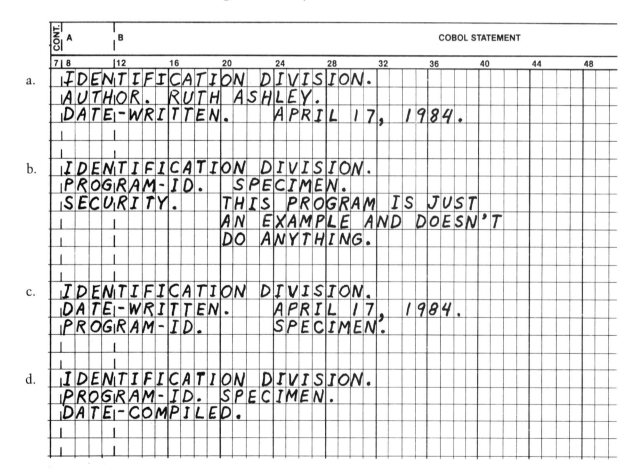

4. What paragraph in the Identification Division may appear in a compiler source listing in a form different from the form in which you coded it in the source program?

_____

5. At which points in the example below could you insert comments or blank lines?

```
a→
      IDENTIFICATION DIVISION.
b→
      PROGRAM-ID.   CH3L1CQ5.
c→
      AUTHOR.       PAUL ASHLEY.
d→
      SECURITY.     NONE.
e→
```

Answers

1. b, e, g   **2.** PROGRAM-ID   **3.** b, d; Here's what's wrong with the others: a—The PROGRAM-ID paragraph is omitted. c—The paragraphs are not in the correct order. **4.** DATE-COMPILED   **5.** b, c, d, e

Application Questions

1. Write Identification Division entries as needed for each situation below.

a. The name of the program is SORTPAY.

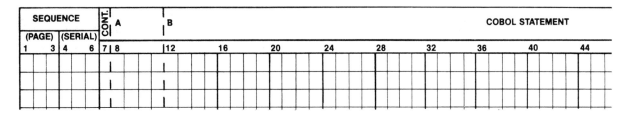

b. The program was written by David McDonell, who can be reached at 555-7888.

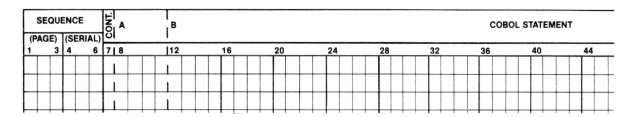

c. David works for DuoTech, Inc., in San Diego.

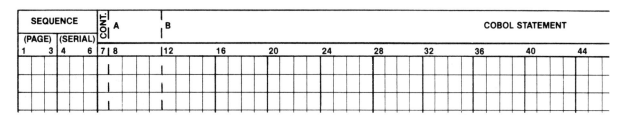

d. The program will sort the employee records in order of anticipated gross salary for the year.

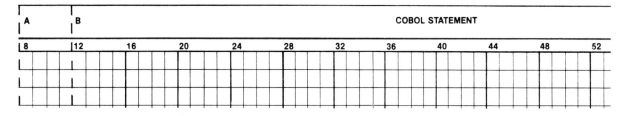

e. The program was written on June 7, 1989.

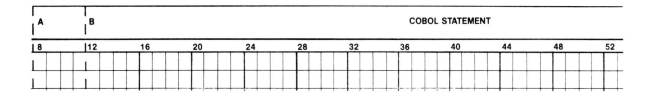

2. Now write a complete Identification Division for a program named CH3L1AQ2. Use as many of the optional paragraphs as you can. Use information specific to you and your company.

SEQUENCE		CONT.	A	B								COBOL STATEMENT
(PAGE)	(SERIAL)											
1 3	4 6	7 8	12	16	20	24	28	32	36	40	44	

Answers

Be very picky in checking your answers. Be sure you started the division header and each paragraph-name in area A and ended each with a period. Be sure the division header is on a separate line. Paragraph-names may be on a separate line from entries. The program-name must be valid. It and all the comment-entries must be completely contained in area B. Each comment-entry must end with a period.

1. a.

```
PROGRAM-ID.  SORTPAY.
```

b.

```
AUTHOR.  DAVID MCDONELL
         PHONE 555-7888
```

c.

```
INSTALLATION.  DUOTECH, INC.
               SAN DIEGO, CA.
```

d.

CONT.	A	B	COBOL STATEMENT								
7|8	|12	16	20	24	28	32	36	40	44	48	
*		THIS PROGRAM SORTS EMPLOYEE RECORDS									
*		BY ANTICIPATED GROSS SALARY.									

e.

DATE-WRITTEN. JUNE 7, 1984.											

2.

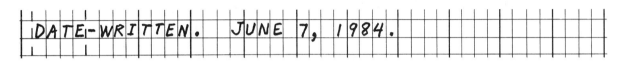

SEQUENCE		CONT.	A	B	COBOL STATEMENT							
(PAGE)	(SERIAL)											
1 3	4 6	7|8	|12	16	20	24	28	32	36	40	44	
		IDENTIFICATION DIVISION.										
		PROGRAM-ID. CH3L1AQ2.										
		AUTHOR. RUTH ASHLEY.										
		INSTALLATION. DUOTECH, INC.										
		SAN DIEGO, CA.										
		DATE-WRITTEN. 2/15/84.										
		DATE-COMPILED. 2/15/84.										
		SECURITY. THIS PROGRAM REQUIRES										
		NO SPECIAL CONSIDERATIONS.										

The Environment Division

The Environment Division is used to describe the computer and equipment required by the program. It is the most installation-dependent COBOL division.

Objectives   By the time you finish studying this lesson, you will be able to code a basic Environment Division for a COBOL program, including the Configuration Section and two of its paragraphs.

Rationale   The Environment Division is the second division in most COBOL programs. Many compilers have made the entire division optional for some programs. However, you will see Environment Division entries in most COBOL programs you encounter; thus, you need to know the basic coding of such entries.

Division Structure

The Environment Division can contain up to two sections. One section is needed only when the program uses files; we'll get to that section later in the book.

The other section is called the Configuration Section. It is used to provide the configuration (that is, the physical setup) of computers and peripheral equipment on which the program will run. It can also be used to provide special names for some devices.

Figure 3.3 shows the basic Environment Division structure for a program. The Input-Output Section is included only when a program uses files; it is shown here for completeness.

Figure 3.3 Basic Environment Division Structure

Format:
```
ENVIRONMENT DIVISION.
[CONFIGURATION SECTION.
[SOURCE-COMPUTER.  [source-computer-entry.]]
[OBJECT-COMPUTER.  [object-computer-entry.]]]
[INPUT-OUTPUT SECTION.
        file-related-entries]
```

Examples:
```
ENVIRONMENT DIVISION.
CONFIGURATION SECTION.
SOURCE-COMPUTER.  IBM-370.
OBJECT-COMPUTER.  IBM-370.

ENVIRONMENT DIVISION.
```

Notes:
1. The division header is required by most compilers, even if the rest of the division is omitted.
2. Some compilers allow the Configuration Section to be omitted.
3. Entries are computer-specific.
4. The Input-Output Section is used to describe files.

Many programmers write a basic Environment Division early in their careers, then simply copy it and modify it as needed as long as they remain at the same installation.

Division Header   The Environment Division header is generally required in a COBOL program; however, the entire division may be omitted in a few compilers. Like other headers, it must begin in area A, occupy a line by itself, and end with a period. Also, like other COBOL entries, it must be spelled correctly.

Configuration Section   The entire Configuration Section is optional in some compilers. If you code this section, code the section header on a separate line, beginning in area A.

Paragraphs in the Configuration Section   As you know, the program you write is called the source program. The computer on which a source program is compiled is called the source computer. The SOURCE-COMPUTER paragraph is used to name that computer. It might be IBM-370, ACS-8000, or any other name the compiler accepts. In many compilers you can enter anything you want in this paragraph, because the data is treated as a comment and used only for documentation.

Once the source program is compiled, an object program may be produced. This object module is executed by the object computer. The OBJECT-COMPUTER paragraph is used to name that computer.

Again, the name can be anything the compiler accepts. Some compilers accept any comment-entry here, but some are pickier. Since most programs are compiled and run on the same computer, you may have the same entry in each paragraph.

As you can tell from the format statement, you may use the section header without any paragraphs. You may also use either paragraph-name without any entry. If a computer name entry is used, it must be entirely within area B. If neither your compiler nor your installation standards require these paragraphs, you should omit them. The section and paragraph-names are not self-explanatory, so they may confuse more than they help.

Summary   In the Environment Division you code the entries required by your compiler or preferred by your installation. If you include the division, you must include the division header. Some compilers require a Configuration Section to describe the source and object computers. The SOURCE-COMPUTER paragraph in this section names the computer that will compile the program, and the OBJECT-COMPUTER paragraph names the computer that will execute the program. The Input-Output Section is used if the program involves files. You'll learn to use more Environment Division entries later in this book.

Comprehension Questions

1. Under what circumstances can you omit the Environment Division header?

   a. Never
   b. If the program uses no files
   c. If the compiler permits it and you're omitting the division
   d. If the program is to be compiled and run on the same computer
   e. Anytime you want

2. Under what circumstances can you omit the Configuration Section?

   a. Never
   b. If the program uses no files
   c. If the compiler permits it
   d. If the program is to be compiled and run on the same computer
   e. Anytime you want

3. Under what circumstances can you omit the name of the source computer?

   a. Never
   b. If the program uses no files
   c. If the compiler permits it
   d. If the program is to be compiled and run on the same computer
   e. Anytime you want

4. Which of the following shows a valid Environment Division?

```
a. ENVIRONMENT DIVISION.           c. ENVIRONMENT DIVISION.
                                      CONFIGURATION SECTION.


b. ENVIRONMENT DIVISION.
   SOURCE-COMPUTER. UNIVAC.
```

5. Get out your system's COBOL programmer's reference manual or installation standards and look up the Environment Division. Then answer these questions.

   a. Does your compiler require the Environment Division? _____

   b. Does it require the Configuration Section? _____

   c. Does it require the SOURCE-COMPUTER paragraph? _____
      If so, what name should you use for the source computer?

      _____

   d. Does it require the OBJECT-COMPUTER paragraph? _____
      If so, what name should you use for the object computer?

      _____

Answers

1. c **2.** c **3.** c **4.** a, c. b is wrong because you can't code the SOURCE-COMPUTER paragraph unless you code the Configuration Section header. **5.** The correct answers depend on your compiler and installation standards.

Application Questions

1. Code a header for the second division of a COBOL program.

SEQUENCE		CONT.	A	B	COBOL STATEMENT
(PAGE)	(SERIAL)				
1 3	4 6	7	8 12	16 20 24 28 32 36 40 44	

2. Code the header for the section that includes the name of the computer on which the program will be compiled.

SEQUENCE		CONT.	A	B	COBOL STATEMENT
(PAGE)	(SERIAL)				
1 3	4 6	7	8 12	16 20 24 28 32 36 40 44	

3. Code the entry that specifies that the program is to be compiled on an IBM-4341 computer.

SEQUENCE		CONT.	A	B	COBOL STATEMENT
(PAGE)	(SERIAL)				
1 3	4 6	7	8 12	16 20 24 28 32 36 40 44	

4. A program named CH3L2AQ4 is to be compiled and run on an IBM-370 computer. Code the first two divisions of the program, including information about the programmer.

SEQUENCE		CONT.	A	B	COBOL STATEMENT
(PAGE)	(SERIAL)				
1 3	4 6	7	8 12	16 20 24 28 32 36 40 44	

Answers

Again, be sure to check margins and periods.

1.

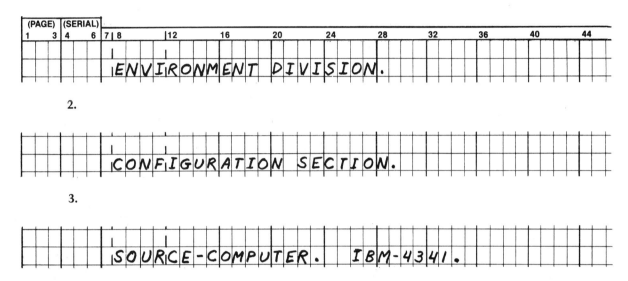

2.

3.

4.

SEQUENCE			CONT.	A	B								COBOL STATEMENT	
(PAGE)	(SERIAL)													
1	3	4	6	7	8	12	16	20	24	28	32	36	40	44

(Coding form contents:)

```
IDENTIFICATION DIVISION.
PROGRAM-ID. CH3L2AQ4.
AUTHOR.    RUTH ASHLEY
           FINANCE DEPARTMENT.

ENVIRONMENT DIVISION.
CONFIGURATION SECTION.
SOURCE-COMPUTER.  IBM-370.
OBJECT-COMPUTER.  IBM-370.
```

You could omit the last three lines. Check the layout, spacing, and punctuation, especially:

- Begin division headers, section headers, and paragraph names in area A.

- Keep other entries within area B.

- End each entry with a period.

- Use at least one space after each word and period.

- Be sure you included the hyphen if you coded SOURCE-COMPUTER or OBJECT-COMPUTER.

The Data Division

Storage must be allocated for all data that a program will use. Names must be given to any storage areas that will be referred to in the Procedure Division. The Data Division is used to reserve storage, assign names, and describe the layout of the data.

Objectives When you finish studying this lesson, you will be able to code descriptions of data items for use in a COBOL program. You'll also be able to create valid names for data items.

Rationale Every COBOL program requires at least some data. In this lesson you'll learn to code the basic structure of the Data Division, where every piece of data used by a program must be defined. This section deals with programs without files, so we're dealing with entries made in the Working-Storage Section, not the File Section, of the Data Division. However, as you'll learn later, much of what you learn here also applies to the File Section (as well as the other Data Division sections).

Overview of the Working-Storage Section

Almost every program uses some data that is not associated with files. This data is called **working** data. Since COBOL defines it in the Working-Storage Section, people who "speak" only COBOL tend to call it working-storage data.

Some examples of working-storage data are:

- Data to be used as input or output, but not associated with a file;

- Flags used to communicate control information between superior and subordinate routines;

- Intermediate results of computations — sums, products, etc. — stored in the process of calculating the final results;

- Counters used for administrative purposes, such as items that keep track of the number of lines that have been printed so far or the number of records that have been processed so far.

In a COBOL Data Division, storage space for file-associated input and output records must be defined in the File Section. Storage space for working data must be defined in the Working-Storage Section. In this lesson you will learn to define a Working-Storage Section.

Figure 3.4 Partial COBOL Program

```
IDENTIFICATION DIVISION.
PROGRAM-ID. CH3L3.
AUTHOR. R.ASHLEY.

ENVIRONMENT DIVISION.

DATA DIVISION.
WORKING-STORAGE SECTION.
77  END-SIGNAL        PIC X.
01  USER-NAME.
    05  FIRST-NAME     PIC X(12).
    05  LAST-NAME      PIC X(14).
```

COBOL Program Structure

Figure 3.4 shows the first part of a COBOL program, including the first three divisions, in order. The Data Division follows the Environment Division. Like all division headers, the Data Division header starts in area A, is terminated with a period, and occupies a line by itself.

The section header, WORKING-STORAGE SECTION, likewise starts in area A, is terminated with a period, and occupies a line by itself. The entries on the following lines define data items. The first is an **independent** data item. The last three lines represent a **data record**, which is subdivided into two data items.

COBOL Names

Since the Data Division is concerned with naming data, this is a good time to look at rules for naming.

You have to provide names for many items in a COBOL program; all can be referred to as programmer-supplied names. You name the program itself in the PROGRAM-ID paragraph. You also must provide names for every data item and paragraph you use in the Procedure Division, as well as for each file accessed by the program.

Naming Rules The general COBOL rules for forming data-names and paragraph-names are similar to the rules for forming program-names:

- Up to 30 characters

- Made up of letters, digits, hyphens

- Hyphen not first or last

- Data-names must contain at least one letter

- Not a COBOL reserved word

As you know, the compiler may use only the first six or eight characters of a program-name. It will use all the characters of any other names. Most of the names must be unique within the program. We'll give each data item a different name. You should use mnemonic names that will have meaning to human readers. These are all valid COBOL data-names; they can refer to items described in the Data Division:

WITHHOLDING-TAX

IN-LAST-NAME

OUT-ITEM-NUMBER

FIRST-PRINT-LINE

These are not valid COBOL data names:

999 (no letter)

MESSAGE-FOR-USE-IN-COMMUNICATING-WITH-USER (too long)

$AMOUNT (invalid character)

CONFIGURATION (reserved word)

When you create names, be as meaningful as possible without making your names so long you get writer's (or typist's) cramp. Figure 3.4 includes four names. You'll see many more examples of meaningful names as you continue this course.

Reserved Words Some words are reserved for the COBOL compiler to use. Any word that appears in capital letters in any COBOL format statement is a reserved word. You can't use words such as DIVISION, ENVIRONMENT, or DATA as data-names. You can use a name like INPUT-CUSTOMER-DATA, however, since that is not itself a reserved word.

Appendix B includes a list of words reserved by most COBOL compilers. The reference manual for each compiler includes a list of its reserved words. If you scan the list in the Appendix, you'll see that many common words, such as NUMBER, FILE, and ADDRESS, are reserved words. By adding a hyphen and an appropriate prefix or suffix, however, you can make unique names from those words, as in ACCOUNT-NUMBER, EMPLOYEE-FILE, and CUSTOMER-ADDRESS.

Data Item Format

You also need to tell the compiler how to store or interpret each data item. Unless you instruct the compiler otherwise, each character of data occupies one byte in storage (in byte-oriented machines). (This is character format, as described in *Introduction to Computer Programming*. In COBOL it is known as **display** format.) You specify how many bytes and the type of data with a PICTURE clause. Figure 3.4 includes some examples.

Picture-Entries Figure 3.5 shows the basic picture characters. Each of these specifies one byte of storage. X specifies any character at all, 9 specifies a numeric character, and A specifies an alphabetic character. If you use PICTURE XXX or PICTURE X(3), the data item is three bytes long. In most cases, such a data item holds three alphanumeric characters, such as "OUT", "YES", or "6AM". Actually, it can contain anything that fits in three bytes. Thus, you could use X to represent a one-character field, as in the first picture in Figure 3.4. You could use 9 to describe a field that will hold only one digit from 0 to 9, or A to describe a field that will hold either a letter from A to Z (either upper- or lowercase) or a space. In practice, character A is little used. We won't use it in this course.

Figure 3.5 Basic Picture-Entries

Picture character	Each byte contains		
X	Any data (alphanumeric)		
9	A valid digit (0-9)		
A	An alphabetic character (A-Z, space)		

Examples	Means	Valid	Invalid
XXX	3 characters	A#1	nothing
X(3)	3 characters	B27	nothing
99999	5 digits	12345	ABC45
9(5)	5 digits	00000	spaces
AAAA	4 alphabetic characters	ABCD	0ABC
AA99	4 characters	CA01	nothing
99XA	4 characters	16-B	nothing

An item may be described using more than one type of data character. You can describe a field as 99XX, for example. Such a picture would be considered to be alphanumeric by the compiler; it would be treated the same as X(4). You might as well define it with Xs.

You shouldn't write out repeated characters in a picture. XXXX is identical to X(4). X(6) is equivalent to XXXXXX. The abbreviated form is much easier for others to understand.

If you use Xs in a data item definition, the corresponding positions can contain any character. If you use only 9s or A's, errors will occur if the wrong data gets into the storage area for the item. It's most convenient to use Xs when it doesn't matter what the data is. We'll use X for most data in this book. (You'll learn later when it is important to use 9s. A's are never important and are almost never used in practice. We explained them because you may see them in other programs.)

Many additional picture characters can be used in arithmetic data as well as in preparing values for printing or console display, as you'll learn later. You'll need only X, and occasionally 9, in this book.

Some installations prefer that pictures be coded as X(01), X(02), etc. to simplify program maintenance. We will use repeat numbers for any length greater than 2; that is, we'll use XX and X(3). We will use X(3) rather than XXX because this makes the picture length more readily apparent to readers. You should adhere to your installation's guidelines in picture coding.

The PICTURE Clause   The picture-entry is coded as part of the PICTURE clause in the Data Division. Figure 3.6 shows the format of the PICTURE clause.

Notice that you can use either PIC or PICTURE to specify the clause. This book uses PIC for brevity in most programs. We'll use PICTURE in discussions and explanations whenever possible.

Refer to Figure 3.4 again to see the PICTURE clause in the context of the Data Division.

Independent Data Items

Data items in storage may be grouped together into records, or they may be independent. Independent data items stand alone and are not associated with their neighboring items in storage.

Figure 3.6 The PICTURE Clause

Format:

$$\left\{ \begin{array}{l} \underline{PICTURE} \\ \underline{PIC} \end{array} \right\} \ \text{IS picture-entry}$$

Examples:

```
PICTURE IS X(4)

PICTURE 9(4)

PIC X(12)
PIC 9(12)
```

Notes:

1. Use either PIC or PICTURE.
2. IS is optional.
3. Picture-entry shows the length and format of the data item.
4. Picture-entry is made up of Xs, 9s, As, and other characters.
5. Spaces within picture-entry are optional.

Some programming experts feel that all data items should be grouped according to use and placed in records; data-names are easier for other readers to locate that way. Even if your company has that policy, you'll still need to understand independent items when you see them in other people's programs.

Level Numbers Every data item has a **level number**. This is a number that indicates the item's position in a record. Independent data items are given the level number 77 to show that they do not belong to a record or group of items. Level number 77 is coded in area A, while the data-name is entirely within area B. In most compilers, level 77 items must be defined before any other items in the Working-Storage Section. Space in memory is reserved for these items first.

You'll group most data items into records with other related items; this simplifies program maintenance. Levels 01 through 49 are used for items grouped into records.

Data-Name The level number is followed by an entry that names the data item and describes its characteristics. The name must adhere to the rules for forming COBOL names.

Subdivided Data Items

Most data items are related to other items. A name, for example, can be subdivided into first and last names. A print record might be subdivided into individual items such as name, address, phone, balance, and so forth. You subdivide when you need to refer to a smaller item within a larger one. You can also group several data items into a larger one; for example, a program might use six different flags. These can be grouped together rather than defined as independent items. Again, the result is a large item subdivided into smaller ones.

Subdivided items must be defined as part of a data record. Figure 3.4 shows an example in which USER-NAME is subdivided into FIRST-NAME and LAST-NAME. This sets aside memory space that can be referred to as USER-NAME. The first part of that space can be referred to as FIRST-NAME and the second part as LAST-NAME.

Level 01   Each record description begins with level 01, which must be coded in area A. Many compilers allow you to omit leading zeros on level numbers. However, most programmers code them. The name you provide at level 01 is the **record-name**. In Figure 3.4 the record-name is USER-NAME.

Other Levels   In Figure 3.4 USER-NAME is subdivided into two data items named FIRST-NAME and LAST-NAME. We have given these level number 05; you could use 02, 03, 28, or anything up to level 49, as long as you use the same number for each item at the same level. It is very common to use 05 for the first level of subdivision, 10 for the next level, and so forth.

Here's how storage is laid out for the example in Figure 3.4.

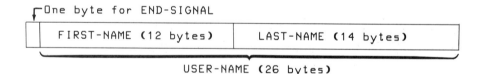

The data-name USER-NAME refers to 26 bytes; it includes both FIRST-NAME and LAST-NAME. USER-NAME is the record-name. Since it is subdivided, it is a **group item**. A group item is never defined with a PICTURE clause. Usually you just code the level number, the data-name, and a period for group items.

Items within a group that are not subdivided are called **elementary items**. FIRST-NAME and LAST-NAME are examples of elementary items. All level 77 items are also elementary items. Each elementary item must have a PICTURE clause. The combined pictures of its elementary items define the size and type of a group item.

Records can have more than two levels, but we'll stick to two for now. You'll learn to define more complex records later.

Defining Records   Suppose the data in another record is laid out like this:

PHONE-LISTINGS		
NAME	AREA-CODE	PHONE-NUMBER
20 characters	3 digits	7 digits

To define the record you need to know how many characters, and what type, make up each elementary item. Here's one way to define the record.

```
01   PHONE-LISTINGS.
     05  PHONE-NAME          PIC X(20).
     05  PHONE-AREA-CODE     PIC 9(3).
     05  PHONE-NUMBER        PIC 9(7).
```

The name PHONE-LISTINGS refers to 30 bytes of data. Notice that each elementary name is prefixed with PHONE-; this technique helps people reading the program to know what record the items belong to. We used level 05 for the elementary names; you could use any level number from 02 to 49 here.

Here's another example:

```
01   BIRTHDAY-FILE.
     05  BIRTHDAY-PERSON     PIC X(26).
     05  BIRTHDAY-SEX        PIC X.
     05  BIRTHDAY-MONTH      PIC 99.
     05  BIRTHDAY-DAY        PIC 99.
     05  BIRTHDAY-YEAR       PIC 99.
```

This record description represents a 33-byte record. The one below represents a 96-byte record. Here a third level is included.

```
01   MAILING-LABEL.
     05  MAIL-NAME           PIC X(24).
     05  MAIL-LINE-1         PIC X(24).
     05  MAIL-LINE-2         PIC X(24).
     05  MAIL-LINE-3.
         10   MAIL-CITY      PIC X(17).
         10   MAIL-STATE     PIC XX.
     05  MAIL-ZIP            PIC X(5).
```

Notice that the group items (MAILING-LABEL and MAIL-LINE-3) do not contain PICTURE clauses.

Defining Unreferenced Fields You must define every position in the record so the compiler can figure out the size of the group item, even though the Procedure Division may not use every position. For example, an input data record may contain only two fields you'll refer to, but you must reserve memory space for the entire record, or the system won't be able to read it properly. If you don't want to bother making up names for items you'll never refer to, you can use the reserved word FILLER to name unreferenced areas. Here's an example:

```
01  EMPLOYEE-DATA.
    05   FILLER            PIC   X(20).
    05   EMPLOYEE-CODE     PIC   9(6).
    05   FILLER            PIC   X(24).
    05   EMPLOYEE-AGE      PIC   99.
    05   FILLER            PIC   X(28).
```

This describes an 80-character record. In this program, EMPLOYEE-DATA will refer to all 80 characters. EMPLOYEE-CODE refers to bytes 21 through 26, and EMPLOYEE-AGE refers to bytes 51 and 52. Other positions cannot be referred to directly. The word FILLER can be used as often as needed in the Data Division, but it can never be referenced directly in the Procedure Division.

Data Division Structure

Now that you can code the details, let's look at the overall structure of the Data Division. Figure 3.7 shows the general format of the Data Division. The File Section is required only when the program accesses files; you'll learn to code it later.

The division header and section names begin in area A, as always. The word WORKING-STORAGE must include the hyphen. Levels 77 and 01 appear in area A. The rest of each data description entry, including other level numbers, appears in area B.

The spacing in data description entries can vary. COBOL requires at least one space separating any two elements. Any place you can use one space, you can use more than one. Most programmers follow a few spacing conventions (not rules) to make their Data Divisions more readable. They indent four spaces to start a new level; they leave two spaces after a level number so that the data-name begins four columns after the beginning of the level number; and they align all the PICTURE clauses. These conventions are used in examples throughout this course. Notice also that each data description entry ends with a period; this is required.

Figure 3.7 Structure of Data Division

Format:

```
DATA DIVISION.
[FILE SECTION.
[file-description-entry
{record-description-entry}...]...]
[WORKING-STORAGE SECTION.
[77  data-description-entry]...
[01  record-description-entry]...]
```

Examples:

```
DATA DIVISION.
WORKING-STORAGE SECTION.
77  SECRET-CODE            PICTURE X(4).
01  COMPANY-DATA.
    05  COMPANY-NAME       PICTURE X(20).
    05  COMPANY-PHONE      PICTURE X(10).


DATA DIVISION.
WORKING-STORAGE SECTION.
01  DEPARTMENT-VALUES.
    05  DEPARTMENT-NAME    PIC X(12).
    05  DEPARTMENT-NUMBER  PIC 9(3).
```

Notes:

1. Division and section headers begin in area A.
2. Levels 77 and 01 must be in area A.
3. Rest of data description may be in area B.
4. PIC or PICTURE describes each elementary data item.
5. A period ends the description of each item.

Data Item Definition Review

Every elementary data item definition includes at least these components: level number, data-name, and PICTURE clause. Let's look at some more examples.

A working-storage data item is needed to hold a two-character code to specify the state. You might use this entry:

```
01  STATE-CODE            PICTURE XX.
```

A working-storage data item is needed to hold the description of an auto accessory; the description can be up to 45 characters long. Also, a field to be used for counting the accessories must allow for a maximum value of 3000. Since these two items are related, they can be defined as one record. Here's one way to do it:

```
01  ACCESSORY-DETAILS
    05  ACCESSORY-DESCRIPTION    PICTURE X(45).
    05  ACCESSORY-COUNT          PICTURE 9(4).
```

Summary   This lesson has shown you how to define a Working-Storage Section in the Data Division. Independent items are elementary items that are not associated with any groups. They are defined as level 77, and their definitions must include PICTURE clauses. All level 77 definitions must precede all record definitions in working storage.

Items that belong to groups are placed in records. Often you can make items easier to locate by grouping them together in records. A record is defined starting at level 01. Subdivisions of the record are defined at levels from 02 through 49; it is common to code the first set of subdivisions on level 05, any subdivisions of the level 05 items on level 10, and so forth.

Items that are subdivided are called group items. Items that are not subdivided are called elementary items. Elementary items must be defined by a PICTURE clause; group items must not be.

Every item must be assigned a data-name, which is used in the Procedure Division to access that item. Data-names may be up to 30 characters long and may use letters, digits, and hyphens. They must contain at least one letter and may not start or end with a hyphen. They cannot be one of the COBOL reserved words. Make names as meaningful as possible, using prefixes and suffixes to show group relationships. FILLER may be used as the name for items that are not to be referenced by the Procedure Division.

The PICTURE clause defines the size and type of an elementary item. Xs indicate alphanumeric data, 9s indicate numeric data, and A's indicate alphabetic data. Numbers in parentheses may be used to indicate how many times the preceding picture character should be repeated.

All division and section headers begin in area A. Level numbers 01 and 77 must be entirely contained in area A. Everything else (all data-names and PICTURE clauses and all other level numbers) may be contained in area B. Use extra spaces to align descriptions to make them easier to read and to depict physically the subdivisions of a record.

Comprehension Questions

1. Independent data items are defined in:

　a. What division? _____

　b. What section? _____

2. What level number is used for:

　a. Independent data items? _____

　b. Record-names? _____

3. FILLER items are coded in which division(s)?

_____

4. Which of the following are valid names for COBOL data items?

　a. #TIME-OUT
　b. TIME-IN
　c. CELEBRATION-OF-TRICENTENNIAL-PLANNING-STATUS
　d. PLANNING-STATUS
　e. CONFIGURATION
　f. 555-1212

5. What is wrong with each invalid name in question 4? *Write "nothing" for those that are valid.*

　a. _____
　b. _____
　c. _____
　d. _____
　e. _____
　f. _____

6. Which are valid PICTURE clauses?

　a. PICTURE XX
　b. PIC X(28)
　c. PIC (28)X
　d. PIC 28(X)
　e. PIC XX

7. Which of these are valid values for a data item described with PIC X(4)?

　a. BILL
　b. 4798
　c. any value up to four bytes long

8. Which of these are valid values for a data item described with PIC 999?

   a. 000
   b. ƀƀƀ (spaces)
   c. 012
   d. CAT

9. Which of the elements below are coded beginning in area A?

   a. Data Division header
   b. Working-Storage Section header
   c. Level number 77
   d. Data-name
   e. PICTURE clause

10. Which of the following is a valid record description?

```
a.  77   USER-DATA.
         01    USER-CODE        PIC 9(4).
         01    USER-NAME        PIC X(25).

b.  01   USER-DATA.
         77    USER-CODE        PIC 9(4).
         77    USER-NAME        PIC X(25).

c.  01   USER-DATA.
         02    USER-CODE        PIC 9(4).
         05    USER-NAME        PIC X(25).

d.  01   USER-DATA.
         05    USER-CODE        PIC 9(4).
         05    USER-NAME        PIC X(25).
```

Answers

1. a. Data Division b. Working-Storage Section   **2.** a. 77 b. 01   **3.** Data Division only   **4.** b, d   **5.** a. Contains an invalid character (#) c. More than 30 characters e. Reserved word f. doesn't contain a letter   **6.** a, b, e   **7.** a, b, c (any value that will fit in four bytes)   **8.** a, c   **9.** a, b, c   **10.** d. Here's what's wrong with the others: a - 1) An independent item cannot be subdivided. 2) Level 77 items must be defined with PICTURE clauses. 3) Level number 01 must be contained in area A. b - 1) A record cannot contain level 77 items, which must be independent. 2) All level 77 definitions must precede all record (level 01) definitions. 3) Level number 77 must be contained within area A. c - USER-NAME has a higher level number than USER-CODE, meaning that it is a subdivision of USER-CODE. Thus, USER-CODE is a group item and must not have a PICTURE clause.

Application Questions

1. Code picture specifications for the following:

   a. A city name field that must hold names as long as "San Bernardino".

   _____

   b. A quantity field that must contain a numeric value up to 8500.

   _____

2. Code an elementary data item definition (level 05) for a first name field. Allow for a first name as long as 15 letters.

3. Code an independent data item definition for a one-byte flag that will be used to indicate the end of file.

4. Code a record description to be laid out like this:

INVENTORY-DATA		
PART-NUMBER	PART-NAME	QUANTITY
6 characters	15 characters	3 digits

5. Code the entries needed to define a Data Division and specify two elementary data items. One describes a six-character date. The other describes a one-character inquiry code.

6. Code a 70-byte record description to be laid out like this:

BOOK-DATA					
Call Number	Author	Title	Quantity must be digits	Condition	Other
1 6	7 30	31 60	61 62	63 65	66 70

The program will refer to only the title and quantity fields.

Answers

1. a. X(14) b. 9(4) (9999 is also correct, but the abbreviation is preferred)

2. `05  FIRST-NAME        PIC X(15).`

You could use a different data-name. You could use PICTURE [IS] instead of PIC.

3. `77 END-OF-FILE-FLAG        PIC X.`

4.
```
01   INVENTORY-DATA.
     05   INVENTORY-PART-NUMBER    PIC X(6).
     05   INVENTORY-PART-NAME      PIC X(15).
     05   INVENTORY-QUANTITY       PIC 9(3).
```

5.
```
DATA DIVISION.
WORKING-STORAGE SECTION.
01   SPECIAL-FIELDS.
     05   DATE-FIELD          PIC X(6).
     05   INQUIRY-CODE        PIC X.
```

The division and section headers must be on separate lines. Each must begin in area A and be terminated by a period. Level number 01 must be within area A. All data-names and other levels must be within area B. You could use PICTURE instead of PIC. You could include IS. You could use a string of Xs instead of the abbreviation. Each data description entry must be terminated with a period. Be sure you didn't use DATE as a data-name.

6.
```
01   BOOK-DATA.
     05   FILLER             PIC X(30).
     05   BOOK-TITLE         PIC X(30).
     05   BOOK-QUANTITY      PIC 99.
     05   FILLER             PIC X(8).
```

You could also code it like this:

```
01   BOOK-DATA.
     05   FILLER             PIC X(6).
     05   FILLER             PIC X(24).
     05   BOOK-TITLE         PIC X(30).
     05   BOOK-QUANTITY      PIC 99.
     05   FILLER             PIC X(3).
     05   FILLER             PIC X(5).
```

Alternatively, you could have used unique data-names for each field.

Chapter Review Questions

1. What paragraph is required in the Identification Division?

   _____

2. What Environment Division section can you use to define the computer(s) the program is intended for?

   _____

3. Suppose your installation requires that you code the name of the computer on which the program will be compiled. What paragraph would you use?

   _____

4. In what Data Division section do you define data items that are not associated with files?

   _____

5. What level number would you code to indicate each of these:

   a. Independent data item   _____

   b. Record   _____

   c. Subdivision of a record   _____

   d. Elementary data item   _____

6. Code picture specifications for each of these:

   a. A name field that will hold 40 characters _____

   b. A date field that will hold a date in this format: 01/28/83

   _____

   c. A year field that will hold four digits _____

   d. An employee-code field that will hold nine digits _____

7. Which of these data-names are valid?

   a. EMPLOYEE-#
   b. EMPLOYEE NUMBER
   c. EMPLOYEE-NUMBER
   d. 67890
   e. THE-OFFICIAL-EMPLOYEE-IDENTIFICATION-NUMBER

8. Give the reason each invalid name above isn't valid.

   a. _____

   b. _____

   c. _____

   d. _____

   e. _____

9. You need to define a record and an independent data item for a program. Here's the record format:

CUSTOMER-DATA			
Unused	Last Name	First Name	Unused
1 20	21 35	36 47	48 70

The independent item is a code field that holds three digits. Write the complete Data Division.

10. Code complete Identification and Environment Divisions for a program to be called CH3REV, which will be compiled and executed on a PDP-11. The program uses no files. Code every possible paragraph.

SEQUENCE		CONT.	A	B	COBOL STATEMENT
(PAGE)	(SERIAL)				
1 3	4 6	7 8	12	16 20 24 28 32 36 40 44	

11. What is wrong with each set of lines below? (Assume each starts in the appropriate area.)

```
a. IDENTIFICATION DIVISION.
   AUTHOR.  RUTH ASHLEY.
   PROGRAM-ID.  RA733.
```

```
b. ENVIROMENT DIVISION.
   CONFIGURATION SECTION.
   SOURCE-COMPUTER.  3033.
```

```
c. DATA DIVISION.
   WORKING STORAGE SECTION.
   01    INPUT-INVENTORY.
```

```
d. 01    MEMBERSHIP-RECORD       PIC X(80).
      05    MEMBER-NAME          PIC X(24).
      05    MEMBER-NUMBER        PIC 9(3).
```

Answers

1. PROGRAM-ID 2. CONFIGURATION SECTION 3. SOURCE-COMPUTER 4. WORKING-STORAGE SECTION 5. a. 77 b. 01 c. 05 (or any level number from 02 through 49) d. anything from 01 through 49 6. a. X(40) b. X(8) or 99X99X99 c. 9(4) or 9999 d. 9(9) 7. c 8. a. invalid character (#) b. invalid character (space) d. needs a letter e. too long

9.
```
DATA DIVISION.
 WORKING-STORAGE SECTION.

 77   CODE-FIELD       PIC   999.
 01   CUSTOMER-DATA.
      05   FILLER       PIC   X(20).
      05   LAST-NAME    PIC   X(15).
      05   FIRST-NAME   PIC   X(12).
      05   FILLER       PIC   X(23).
```

10.
```
IDENTIFICATION DIVISION.
 PROGRAM-ID.  CH3REV.
 AUTHOR.   YOUR NAME.
 INSTALLATION.   YOUR INSTALLATION.
 DATE-WRITTEN.   TODAY'S DATE.
 DATE-COMPILED.   ANYTHING YOU WANT.
 SECURITY.   NONE.

 ENVIRONMENT DIVISION.
 CONFIGURATION SECTION.
 SOURCE-COMPUTER.   PDP-11.
 OBJECT-COMPUTER.   PDP-11.
```

11. a. PROGRAM-ID paragraph must be first. b. ENVIRONMENT is spelled wrong. c. WORKING-STORAGE must contain a hyphen. d. Group items (MEMBERSHIP-RECORD) don't get a PICTURE clause.

Chapter 4

Sequence Structures in the Procedure Division

You have learned to code basic entries in the first three divisions of a COBOL program. These entries are useless without the Procedure Division. This chapter teaches you the basic entries for the Procedure Division. You'll learn to code the statements needed for simple sequence structures.

File processing requires a great deal more coding than the statements you'll be using here. After you have successfully run a program that uses no files, you'll be in a better position to deal with the intricacies of file handling.

This chapter consists of five lessons:

Lesson 4.1: Procedure Division Concepts
Lesson 4.2: A Sequence Structure in COBOL
Lesson 4.3: Using Constants in COBOL Programs
Lesson 4.4: The MOVE Statement
Lesson 4.5: ACCEPT and DISPLAY Statement Options

Procedure Division Concepts

The Procedure Division is the heart of a COBOL program. The program's logic is encoded into the statements of the Procedure Division.

Objectives You will be able to code the beginning of a Procedure Division, recognize a correctly formatted Procedure Division, and create valid paragraph-names.

Rationale The format and structure of the Procedure Division are the environment in which you will build your sequence, decision, and repetition structures.

Procedure Division Structure

As you know, the Procedure Division is the last division of a COBOL program. It may contain sections and paragraphs. You won't be using sections until very late in this course. Every Procedure Division, however, includes paragraphs. Every paragraph includes one or more statements, most of which may have optional clauses.

Paragraphs As the programmer, you are responsible for providing paragraph-names. These names are formed according to the standard COBOL naming rules you've already learned, except they needn't start with a letter. You'll be able to convert pseudocode routine names to paragraph-names. Figure 4.1 shows an example. Keep the names meaningful, and use hyphens liberally.

Many programmers like to begin each paragraph-name with a hierarchical number, such as 0000-MAIN-LOGIC, 1000-PROCESS-RECORDS, and 1100-READ-RECORD. The paragraphs are stored in numerical order in a manner similar to the system we have been using for pseudocode. This shows where paragraphs fit into programs and helps readers find subordinate routines in a long listing. We'll use numbered paragraphs later in the course when the programs are quite long.

Every statement in the Procedure Division must be included in a paragraph. This means that your first entry following the division header must be a paragraph-name. Like the division header, paragraph-names must begin in area A.

Figure 4.1 Naming Paragraphs

Pseudocode	Paragraph-names
0 - Control routine	CONTROL-ROUTINE
set up files	
read one record	
DO UNTIL no more records	
list records (1)	
ENDO	
close files	
STOP	
1 - List records	LIST-RECORDS
write record	
read one record	READ-ONE-RECORD

Statements   COBOL statements in the Procedure Division always start with a COBOL verb, such as ADD, PERFORM, MOVE, or IF. (Although IF isn't a verb in English, the COBOL compiler treats it as a verb.) You'll learn how and why to code statements throughout this course.

Each COBOL statement is either imperative or conditional. An **imperative** statement specifies an unconditional action, such as MOVE or ADD. A **conditional** statement includes a condition that determines whether some action is carried out. IF is the classic example of a conditional statement, but COBOL has others as well.

The difference between imperative and conditional statements is important in both control logic and punctuation. You don't need to include a period after each imperative statement; control will automatically continue to the next statement in sequence. Period placement is critical following conditional statements, however, since the system needs to know how much to skip if the condition is false.

Conditional statements frequently combine with imperative statements to form sentences. For example:

```
IF PARTS-ON-HAND GREATER THAN CUT-OFF-POINT
   ADD 1 TO OVER-SUPPLY-COUNT.
```

Here IF is a conditional statement that determines whether the imperative statement (ADD) will be executed. The period at the end of the ADD statement marks the end of the IF statement also.

A COBOL **sentence** is a series of one or more statements that ends with a period. Even a single statement is a sentence if it ends with a period. The example above is more properly referred to as an IF sentence, but you can use common jargon and call such sentences IF statements.

Relation to Pseudocode

The pseudocode you use in designing a program can be translated into COBOL statements that become the Procedure Division. The detail with which the pseudocode is written determines how easy the translation is. Extremely detailed pseudocode can result in a line-for-line COBOL Procedure Division. Vague pseudocode will require much thought and more coding. Most beginning programmers find it more efficient to be quite detailed in pseudocode. The detail you need will decrease as you get more experienced (although you will still want the detail for walkthroughs). You'll always need to detail the control logic, however, even when you don't itemize processing details.

Figure 4.2 shows the program structure and the pseudocode from Figure 4.1 with the corresponding Procedure Division. Don't get caught up in the statement details, but notice that most pseudocode lines result in a single COBOL statement.

Coding the Procedure Division

Notice how the coding is laid out in Figure 4.2. Paragraph-names begin in area A. The indentation corresponds to that in the pseudocode. As long as each statement is entirely within area B, any indentation is permissible.

Notice that each word is separated from the next by at least one space. Notice, too, that only one statement or major part of a statement is coded on each line. This not only makes the program easy to read but also means that each line number refers to a specific statement or clause. This can help with debugging.

We have included a period after each statement. While this isn't essential to coding, it is a good practice.

Notice the paragraph-names again. Each PERFORM statement calls a paragraph by name. The name must be spelled exactly the same when referenced as when used to label the paragraph. Otherwise, the compiler won't be able to locate the paragraph referred to. Each letter, digit, and hyphen is critical. Avoid abbreviations. If you must abbreviate, be consistent; don't use STU as an abbreviation for "student" in one place in a program and STUD or STDNT in another. It also helps if abbreviations are pronounceable.

Using Data Items in the Procedure Division

The sample Procedure Division in Figure 4.2 refers to data items that have been defined in the Data Division. Every data item a program refers to must be defined. Every data-name must be spelled exactly

Figure 4.2 Pseudocode-to-COBOL Translation

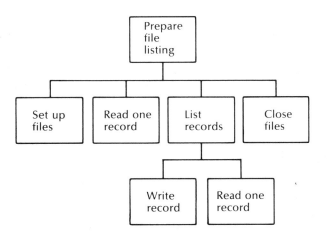

```
0 - Control routine
        set up files
        read one record
        DO UNTIL no more records
            list records (1)
        ENDO
        close files
        STOP
1 - List records
        write record
        read one record
```

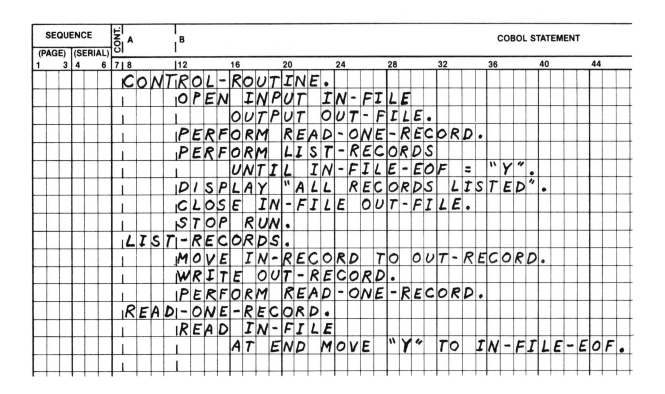

SEQUENCE		CONT.	A	B	COBOL STATEMENT

```
CONTROL-ROUTINE.
        OPEN INPUT IN-FILE
             OUTPUT OUT-FILE.
        PERFORM READ-ONE-RECORD.
        PERFORM LIST-RECORDS
             UNTIL IN-FILE-EOF = "Y".
        DISPLAY "ALL RECORDS LISTED".
        CLOSE IN-FILE OUT-FILE.
        STOP RUN.
LIST-RECORDS.
        MOVE IN-RECORD TO OUT-RECORD.
        WRITE OUT-RECORD.
        PERFORM READ-ONE-RECORD.
READ-ONE-RECORD.
        READ IN-FILE
             AT END MOVE "Y" TO IN-FILE-EOF.
```

the same wherever it is defined or used. Here again, if you must abbreviate, be very consistent in your abbreviations.

If a statement refers to any undefined data items, the compiler will refuse to compile the program. It will list messages indicating which data-names could not be found.

Programming Practices

Unfortunately, most COBOL code can be written and compiled without concern for good programming style and practices. This is especially true in simple programs such as those you'll be learning to code in the early part of this book. It is not so true in complex programs.

You'll see well-structured code, meaningful names, and clearly laid out structures in all examples and sample answers. Your coding may be different and still be correct. However, we suggest you adhere to the style shown, at least during the learning phase of your programming career; and if you want to get ahead, learn your company's programming standards and stick to them.

Summary   The Procedure Division contains statements that are organized into paragraphs (and perhaps sections). Each statement begins with a COBOL verb. Imperative statements specify direct actions. Conditional statements include a condition that controls execution. A series of one or more statements terminated by a period is a sentence. Imperative statements need not end with a period, but conditional statements must always do so.

You can translate from detailed pseudocode almost directly into COBOL. Less detailed pseudocode might take a little more work.

Names used in the Procedure Division must have been defined in the Data Division and must be spelled consistently. The compiler will reject any programs that contain undefined names.

As you study, try to develop good programming practices. Copy the style used here and learn your company's standards.

Comprehension Questions

1. Identify the coding rules that apply to each of the following. *More than one may apply.*

   _____ A. Procedure Division header   a. Always followed by a period.

   _____ B. Paragraph-name   b. Space separates adjacent words

   _____ C. Statement   c. Begins in area A

   _____ D. Sentence   d. Completely in area B

2. Which of the following is true?

   a. A conditional statement is executed if no condition is specified.
   b. A conditional statement may include an imperative statement.
   c. An imperative statement is always executed, even if it occurs within a conditional statement.

3. Pseudocode can be translated into entries for the:

   a. Identification Division
   b. Environment Division
   c. Data Division
   d. Procedure Division

4. Suppose a Data Division contains only this coding:

```
01   INDIVIDUAL-DATA.
     05   FIRST-NAME      PICTURE X(12).
     05   LAST-NAME       PICTURE X(12).
     05   PRESENT-AGE     PICTURE 99.
```

   Which of the following could be referenced in the Procedure Division?

   a. NAME-FIRST
   b. AGE
   c. PRESENT AGE
   d. LAST-NAME

Answers

1. A. a, b, c B. a, c (No spaces are allowed in names.) C. b, d D. a, b, d **2.** b **3.** d
4. d (Identical spelling is required.)

Application Questions

1. Code the first two lines of a Procedure Division below. Create a valid paragraph-name.

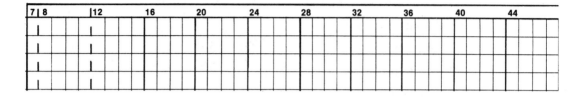

2. Suppose you want to use a data item called STREET-ADDRESS in the Procedure Division. Where would you define the item?

_____

3. Which of the following could be correct coding to begin the Procedure Division?

a. ```
PROCEDURE DIVISION.
FIRST-PARAGRAPH.
PERFORM SET-UP-FILES.
```

b. ```
PROCEDURE DIVISION.
    FIRST-PARAGRAPH.
    PERFORM SET-UP-FILES.
```

c. ```
PROCEDURE DIVISION.
FIRST-PARAGRAPH.
    PERFORM SET-UP-FILES.
```

**4.** Name a paragraph that would be included in the Procedure Division correctly begun above.

_____

**Answers**

**1.** ```
PROCEDURE DIVISION
FIRST-PARAGRAPH-NAME.
```

Be sure you started each line in area A.

2. Data Division   **3.** c. Here's what's wrong with the others: a - The PERFORM statement must be indented to start in area B. b - The FIRST-PARAGRAPH paragraph-name must start in area A.   **4.** FIRST-PARAGRAPH or SET-UP-FILES

A Sequence Structure in COBOL

In this lesson you'll learn to code a complete COBOL Procedure Division using a sequence structure; that is, a structure in which the statements will be executed in the sequence they are coded. All statements will be imperative statements.

Every COBOL program involves input and output. In this chapter you'll use statements for low-volume I/O, not using files.

Objectives When you finish this lesson, you'll be able to code a complete COBOL sequence structure using low-volume I/O. You'll be able to code simple forms of these statements: ACCEPT, DISPLAY, STOP RUN, and GOBACK.

Rationale ACCEPT and DISPLAY statements are used in many programs to handle low-volume I/O. DISPLAY is especially common as a way to print messages. Every program ends with a STOP RUN or GOBACK statement. When you have learned to code these statements, you will be able to code a complete (though short) COBOL program.

The DISPLAY Statement

The DISPLAY statement is used to display a message or value. In most cases the output appears on the system printer. You'll learn later to control where the output is displayed.

Figure 4.3 shows the basic format of the DISPLAY statement. You can display a literal or the value of a data item from memory. To display the value of a data item, you use its data-name in the DISPLAY statement. The data-name must have been defined in the Data Division.

Figure 4.3 Basic DISPLAY Statement

Format:

```
DISPLAY  { literal   } ...
         { data-name }
```

Examples:

```
DISPLAY "GOOD MORNING"
DISPLAY CURRENT-VALUE.
DISPLAY "GOOD MORNING, "  FIRST-NAME.
DISPLAY PART-NUMBER " IS NOT AVAILABLE.".
DISPLAY FIRST-NAME LAST-NAME CURRENT-AGE.
```

Notes:
1. Literal may be anything enclosed in quotes.
2. The value of any defined data-name may be displayed.
3. You can use a comma and/or space to separate literals and data-names.

The COBOL compiler uses the Data Division to determine exactly what memory addresses are associated with a data-name. The contents of those addresses are displayed whenever the DISPLAY statement is executed.

At this point, consider a literal to be anything at all that you enclose in quotes (except another quote). You'll learn more about literals in the next lesson.

Notice the examples in the figure. The first example shows a literal; when it is executed, the words GOOD MORNING will be printed on the printer.

When the second example is executed, the value of the data item CURRENT-VALUE will be printed, but the name of the item won't be. Suppose the compiler has determined that the name CURRENT-VALUE refers to memory addresses 1020 through 1024. Suppose that those bytes contain 15432 when the DISPLAY statement is executed. The value 15432 will be printed on the printer.

You can combine literals and data-names in one DISPLAY statement. You might want to do this to label items being displayed, a very friendly thing to do. For example, you could use DISPLAY "THE CURRENT VALUE IS " CURRENT-VALUE instead of just displaying CURRENT-VALUE. Then the output would be THE CURRENT VALUE IS 15432. Notice the trailing space in the literal. This ensures that a space appears before the value in the printed result; otherwise the output would be THE CURRENT VALUE IS15432, which isn't easy to read.

In a DISPLAY statement you may want to use a literal longer than the B area. The easiest way to deal with this is to divide a long literal into several shorter ones and code the separate literals on separate lines. Here's an example:

```
DISPLAY "THE RESULT OF THE UPDATE OPERATION "
        "WAS NOT SUCCESSFUL.  CHECK OUT THE "
        "INPUT DATA.".
```

This message will appear on a single line. Notice how trailing spaces ensure proper spacing when the three literals are printed one after the other.

Examine the fourth example in Figure 4.3 carefully. Notice the periods before and after the ending quote. The period before the quote is part of the literal and will be displayed. To the compiler, this period is simply another character to be displayed; the compiler does not see it as a period that ends the DISPLAY sentence. That's why another period follows the quote.

The ACCEPT Statement

The ACCEPT statement is used to receive low-volume input from a device. Your compiler determines what device to use. Large systems, which tend to be batch-oriented, may accept data by reading one record from the system's main input device. In the old days this device was usually a card reader. Nowadays it's frequently a disk file or disk input queue that holds card-image records. Most microcomputers, which tend to be online-oriented, accept input directly from the user at the terminal. This isn't feasible in large batch systems, where one slow user could tie up the system for an unreasonable time. Some installations do not permit you to use ACCEPT to receive input data from the user. We won't ask you to use ACCEPT in programs you will run, but you should know how it works.

Figure 4.4 shows the basic format of the ACCEPT statement. Notice that you provide one or more data-names here; no literals are allowed. Some compilers restrict you to a single data-name per AC-CEPT statement.

Figure 4.4 Basic ACCEPT Statement

Format:
```
ACCEPT {data-name}...
```

Examples:
```
ACCEPT PART-NUMBER.
ACCEPT FIRST-NAME LAST-NAME.
ACCEPT AMOUNT-PAID, AMOUNT-OWED, AMOUNT-LEFT.
```

Notes:
1. Data-names must be defined in the Data Division.
2. Use commas or spaces to separate data-names.

Assigning Values to Data Items   Suppose the Data Division includes these definitions:

```
01  CURRENT-AGE          PICTURE 99.
01  USER-NAME.
    05  FIRST-NAME       PICTURE X(12).
    05  LAST-NAME        PICTURE X(12).
```

The statement ACCEPT CURRENT-AGE would cause data to be read from the main input device. The first two characters would be assigned to CURRENT-AGE. Anything else in the input data is ignored. If those two characters aren't digits, there may be problems.

The statement ACCEPT FIRST-NAME LAST-NAME also causes data to be read from the input device. Now the first 24 characters are read; the first 12 are assigned to FIRST-NAME, the last 12 to LAST-NAME. You can get the same effect with ACCEPT USER-NAME.

Here are some sample records; assume that each contains spaces on the right to fill out the 24 positions.

```
RUTH ASHLEY
AGAMEMNON SHARPO
```

When the first record is accepted, "RUTH ASHLEY " is assigned to FIRST-NAME. Twelve spaces are assigned to LAST-NAME. When the second record is accepted, "AGAMEMNON SH" is assigned to FIRST-NAME and "ARPO   " is assigned to LAST-NAME. The values accepted are assigned to data items based on length only; thus, you must be cautious in preparing data for input via ACCEPT statements.

Data Format   When data items are described with Xs, they can hold any characters. If they are described with only 9s or A's, however, you need to be careful of the data you assign to them. For instance, in the preceding examples, CURRENT-AGE is defined with 99. ACCEPT CURRENT-AGE will assign two characters from the next line of the input device to CURRENT-AGE. However, in many systems they must be *numeric*; that is, they must be digits. (The user might be able to include a sign and/or decimal point. We'll discuss that later.)

Different systems respond in different ways to invalid ACCEPT data. Some systems will ignore the problem, store the data, and move right along to the next statement. Others will cause the program to bomb. This is just one reason why we won't ask you to use ACCEPT to receive user-entered data in this course.

One way to avoid such problems is to define all ACCEPT fields with Xs, validate the input data in your program, and handle invalid data by displaying appropriate reject messages. You'll want to display messages that mean more than "INVALID DATA TYPE".

Some online-oriented systems that accept data directly from users do very interactive processing. If the user enters invalid data, they automatically display an error message and wait for the user to re-enter the data. Systems like this make it very easy to accept numeric and alphabetic data.

If ACCEPT is used in your installation, you should learn exactly how it functions and how you can use it.

The STOP RUN Statement

Each program needs an ending; STOP RUN is the standard last logical line in a COBOL program. Figure 4.5 shows the STOP RUN statement.

Figure 4.5 STOP RUN Statement

Format:
```
STOP RUN.
```

Example:
```
STOP RUN.
```

Notes:
1. STOP RUN terminates the program.
2. Some systems require that you use GOBACK instead.

Some installations, because of other programs that are running at the same time, require that you use GOBACK instead of STOP RUN. GOBACK returns control to a higher-level program instead of just terminating the current program. STOP RUN is used in this course, but use GOBACK if your installation prefers.

Complete Program

Now let's look at a complete program and see how the statements covered in this lesson are used in it. Figure 4.6 shows the program and the data to be accepted.

Figure 4.6 Sample Program

Program:

```
IDENTIFICATION DIVISION.
PROGRAM-ID.  CH4L2.

ENVIRONMENT DIVISION.

DATA DIVISION.
WORKING-STORAGE SECTION.
01  PART-DATA.
    05  PART-NUMBER     PIC 9(5).
    05  PART-NAME       PIC X(30).

PROCEDURE DIVISION.
SHOW-LINE.
    DISPLAY "THIS IS A SAMPLE PROGRAM.".
    ACCEPT PART-DATA.
    DISPLAY " ".
    DISPLAY "THE NUMBER OF " PART-NAME
            " IS " PART-NUMBER.
    STOP RUN.
```

Data:

```
03700PHILLIPS-HEAD SCREWDRIVER
```

Notice that the Procedure Division begins with a paragraph-name. When this program is run, here is what will appear on the printer:

```
THIS IS A SAMPLE PROGRAM.
(blank line)
THE NUMBER OF PHILLIPS-HEAD SCREWDRIVER      IS 03700
```

Notice that each DISPLAY statement starts a new line on the output device, so that if you specify a single space as the only item to be displayed, the output is a blank line.

When the ACCEPT statement is executed, the value of the data is stored in the area reserved for PART-DATA. The first five characters are associated with the name PART-NUMBER, while the next 30 are associated with the name PART-NAME. Extra spaces may follow a value. If only 25 characters of data are accepted into PART-NAME, the rest of the field (on the right) is automatically filled with blanks. The entire item, including the blanks, is then displayed.

Notice that the group name is used in the ACCEPT statement and elementary names in the DISPLAY statement. ACCEPT PART-NUMBER PART-NAME would be valid in most compilers; the effect would have been the same. On the other hand, the elementary names must be used in the DISPLAY statement to rearrange the two values.

Summary The four COBOL statements you studied in this lesson accomplish three important program functions: input, output, and termination. ACCEPT reads one record from an input device designated by the compiler. ACCEPT is not used in many installations, but you may see it in programs. DISPLAY writes a message or data item value on an output device designated by the compiler. STOP RUN terminates the program; your installation may prefer to use GOBACK for this purpose.

Comprehension Questions

1. Which of the following can be specified in an ACCEPT statement?

   a. A quoted literal
   b. A data-name
   c. STOP RUN

2. Which of the following can be specified in a DISPLAY statement?

   a. A quoted literal
   b. A data-name
   c. STOP RUN

3. Which of the following statements are coded correctly?

   a. STOPRUN.
   b. ACCEPT "NAME"
   c. ACCEPT STREET, CITY.
   d. DISPLAY "NAME: ", USER-NAME.
   e. DISPLAY NUMBER-OF-ACCESSORIES-CURRENTLY-IN-STOCK.

4. Where will data resulting from DISPLAY appear?

   a. On the main printer
   b. At the operator's console
   c. On the user's terminal
   d. It depends on the compiler

5. Where does the ACCEPT statement look for data?

   a. The operator's console
   b. The user's terminal
   c. The system card reader
   d. It depends on the compiler

6. What will the statement DISPLAY "NEW-ITEM" cause to be displayed?

   a. The word NEW-ITEM
   b. The value of the memory area defined as NEW-ITEM in the Data Division
   c. An error message

7. What will the statement DISPLAY NEW-ITEM cause to be displayed?

   a. The word NEW-ITEM
   b. The value of the memory area defined as NEW-ITEM in the Data Division
   c. An error message

8. Suppose the memory area called NEW-ITEM currently has a value of 416. What will be displayed by the statement DISPLAY "NEW-ITEM" NEW-ITEM?

   a. NEW-ITEM 416
   b. NEW-ITEM416
   c. 416NEW-ITEM
   d. 416 NEW-ITEM
   e. 416 416
   f. 416416
   g. An error message

9. Suppose INPUT-YEAR is defined with PICTURE 9(4). If the statement ACCEPT INPUT-YEAR is processed and the input value is ABCD, what will happen?

    a. ABCD will be stored in the memory area assigned to INPUT-YEAR, and the system will go on to the next statement.

    b. The program will be terminated with a DATA TYPE error message.

    c. The input data will be rejected; the system will display an error message and accept another input value.

    d. Any of the above might happen; it depends on the compiler.

10. Suppose you want to display the words STUDENT NAME: on one line and the value of STUDENT-NAME on the next line, like this:

```
STUDENT NAME:
ELEANOR MARTINSON
```

Which of the following routines is correct?

```
a. DISPLAY "STUDENT NAME:" STUDENT-NAME.
b. DISPLAY "STUDENT NAME:" " " STUDENT-NAME.
c. DISPLAY "STUDENT NAME:".
   DISPLAY STUDENT-NAME.
d. DISPLAY "STUDENT NAME:"
          STUDENT-NAME.
```

11. Rewrite the preceding correct answer so a blank line will be displayed before the student name, like this:

```
STUDENT NAME:

LEROY CANTONELLI
```

_____

_____

_____

12. Suppose you want to display the words PAGE NUMBER: followed on the same line by the value of the PAGE-NUMBER field. A space should separate the colon and the first digit of the PAGE-NUMBER field, as in PAGE NUMBER: 241.

    Which of the following routines would do it? _More than one is correct._

```
a. DISPLAY "PAGE NUMBER: " PAGE-NUMBER.
b. DISPLAY "PAGE NUMBER:" PAGE-NUMBER.
c. DISPLAY "PAGE NUMBER:" " " PAGE-NUMBER.
d. DISPLAY "PAGE NUMBER:", PAGE-NUMBER.
e. DISPLAY "PAGE NUMBER:"
          PAGE-NUMBER.
f. DISPLAY "PAGE NUMBER:".
   DISPLAY " ".
   DISPLAY PAGE-NUMBER.
```

13. You want to display this message:

```
PLEASE CONTACT YOUR SUPERVISOR.
```

Notice that the message ends with a period. Which of the following statements is correct?

```
a. DISPLAY "PLEASE CONTACT YOUR SUPERVISOR"
b. DISPLAY "PLEASE CONTACT YOUR SUPERVISOR.".
c. DISPLAY "PLEASE CONTACT YOUR SUPERVISOR".
```

14. Suppose your Data Division contains these definitions:

```
01  USER-DATA.
    05  USER-CODE      PIC X(5).
    05  USER-NAME      PIC X(10).
```

Your Procedure Division contains these statements:

```
ACCEPT USER-DATA.
DISPLAY USER-CODE.
DISPLAY USER-NAME.
```

The input record looks like this:

```
FERNANDEZ 10125
```

a. What will be displayed by DISPLAY USER-CODE?

b. What will be displayed by DISPLAY USER-NAME?

15. Which of the following will print a single row of 80 asterisks?

```
a. DISPLAY "........................................................................".
b. DISPLAY ".............................................."
           "..............................................".
c. DISPLAY "*"(80).
```

Answers

1. b **2.** a, b **3.** c, d. Here's what's wrong with the others: a - STOP RUN is two words. b - You cannot ACCEPT a literal. e - This data-name is longer than 30 characters. **4.** d **5.** d **6.** a **7.** b **8.** b **9.** d **10.** c. Here's what's wrong with the others: a - Since they're both in the same DISPLAY statement, both items will be displayed on the same line. b - All these items will be displayed on the same line. d - Starting a new line in the DISPLAY statement doesn't make any difference; both items still will be displayed on the same line.
11. `DISPLAY "STUDENT NAME:".`
`DISPLAY " ".`
`DISPLAY STUDENT-NAME.`
12. a, c. Here's what's wrong with the others: b - This doesn't put a space after the colon. d - Neither does this. e - Starting a new line in the DISPLAY statement doesn't make any difference; there's still no space after the colon. f - This would display the items on two different lines. **13.** b **14.** a. FERNA b. NDEZ 10125 **15.** b. Here's what's wrong with the others: a - This line is too long to fit in area B. c - The format for the DISPLAY statement does not include elements such as (80).

Application Questions

The Working-Storage Section includes these definitions:

```
01  MEMBER-NAME           PIC X(24).
01  PHONE-DATA.
     05  HOME-PHONE        PIC X(8).
     05  OFFICE-EXTENSION  PIC 999.
```

The data is in two separate records:

```
JUDI N. FERNANDEZ
555-1212666
```

Use this information to answer questions 1 through 4.

1. Write a statement to accept the name field.

2. Write a statement to accept the next two values.

3. Write a statement to print a message like this:

   NAME: value of member name

4. Write a statement to print a message like this:

   HOME PHONE: phone number   OFFICE EXTENSION: extension

5. Write a statement to print a blank line.

6. Write a statement to print the message "END OF PROGRAM".

7. Write a statement to terminate the program.

8. The following questions are about the system you work with. You'll need to use your COBOL compiler reference manual to answer them. You might also need the help of someone who knows your system.

    a. Look up the ACCEPT statement. (Don't worry about optional clauses you see that haven't been discussed yet.) From what device does your system read data in response to a statement like ACCEPT NEW-NAME?

_____

    b. Does your installation allow the use of ACCEPT for input data?

_____

    c. Does your system check input data for numeric and alphabetic items?

_____

    If so, what does it do if an input value is invalid? _____

_____

    d. Look up the DISPLAY statement. On what device will your system write data in response to a statement like DISPLAY NEW-NAME?

_____

Answers

1. `ACCEPT MEMBER-NAME.`

2. `ACCEPT PHONE-DATA or ACCEPT HOME-PHONE, OFFICE-EXTENSION.`

3. `DISPLAY "NAME: ", MEMBER-NAME.`

4. `DISPLAY "HOME PHONE: ", HOME-PHONE,`
   `        " OFFICE EXTENSION: ", OFFICE-EXTENSION.`

5. `DISPLAY " ".`

6. `DISPLAY "END OF PROGRAM".`

7. `STOP RUN. (or GOBACK.)`

8. The answers depend on your system.

Using Constants in COBOL Programs

One type of data your programs will use is a constant—a value that doesn't change. You used one type of constant when you displayed a literal in quotes. In this lesson, you'll learn more about literals in quotes. You will also learn about other types of constants and see how they can be used in your programs.

Objectives   When you finish this lesson, you will be able to assign values to data items using the VALUE clause. You will also be able to create and use all the types of COBOL constants.

Rationale   Most programs use many constants. You must understand them when you see them in other programs, and you need to use them in your own programs. If you don't use them properly, your programs may bomb or put bad data in your company's files. This lesson shows you how to avoid such consequences.

Variables and Constants

A program uses two major types of data: variables and constants. A **variable** is an item whose value may change during the run of the program, and a constant is an item whose value may not change. Technically, any named item is a variable, even though it might not actually be changed in a single program run. (A program **run** is one execution of the program, from the time that it is loaded and given control until it terminates and returns control.) For example, look at the following pseudocode routine:

```
0 - Double Numbers
      get number from user
      DO UNTIL user enters "QUIT"
          double = number * 2
          display double
          get number from user
      ENDO
      display "GOODBYE"
      STOP
```

This online program doubles numbers and displays the results until the user enters the word "QUIT". Then it terminates. One run of the program would start by getting the first number from the user and would continue until the word "GOODBYE" is displayed and the program ends. During the run, the program might calculate and display any number of doubles.

The first data item in the program is the number the user enters. In COBOL this item is named something like USERS-INPUT-NUMBER. Can its value change during one run of the program? Yes. Every time the program gets a number from the user, this value changes. USERS-INPUT-NUMBER is an input item, and *all input items are variables*. The very act of accepting or reading a value causes the memory item to be changed, so all such items must be variables.

Now look at the item that holds the double. This item could be named DOUBLE. Every time the double is calculated, the value of this item changes, so it is a variable. All result fields in a COBOL program must be variables.

Now look at the value 2 used to multiply the USERS-INPUT-NUMBER by. Does it change during the run? No. No matter how many numbers the user enters, they are always multiplied by 2. The 2 is a constant value.

This routine uses two literals in quotes: "QUIT" and "GOODBYE". These two values are constants; there is no way they can be changed while the program is running. Note that *all literals are constants*.

Constant Values in a COBOL Program

Almost every COBOL program uses constants. Most constants are defined in the Data Division; a few are coded directly in the Procedure Division as literals. Some literals are used so often they are represented by special COBOL words. This lesson examines the three types of literals: nonnumeric literals, numeric literals, and figurative constants. Then you'll see how you can give constant values to items in the Data Division.

Nonnumeric Literals Any string of characters (up to 120) that you enclose in quotation marks is a nonnumeric literal. Many compilers allow you to use either double or single quotes. A single quote is actually an apostrophe ('). Double quotes are used in this course because they are accepted by most COBOL compilers. Some compilers, notably IBM, require single quotes instead. You'll have to check your compiler (or installation) requirements here and use quotes appropriate for your system.

The system will use a quoted literal as it is. If you include spaces or periods inside the quotes, they are part of the literal. The only thing you can't include in a nonnumeric literal is another quotation mark. Here are some examples:

```
"GOOD MORNING"    (12 characters)
"IBM"             (3 characters)
"1928 "           (5 characters)
"O'CONNOR"        (8 characters)
```

You have already seen how nonnumeric literals can be used in the DISPLAY statement, as in:

```
DISPLAY "GOODBYE".
```

Later you'll also learn how to use them in other statements, as in:

```
MOVE "N" TO MASTER-FILE-EOF-FLAG.
```

Numeric Literals   Numeric literals consist of up to 18 digits; a leading sign and a decimal point also can be included if appropriate. You cannot use commas or spaces, however. No quotes are used with numeric literals. Here are some examples:

```
67
+28.2
6000
−43
```

The system will store and use the numeric literal's value as a number (an algebraic quantity).

You can use numeric literals in the DISPLAY and MOVE statements, as in:

```
DISPLAY 98.6.
MOVE 0 TO LINE-COUNT.
```

Figurative Constants   A figurative constant is a special COBOL name that represents a constant value. Figure 4.7 lists all the figurative constants. SPACE and SPACES are equivalent, as are ZERO, ZEROS, and ZEROES. They are the two constants you'll use most often.

Figure 4.7 Figurative Constants

Reserved word	Value	Type
ZERO/ZEROS/ZEROES	All zeros	Numeric
SPACE/SPACES	All spaces	Alphabetic or alphanumeric
QUOTE/QUOTES	Quotes	Alphanumeric
ALL literal	The whole item is filled with the specified literal	Alphanumeric
HIGH-VALUE/HIGH-VALUES	Highest value in collating sequence (hex 'FF' in EBCDIC)	Alphanumeric
LOW-VALUE/LOW-VALUES	Lowest value in collating sequence (hex '00')	Alphanumeric

The QUOTE figurative constant can be used to insert quotation marks in a nonnumeric literal. Here's an example:

```
DISPLAY QUOTE, "THE PATHFINDER", QUOTE, " BY COOPER".
```

will display

```
"THE PATHFINDER" BY COOPER
```

The ALL figurative constant is used in conjunction with a one-byte quoted literal. ALL " " has the same effect as SPACES. ALL "*" would fill a data item with asterisks. ALL "_" can be used to underline a field.

HIGH-VALUE and LOW-VALUE have special uses we aren't concerned with now.

Figurative constants may be used in any place that nonnumeric and numeric literals may. You can DISPLAY them, although most of them make no sense. However, DISPLAY SPACES can be used instead of DISPLAY " " to skip a line. You will learn to use figurative constants in MOVE statements, as in:

```
MOVE ZERO TO LINE-COUNT.
```

Summary of Constants   Nonnumeric literals, numeric literals, and figurative constants are all constants that can be used in COBOL statements such as DISPLAY and MOVE.

Initializing Data in Working Storage

Items defined in the Working-Storage Section may be given initial values. An **initial value** is a value that is stored for the item as the program is loaded and before it begins executing. (This is called **initializing** an item.) Most constants you'll use in a program should be defined and initialized in working storage. This simplifies coding and makes program maintenance easier.

If you don't initialize an item, its initial value will be whatever data was left over in memory from the previous program. In most systems, memory is not cleared when a new program is loaded and given control. Such accidental initial values are called **garbage**.

You have already learned to define data items in the Working-Storage Section. Any elementary item defined in this section can be given an initial value with the VALUE clause. Figure 4.8 shows the format.

If you use a VALUE clause, you must specify a literal; nonnumeric, numeric, and figurative constants may be used. The literal specified in the VALUE clause should match the item type. If the data item was given a picture of 9(3), you could assign a value of ZEROS, 123, 6, and so on, but you couldn't assign a value of "ABC" or SPACES. Some compilers would accept the nonnumeric literal "123"; some wouldn't. Stick to numeric literals (including the figurative constant ZEROS) for numeric items.

A data item described with Xs can receive any type of characters. You'll use SPACES or quoted literals to assign values to such data items.

Here's how the VALUE clause looks in a program:

```
WORKING-STORAGE SECTION.
01   CURRENT-DETAILS.
     05   CURRENT-AGE      PIC 99    VALUE 5.
     05   FIRST-NAME       PIC X(12) VALUE "RUTH".
```

When the literal specified is shorter than the data item, the data item is **padded**. If the data item is numeric, as in the first item above, the data is aligned on the right (or at the decimal point if there is one). Then any unfilled positions are padded with zeros. For example, since its picture is 99, CURRENT-AGE is a two-digit number. The

Figure 4.8 VALUE Clause

Format:
```
VALUE IS literal
```

Examples:
```
VALUE IS "ADDRESS"
VALUE IS 1986
VALUE IS ZEROS
VALUE SPACES
VALUE ZERO
```

Notes:

1. Any item in working storage that has a PICTURE clause can have a VALUE clause.
2. Any type of literal can be used in a VALUE clause.
3. Literal type must match data type as specified in the PICTURE clause.

initial value will be stored as 05. Nonnumeric values, such as FIRST-NAME above, are aligned on the left and padded with blanks on the right. The value established for FIRST-NAME is "RUTH   ", since the picture is X(12).

If a literal specified in a VALUE clause is too long, you'll probably get a message at compilation time so you can correct it.

Using Initialized Items   When do you need to initialize items and when not? Input variables do not need to be initialized, since the first input statement (such as ACCEPT) will overlay the initial garbage with real values.

Working-storage items may or may not need to be initialized. It depends on how they are used in the Procedure Division. If they are intended to hold constant values, they should be initialized; for example, a constant page size might be set to 66 lines. If they are intended as variables, you must decide if they need initializing by examining your program logic. Many times, flags need an initial value of N to avoid an accidental initial value of Y. (It is good practice to initialize all flags routinely, even when the program logic doesn't depend on it.) Other types of items might also need initial values. Many numeric fields should be initialized to zero, for example.

When you code a Working-Storage Section, question each elementary item you define: Does it need to be initialized or not? Check your program logic to see. When in doubt, always initialize. It never hurts.

Defining Constant Messages   A program usually uses several constant messages: report headings, error messages, and so forth. When you use the DISPLAY statement, you can build the messages right into the statement as literals, as in this heading:

```
DISPLAY "EMPLOYEE NAME:          ADDRESS:"
        "                     PHONE:".
```

You can also define the constant messages in working storage and display them from there, as in:

```
01  HEADING-LINE.
    05  FILLER      PIC X(14)    VALUE "EMPLOYEE NAME:".
    05  FILLER      PIC X(16)    VALUE SPACES.
    05  FILLER      PIC X(8)     VALUE "ADDRESS:".
    05  FILLER      PIC X(22)    VALUE SPACES.
    05  FILLER      PIC X(6)     VALUE "PHONE:".
         .
         .
         .
    DISPLAY HEADING-LINE.
```

Doing it this way has three main advantages. First, it's easier to define the spacing this way than in Procedure Division literals. Second, it's easier to change when the user decides (for example) to include the employee's identification number as the first column of the report. Notice that FILLER is used for each item here. This record will be referred to as HEADING-LINE; the subdivisions will never be referred to separately. Third, it's easier to use the same literal in different parts of the program.

Example   Figure 4.9 shows how the program in Figure 4.6 can be coded using literals defined in working storage.

Notice that each display line is given an appropriate name and initialized. The DISPLAY statements now specify data items rather than literals. Notice that each data item that will be used directly still has a unique name. FILLER is used for unreferenced areas. The next lesson will show you how to code the MOVE statements you see in the figure.

Summary   In this lesson you have seen how to define and use literal values in a COBOL program. Nonnumeric literals are enclosed in quotes and may be used anywhere that nonnumeric values are appropriate. Numeric literals are not enclosed in quotes; they are made up of the ten decimal digits, possibly with one decimal point and/or one sign. They may be used wherever numeric values are appropriate; numeric literals without signs or decimal points may also be used wherever alphanumeric (but not alphabetic) values are appropriate.

Figure 4.9 Sample Program

Program:

```
IDENTIFICATION DIVISION.
PROGRAM-ID.  CH4L2.

ENVIRONMENT DIVISION.

DATA DIVISION.
WORKING-STORAGE SECTION.
01  PART-DATA.
    05  PART-NUMBER          PIC 9(5).
    05  PART-NAME            PIC X(30).
01  DISPLAY-LINES.
    05  FIRST-LINE           PIC X(25)
                             VALUE "THIS IS A SAMPLE PROGRAM".
    05  SECOND-LINE          PIC X         VALUE SPACES.
    05  THIRD-LINE.
        10  FILLER           PIC X(14)
                             VALUE "THE NUMBER OF ".
        10  PART-NAME-OUT    PIC X(30).
        10  FILLER           PIC X(3)    VALUE " IS ".
        10  PART-NUMBER-OUT  PIC X(5).

PROCEDURE DIVISION.
SHOW-LINE.
    DISPLAY FIRST-LINE.
    ACCEPT PART-DATA.
    DISPLAY SECOND-LINE.
    MOVE PART-NUMBER TO PART-NUMBER-OUT.
    MOVE PART-NAME TO PART-NAME-OUT.
    DISPLAY THIRD-LINE.
    STOP RUN.
```

Figurative constants are a set of COBOL reserved words that may be used in place of certain literals. The most commonly used figurative constants are ZERO (also called ZEROS or ZEROES), which is a numeric literal, and SPACE (also called SPACES), which is an alphabetic or alphanumeric literal.

You can initialize any elementary item in the Working-Storage Section using the VALUE clause. The type of literal used in the VALUE clause must match the data type of the item. Flags and constant messages are generally initialized; other kinds of working-storage items may also be initialized.

Comprehension Questions

1. Identify each of the following:

   _____ A. 68

   _____ B. "68"

   _____ C. "ZERO"

   _____ D. ZERO

   _____ E. BLANK

   _____ F. "SPACE"

   _____ G. "EMPTY SPACE"

   _____ H. 497.2

   _____ I. 0

   _____ J. 48+3

   _____ K. $12.98

   a. Figurative constant
   b. Numeric literal
   c. Nonnumeric literal
   d. Not a valid literal of any type

2. Which of the entries below are valid data item definitions?

```
a. 05  FIELD-ONE      PIC XXX      VALUE SPACE.
b. 05  FIELD-TWO      PIC XXX      VALUE ZERO.
c. 05  FIELD-THREE    PIC 999      VALUE IS SPACES.
d. 05  FIELD-FOUR     PIC 999      VALUE IS ZEROES.
```

3. Select the best definition of the term "variable."

   a. Any data item or record used by a program
   b. Any data item used in a Procedure Division statement
   c. Any data item whose value may change during one run of a program
   d. Any data item that is not initialized when the program is loaded

4. Which of the following describes a constant value?

   a. A data item that is initialized when the program is loaded
   b. A data item whose value does not change during the run of the program
   c. A data item that is used in the Procedure Division without being defined in the Data Division
   d. A data item defined on level 77 in the Data Division

5. What is the maximum size of a nonnumeric literal? _____ characters

6. What is the maximum size of a numeric literal? _____ digits

7. Which of the following would cause this message to be displayed:

   ENTER "QUIT" TO TERMINATE THE PROGRAM.

   a. DISPLAY "ENTER "QUIT" TO TERMINATE THE PROGRAM.".
   b. DISPLAY 'ENTER "QUIT" TO TERMINATE THE PROGRAM.'.
   c. DISPLAY "ENTER ''QUIT'' TO TERMINATE THE PROGRAM.".
   d. DISPLAY "ENTER " QUOTE "QUIT" QUOTE
          " TO TERMINATE THE PROGRAM.".

8. Which of the following are valid numeric literals?

   a. 29
   b. 61.5
   c. −201
   d. 316.3-
   e. 418.61CR
   f. 16.29.403

9. Name the figurative constants described below.

   a. Fills the item with the designated character:

   _____

   b. Fills the item with blanks: _____

   c. Fills the item with zeros: _____

   d. Puts a quotation mark in a nonnumeric literal:

   _____

10. Can you include the following definition in your Data Division? _____

       05   LOW-VALUE   PIC 9   VALUE 0.

11. Fill in the boxes to show what value each item will have.

    a. 05   NEW-ACCOUNT   PIC 9(5)   VALUE ZERO.
    b. 05   LIST-TOP   PIC X(5)   VALUE "*".
    c. 05   LIST-TOP   PIC X(5)   VALUE ALL "*".
    d. 05   LOSS-FACTOR   PIC 9(3)   VALUE 1.

12. Which of the following statements is true?

    a. Memory is cleared (set to all low values) before a program is loaded.
    b. Garbage from a previous program may be left over in memory when a new program is loaded.

13. Which of the following statements is true?

 a. All working-storage items should be initialized.
 b. All data items should be initialized.
 c. You should check your program logic to see whether a working-storage item needs to be initialized.

14. Which of the following is a better way of handling a constant message?

```
a. 01   INSTRUCTIONS.
      05   FILLER   PIC X(35)
                      VALUE "PLEASE ENTER THE FOLLOWING ITEMS...".
      05   FILLER   PIC X(10)  VALUE SPACES.
      05   FILLER   PIC X(5)   VALUE "DATE:".
      05   FILLER   PIC X(10)  VALUE SPACES.
      05   FILLER   PIC X(5)   VALUE "TIME:".
      .
      .
      .
      DISPLAY INSTRUCTIONS.

b. DISPLAY "PLEASE ENTER THE FOLLOWING ITEMS..."
         "   DATE:           TIME:".
```

Application Questions

1. Code VALUE clauses for the following:

   a. Initialize a field to blanks.

   _____

   b. Initialize a field to zero.

   _____

   c. Initialize a field to LIST OF RECORDS.

   _____

   d. Initialize a numeric field to 66.

   _____

2. Define the following items. Use level 05.

   a. An end-of-data flag with an initial value of N.

   _____

   b. A data item containing the words BOTTOM OF FILE.

   _____

   c. A line counter with an initial value of zero. The maximum value is 60.

   _____

   d. A 30-character error message field with a blank initial value.

   _____

3. Show another way to accomplish the following using a figurative constant.

```
DISPLAY " ".
```

   _____

4. You want to use the statement DISPLAY XMAS-MESSAGE to cause the message MERRY CHRISTMAS TO ALL to be displayed. Code the Data Division entries.

5. Show a better way to accomplish the following. (Use approximate spacing.)

```
DISPLAY "TEST NUMBER          RAW SCORE"
        "           T-SCORE".
```

Answers

1. a. VALUE SPACES or VALUE SPACE (You could include the word IS). b. VALUE ZERO or VALUE ZEROS or VALUE ZEROES c. VALUE "LIST OF RECORDS" d. VALUE 66

2. Suggested answers are shown below. You may have used different data-names, and you may have used 0 or " " instead of the figurative constants. Most programmers use the figurative constants whenever possible.

```
a. 05  END-OF-DATA-FLAG      PIC X     VALUE "N".
b. 05  BOTTOM-MESSAGE        PIC X(14) VALUE "BOTTOM OF FILE".
c. 05  LINE-COUNTER          PIC 99    VALUE ZEROS.
d. 05  ERROR-MESSAGE         PIC X(30) VALUE SPACES.
```

3. DISPLAY SPACES.

4. WORKING-STORAGE SECTION.
```
   01  XMAS-MESSAGE      PIC X(22)
                         VALUE "MERRY CHRISTMAS TO ALL".
```

5. Here's one solution. Yours should reflect the same idea, even if the details are different.

```
   01  COLUMN-HEADINGS.
       05  FILLER  PIC X(11)  VALUE "TEST NUMBER".
       05  FILLER  PIC X(10)  VALUE SPACES.
       05  FILLER  PIC X(9)   VALUE "RAW SCORE".
       05  FILLER  PIC X(10)  VALUE SPACES.
       05  FILLER  PIC X(7)   VALUE "T-SCORE".
        .
        .
        .
       DISPLAY COLUMN-HEADINGS.
```

The MOVE Statement

You have already learned how to accept and display data and how to stop a program. Another important operation, which you will learn in this lesson, is copying a value from one location to another. In COBOL, copying is accomplished with the MOVE statement.

Objectives   When you finish this lesson, you will be able to code the MOVE statement to copy a value into a memory location. You will also be able to state the results of examples of MOVE statements.

Rationale   Moving data is the operation used most in business programs. For every input or output record, a program might execute ten or twenty MOVE statements. You must know how to use the MOVE statement, and you must understand its effect.

MOVE Statement Format

Figure 4.10 shows the basic format of the MOVE statement.
   The MOVE statement causes the data represented by the first data-name or literal to be copied (or duplicated) into the second data-name. The result is to overlay or destroy any previous value in the

Figure 4.10 Basic MOVE Statement

Format:
```
MOVE {literal     } TO {data-name-2}...
     {data-name-1}
```

Examples:
```
MOVE "1982" TO YEAR-FIELD.
MOVE CURRENT-YEAR TO YEAR-FIELD.
MOVE SPACES TO MESSAGE-1 MESSAGE-2.
```

Notes:
1. Any form of literal may be used as sending field.
2. Sending field is unchanged.
3. Receiving field is completely overlaid.
4. Can use multiple receiving fields.

second data-name, which is called the **receiving field**. The first value, called the **sending field**, can be a data-name or any type of literal; its value is unchanged by the MOVE statement.

The literal is just like the ones you can specify in a DISPLAY statement or a VALUE clause. You could code any of these:

```
MOVE ZERO TO LINE-COUNT.

MOVE  "RUTH"  TO FIRST-NAME.

MOVE 28 TO CURRENT-AGE.
```

However, you should avoid using literals in the Procedure Division. Define them in working storage and refer to them thereafter by their data-names.

Effect of MOVEs As you know, data items can be of various types. A data item described with all 9s is a numeric data item; it is treated differently in a MOVE than a nonnumeric data item is. In talking about MOVEs, a nonnumeric item is any of these:

- An alphabetic item (described with all A's)

- An alphanumeric item (described with Xs or with combined A's, Xs, and 9s)

- A group item (even if all its elementary items are numeric)

Nonnumeric MOVEs When the receiving field is nonnumeric, the MOVE is nonnumeric, even if the sending field is numeric. In a nonnumeric move, the value being moved is aligned on the left of the receiving field, and truncated (chopped off) if it is too long or padded with blanks if it does not fill the receiving field. The leftmost character of the sending field is copied into the leftmost position of the receiving field; then the rest of the copy is made from left to right until the receiving field has been completely filled. Here are some examples:

	Sending value	Receiving field (before)	Receiving field (after)
(1)	T U C S O N	M I A M I	T U C S O N
(2)	T U C S O N	H A L L ␢	T U C S O
(3)	T U C S O N	H A R T F O R D	T U C S O N ␣ ␣

In **(1)**, the two fields are the same size, and the data from the sending field completely overlays the data in the receiving field. In **(2)**, the receiving field is shorter than the sending field. The data from the sending field is truncated on the right so it becomes TUCSO in the receiving field. Truncation in a MOVE operation doesn't cause an error message; the system assumes you know what you are doing and lets you truncate the value. In **(3)**, the receiving field is longer than the sending field. This value is padded with two blanks on the right so that it completely overlays the original value in the receiving field.

Numeric MOVEs   When the receiving field is numeric, the MOVE is numeric. The value to be moved is aligned with the decimal point of the receiving field and truncated or padded with zeros if necessary. A field defined with all 9s is assumed to have a decimal point on the right of the field. A nonnumeric literal with no decimal point is assumed to be an integer. If the sending field is nonnumeric and the receiving field is numeric, an error may occur.

Let's look at some examples of numeric MOVEs without decimal points.

	Sending value	Receiving field (before)	Receiving field (after)
(1)	2 3 5 4	4 0 1 3	2 3 5 4
(2)	2 3 5 4	4 0 0 0 1 3	0 0 2 3 5 4
(3)	2 3 5 4	1 6	5 4
(4)	0	6 6 6 3	0 0 0 0

In **(1)**, both fields are the same size. The sending field is copied exactly into the receiving field. In **(2)**, the receiving field is longer than the sending field. Since both fields have an assumed decimal point at their right ends, the sending value is aligned on the right of the receiving field. Then two leading zeros are filled in to complete the receiving field.

In **(3)**, the receiving field is shorter than the sending field. The sending value is aligned on the right of the receiving field (at the location of the assumed decimal point). Then excess digits are truncated from the left. Notice that this changes the meaning of the value; 54 is a significantly different number than 2354. In **(4)**, the entire receiving field is cleared by moving one zero to it. The sending value is aligned on the right and the rest of the receiving field is padded with zeros on the left. Thus, the single zero causes the entire receiving field to be zeroed out.

Notice that in all these moves the zeros are filled in on the left, where they don't change the meaning of the sending value. Only when truncation occurs is the meaning of the value changed.

Using Values in Programs

Figure 4.11 shows part of a program, along with the resulting display. In a real program it would be better to define all messages in working storage, but you can see the effects of MOVE operations more easily this way. Notice that only one data item is defined in the Data Division. Each DISPLAY statement referring to this item will print the then-current value of MESSAGE-LINE.

Figure 4.11 Effects of MOVE Statements

```
DATA DIVISION.
WORKING-STORAGE SECTION.
01  MESSAGE-LINE      PIC X(30)  VALUE
                "THIS IS THE INITIALIZED VALUE.".

PROCEDURE DIVISION.
SHOW-EFFECTS.
    DISPLAY MESSAGE-LINE.
    MOVE SPACES TO MESSAGE-LINE.
    DISPLAY MESSAGE-LINE.
    MOVE "THIS IS A NONNUMERIC LITERAL BEING MOVED."
        TO MESSAGE-LINE.
    DISPLAY MESSAGE-LINE.
    DISPLAY SPACES.
    MOVE "END PROGRAM" TO MESSAGE-LINE.
    DISPLAY MESSAGE-LINE.
    STOP RUN.
```

Resulting print display:

```
    THIS IS THE INITIALIZED VALUE.

    THIS IS A NONNUMERIC LITERAL B

    END PROGRAM
```

Now let's walk through the Procedure Division and see the effect of each line.

```
DISPLAY MESSAGE-LINE.
```

The first DISPLAY statement uses the initialized value from the Data Division, resulting in the first printed line.

```
MOVE SPACES TO MESSAGE-LINE.
DISPLAY MESSAGE-LINE.
```

The MOVE statement uses a figurative constant that fills the receiving field with spaces. This effectively erases the initialized value for the duration of the run. The DISPLAY statement uses the current value, so the result is the first blank line in the printed result.

```
MOVE "THIS IS A NONNUMERIC LITERAL BEING MOVED."
    TO MESSAGE-LINE.
DISPLAY MESSAGE-LINE.
```

This MOVE statement has a sending field value that is longer than the receiving field, which was described as X(30). The value is therefore truncated, as you can see in the displayed result.

```
DISPLAY SPACES.
```

This statement is included to print the second blank line in the result.

```
MOVE "END PROGRAM" TO MESSAGE-LINE.
DISPLAY MESSAGE-LINE.
```

This MOVE statement uses a shorter sending field. The value is padded with spaces on the right in the move so the receiving field contains the value you see displayed as the last line.

This short program has demonstrated the effects of the VALUE clause in the Data Division and MOVE statements in the Procedure Division. Refer back to Figure 4.9 to see how MOVE statements handle data items in a program.

What Can You MOVE to Where?

You need to consider the picture of a field that will receive a moved value, whether from another field or from a literal. You can move almost anything to a field described with all Xs. For example, these are all valid for SAMPLE-X PIC X(3):

```
MOVE ZEROES   TO SAMPLE-X.  (result  0 0 0  )

MOVE 123      TO SAMPLE-X.  (result  1 2 3  )

MOVE  12      TO SAMPLE-X.  (result  1 2    )

MOVE "12"     TO SAMPLE-X.  (result  1 2    )

MOVE 1234     TO SAMPLE-X.  (result  1 2 3  )

MOVE ALL "*"  TO SAMPLE-X.  (result  * * *  )
```

You cannot move 5.8 to a nonnumeric field, but you could move "5.8".

Numeric fields (9s) are more restricted. You can't move spaces to a numeric field. You can move a nonnumeric field to it if the value is numeric. Suppose SAMPLE-9 PICTURE 9 (3) is defined. These are all valid:

```
MOVE "123"  TO SAMPLE-9.  (result  1 2 3  )

MOVE "12"   TO SAMPLE-9.  (result  0 1 2  )

MOVE 4.8    TO SAMPLE-9.  (result  0 0 4  )

MOVE "4.8"  TO SAMPLE-9.  (result  0 0 4  )
```

Notice that the last two MOVEs result in truncation of the decimal portion. The value is aligned at the decimal point of the receiving field—the far right for SAMPLE-9.

All invalid moves of literals generate an error when you compile the program. When you move a data-name, however, you may get data errors later, when the program is running. The compiler assumes the sending data item will contain a numeric value if the receiving field is defined as numeric.

Figure 4.12 summarizes the types of MOVES you can and cannot make. Whenever the receiving field is not numeric, the MOVE is nonnumeric. When both fields are numeric, the MOVE is numeric, and safe. But what happens when the sending field is nonnumeric and the receiving field is numeric or alphabetic? There is danger here.

Figure 4.12 MOVEs

		Sending field		
		Numeric	Alphabetic	Alphanumeric
Receiving field	Numeric	Yes (numeric)	No	Dangerous (Numeric)
	Alphabetic	No	Yes (nonnumeric)	Dangerous (nonnumeric)
	Alphanumeric	Yes (nonnumeric)	Yes (nonnumeric)	Yes (nonnumeric)

Basically, the compiler assumes you know what you are doing and that you will make sure the sending field contains the the proper data before attempting the MOVE, so the compiler will not prevent the MOVE statement.

If your programming is careless and you try to MOVE a nondigit into a numeric field or a nonletter into an alphabetic field, the program will probably bomb. Worse yet, some systems will allow the MOVE, which risks getting garbage into your files and data bases. Avoid this type of MOVE whenever possible.

Your COBOL reference manual should have a chart similar to Figure 4.12. It will be more complicated because it will include additional data types.

Group MOVEs

A group MOVE is any MOVE in which the receiving field is a group item. Such MOVEs are always nonnumeric, no matter how the elementary items are defined. This can have some unfortunate results, as it may allow nonnumeric data into a numeric field or nonalphabetic data into an alphabetic field, which can lead to a bomb or garbage in your files.

Here's an example. Suppose you have these definitions:

```
01   OLD-BALANCES.
     05   OLD-PRINCIPAL-BALANCE       PIC 9(5)   VALUE 11111.
     05   OLD-INTEREST-BALANCE        PIC 9(5)   VALUE 22222.
     05   OLD-TOTAL-BALANCE           PIC 9(5)   VALUE 33333.
01   NEW-BALANCES.
     05   NEW-PRINCIPAL-BALANCE       PIC 9(7).
     05   NEW-INTEREST-BALANCE        PIC 9(7).
     05   NEW-TOTAL-BALANCE           PIC 9(7).
```

If you MOVE all the OLD items to all the NEW items using elementary MOVEs, as in MOVE OLD-PRINCIPAL-BALANCE TO NEW-PRINCIPAL-BALANCE, each MOVE will be numeric. Each resulting value will be converted from five to seven digits with the appropriate leading zeros supplied. After all three MOVEs, the value of NEW-BALANCES will be 001111100222220033333.

If you use a group MOVE — OLD-BALANCES TO NEW-BALANCES — the data will be given nonnumeric treatment. The source value 111112222233333 will be aligned on the left of the receiving field, with spaces filled in on the right. This results in the value of NEW-BALANCES being 111112222233333ƀƀƀƀƀƀ. The resulting value of NEW-PRINCIPAL-BALANCE will be 1111122, NEW-INTEREST-BALANCE will be 2223333, and NEW-TOTAL-BALANCE will be 3ƀƀƀƀƀƀ. These values are erroneous and are going to cause trouble; NEW-TOTAL-BALANCE may cause a bomb.

There's nothing wrong with group MOVEs; we use them all the time, and so will you. But you must be very careful that no numeric MOVEs are needed at the elementary level. If so, use elementary MOVEs instead of a group one.

Summary The MOVE statement copies data into a memory item. The source value is not changed. The receiving field is completely filled with the new value. If the receiving field is nonnumeric or a group item, the MOVE is nonnumeric; the incoming value is aligned on the left and padded with spaces on the right. If the receiving field is numeric, the MOVE is numeric; the incoming value is aligned at the (assumed) decimal point and padded with zeros. Most systems will not let you move nonalphabetic data into an alphabetic field nor nonnumeric data into a numeric field, although you can do so in a group MOVE.

Comprehension Questions

1. Which of the following is/are true of the MOVE statement?

   a. The sending field must be a literal.
   b. The sending field must be a data-name.
   c. The receiving field must be a literal.
   d. The receiving field must be a data-name.

2. Which of the following are valid MOVE statements, given these definitions:

```
01  WORK-RECORD.
    05 DEPARTMENT PIC X(5).
    05 THROUGHPUT PIC 9(7).
```

   a. MOVE ZEROS TO DEPARTMENT.
   b. MOVE ZEROS TO THROUGHPUT.
   c. MOVE SPACES TO DEPARTMENT.
   d. MOVE SPACES TO THROUGHPUT.
   e. MOVE "TAXES" TO DEPARTMENT.
   f. MOVE "TAXES" TO THROUGHPUT.
   g. MOVE "ABC" TO DEPARTMENT.
   h. MOVE "ABC" TO THROUGHPUT.
   i. MOVE "2150000" TO DEPARTMENT.
   j. MOVE "2150000" TO THROUGHPUT.
   k. MOVE 14.25 TO DEPARTMENT.
   l. MOVE 14.25 TO THROUGHPUT.
   m. MOVE 0 TO DEPARTMENT.
   n. MOVE 0 TO THROUGHPUT.

Answers

1. d **2.** a, b, c, e, g, i, j, l, m, n. Here's what's wrong with the others: d, f, and h - All these statements attempt to move nonnumeric data into a numeric field. k - This statement attempts to move a numeric literal with a decimal point into a nonnumeric field.

Application Questions

1. Code Procedure Division statements to do the following:

a. Give the value 1 to SKIP-LINES, described as PIC 9.

_____

b. Give the value "Y" to EOF-INPUT-FLAG, described as PIC X.

_____

c. Give the value of item FIELD-ONE (PIC XX) to FIELD-TWO (PIC X(20)).

_____

2. Before your statement in (c) above is executed, FIELD-ONE contains the value "X3", and FIELD-TWO contains the value "XXX333XXX333XXX333X3". What is the final value of

a. FIELD-ONE _____

b. FIELD-TWO _____

3. Suppose you execute the following statement under the same conditions as question 2 above: MOVE FIELD-TWO TO FIELD-ONE. What is the resulting value in

a. FIELD-ONE _____

b. FIELD-TWO _____

4. Now write a complete COBOL program, to produce output like this:

```
* * * * * * * * * * * * * * * * * * * * * * * *
MY NAME IS  your name
* * * * * * * * * * * * * * * * * * * * * * * *
```

Initialize all the data in working storage. You'll run this program a bit later. For now, check your coding and continue with the next lesson.

Answers

1. a. MOVE 1 TO SKIP-LINES. b. MOVE "Y" TO EOF-INPUT-FLAG. c. MOVE FIELD-ONE TO FIELD-TWO.   **2.** a. X3 b. X3 followed by 18 spaces   **3.** a. XX
b. XXX333XXX333XXX333X3

4.
```
    IDENTIFICATION DIVISION.
    PROGRAM-ID.
        FIRST.
    ENVIRONMENT DIVISION.
    DATA DIVISION.
    WORKING-STORAGE SECTION.
    01  DISPLAY-LINES.
        05   ASTERISK-LINE      PIC X(25)    VALUE ALL "*".
        05   SPACE-LINE         PIC X        VALUE SPACE.
        05   NAME-LINE          PIC X(23)
                                VALUE "MY NAME IS RUTH ASHLEY.".
    PROCEDURE DIVISION.
    PRACTICE-DISPLAY.
        DISPLAY ASTERISK-LINE.
        DISPLAY SPACE-LINE.
        DISPLAY NAME-LINE.
        DISPLAY SPACE-LINE.
        DISPLAY ASTERISK-LINE.
        STOP RUN.
```

Check your coding carefully. You could have used different data-names, of course. Be sure you used the same names in the DISPLAY statements as in the Working-Storage Section. Check your spacing and punctuation. You could have used "*************************." instead of ALL "*". You could have used " " or SPACES instead of SPACE.

ACCEPT and DISPLAY Statement Options

The ACCEPT and DISPLAY statements can be used for input or output from other than the default devices in most compilers. In addition, you can use ACCEPT to get values such as the current date and time from the operating system.

This lesson focuses on techniques for accessing values from the operating system. All installations allow this use of ACCEPT.

Objectives When you finish this lesson, you'll be able to code all the options of the ACCEPT and DISPLAY statements, as well as supporting Environment Division entries.

Rationale Many programs have a use for the exact time or the current date. You may want to include the time in a displayed message, for example. Most operating systems know the exact time. One format of the ACCEPT statement lets the program access this value; some compilers use a special MOVE statement for this purpose.

You may also need to control where an item is accepted from or displayed to. For example, it is sometimes desirable to have a displayed message appear on the operator's console or to allow data entry from the operator's console. Changes in assignment of input and output devices are permitted by some compilers. Some installations allow you to define a nondefault I/O device as the source of an ACCEPT statement or the destination of a DISPLAY statement.

Using Nondefault Devices

Your installation has a default location for ACCEPT (usually the main input device) and DISPLAY (usually the standard output printer). When you use a basic ACCEPT or DISPLAY statement, that source or destination is used.

Most compilers allow you to define another device as source or destination instead. The most commonly used device is the main computer console used by the computer operator, referred to as CONSOLE. You name this device in the Environment Division and tell the compiler what you will call it. Then you can refer to the device in ACCEPT or DISPLAY statements as needed.

Figure 4.13 SPECIAL-NAMES Paragraph

Format:

```
ENVIRONMENT DIVISION.
[CONFIGURATION SECTION.
[SOURCE-COMPUTER. computer-name.]
[OBJECT-COMPUTER. computer-name.]
[SPECIAL-NAMES. installation-defined-name IS mnemonic-name.] ]
```

Example:

```
ENVIRONMENT DIVISION.
CONFIGURATION SECTION.
SPECIAL-NAMES. CONSOLE IS CRT-SCREEN.
```

Notes:

1. Possible entries for installation defined name are set by each compiler.
2. Mnemonic-name is supplied by programmer and used in the Procedure Division.
3. Some compilers allow you to omit SPECIAL-NAMES and use the installation defined name in the Procedure Division.
4. The names allowed by your compiler for use in ACCEPT and DISPLAY statements are: (fill in)

name	result

The SPECIAL-NAMES Paragraph   Figure 4.13 shows an expanded format of the Configuration Section of the Environment Division. You'll use the SPECIAL-NAMES paragraph only in certain situations, such as specifying a nondefault source for an ACCEPT statement or destination for a DISPLAY statement.

Since SPECIAL-NAMES is in the Environment Division, it has installation- or compiler-specific entries. The format is always the same, however. You use the name the system knows, followed by the keyword IS, followed by the name you will call that entity in the Procedure Division. You use a mnemonic-name in the Procedure Division. We used CRT-SCREEN in the example.

CONSOLE is a typical installation defined name. The compiler defines what CONSOLE means; typically, it refers to the computer operator's console. The special names you can define will depend on the defaults for your compiler.

Take time to check with a knowledgeable programmer or refer to your compiler's reference manual and complete the figure for your own benefit.

You may be wondering why you must go through the bother of defining mnemonic-names in the Environment Division. Why not just use the installation defined names in the ACCEPT and DISPLAY statements? The answer lies in the concept of maintainability. If the

Procedure Division refers to the console 20 times, and you want to convert this program to run on a system that calls the operator's console TERMINAL-0, it's easier to change

```
CONSOLE IS SCREEN
```

to

```
TERMINAL-0 IS SCREEN
```

than to find and make 20 changes in the Procedure Division. (Actually, with a good online editor, it's just as easy to make the 20 changes. But in the days when COBOL was developed, it was much, much easier to make the single Environment Division change.)

Expanded DISPLAY Statement   You can use a mnemonic name in a DISPLAY statement if you use this format:

$$\underline{\text{DISPLAY}} \begin{Bmatrix} \text{literal} \\ \text{data-name} \end{Bmatrix} \dots [\underline{\text{UPON}} \text{ mnemonic-name}]$$

The values will then appear on the device associated with that mnemonic-name. Some compilers, notably IBM compilers for large systems, allow you to use an installation defined name directly in the UPON clause of a DISPLAY statement. With IBM COBOL you can use DISPLAY ALERT-MESSAGE UPON CONSOLE without using the SPECIAL-NAMES paragraph, for example. If you used a specification like the one in Figure 4.12, you could code UPON CRT-SCREEN. The value would be displayed on the main computer operator's console.

By the way, exercise some caution in sending messages to the operator's console. For some types of applications it may be useful to do so. In large, batch-oriented installations, however, you need to be selective about what you send to the operator's console. Computer operators are busy people who can't (and don't) spend a lot of time reading messages. Many installations don't permit you to send such messages from COBOL programs.

Some compilers use CONSOLE or a similar word to refer to the online terminal from which a program was run. That is, if user A sitting at terminal B asks for program C to be executed, then all ACCEPT ... FROM CONSOLE and DISPLAY ... UPON CONSOLE statements in program C will refer to terminal B. Thus the program can interact directly with a particular user at his or her terminal.

Some compilers, especially those for microcomputers, default to a console of some sort for a basic DISPLAY statement (one with no UPON option). These compilers may use PRINTER or a similar word for you to associate with a mnemonic-name and include in DISPLAY statements when you want to print a message rather than display it on the default console.

Expanded ACCEPT Statement   You can also use a mnemonic-name in an ACCEPT statement if you use this format:

```
ACCEPT {data-name} ... [FROM mnemonic-name]
```

The mnemonic-name is defined in the SPECIAL-NAMES paragraph, just as it was for the DISPLAY statement. As with DISPLAY, some compilers allow you to name a device such as CONSOLE directly. Again, you must know what the effect is for your system. Most large, batch-oriented installations do not want you asking the computer operator to enter data; it slows down the system and the operator. In other installations, mostly small, online ones, the user is at a terminal and can enter small amounts of data easily.

Summary of Nondefault Devices   The SPECIAL-NAMES paragraph associates a mnemonic-name with a source device for an ACCEPT statement and/or a destination device for a DISPLAY statement. This can be used in the FROM or UPON clause to access a nondefault device.

Check your installation's acceptable devices to see what options, if any, are available for programs you write.

Using Your Computer's Special Registers

Most computer systems include special information that can be used by any programs. When the computer system is turned on, the current time and the current date are set. An internal clock incorporated into the CPU maintains these values and keeps them accurate. The time and date are stored in special registers (or storage fields) that any COBOL program may access by using the ACCEPT statement. Some compilers allow to you use a MOVE statement to access data from the special registers. You'll see how to do that as well.

ACCEPT Statement   Figure 4.14 shows the format of the ACCEPT statement in which you access a special register. The special register names are known to the compiler already. They are reserved words,

Figure 4.14 ACCEPT FROM Special Registers

Format:

```
ACCEPT data-name FROM {DATE}
                       {DAY }
                       {TIME}
```

EXAMPLES:

```
ACCEPT TODAYS-DATE FROM DATE.
ACCEPT JULIAN-DATE FROM DAY.
ACCEPT EXACT-TIME FROM TIME.
```

Notes:

1. Do not define DATE, DAY, or TIME. They can be used only in ACCEPT statements.
2. Data-name must be defined in the Data Division.
3. DATE is in 9(6) format. The digits are *yymmdd* (year month day). February 14, 1986, would be 860214.
4. DAY is in (9)5 format. The digits are *yyddd* (year day). February 14, 1984, would be 84045.
5. TIME is in (9)8 format. The digits are *hhmmsshh* (hours minutes seconds hundredths). 2:35 would be 02350000.

so you never have to define them. When the statement is executed, the value in the special register is moved to the data-name you specify.

DATE Special Register   The DATE value is stored in 9(6) format; it includes two digits for the year of the century, two for the month of the year, and two for the day of the month.

If your data-name is defined as 9(6) or X(6), the entire value of the DATE special register is moved to it. If your field is defined differently, the result will be different. Suppose DATE contains 840130. Here is the effect of ACCEPTing it into each of four differently defined items.

```
    definition                      result

05  TODAYS-DATE-1    PIC X(10).     840130ƀƀƀƀ
05  TODAYS-DATE-2    PIC X(4).      8401
05  TODAYS-DATE-3    PIC 9(10).     0000840130
05  TODAYS-DATE-4    PIC 9(4).      0130
```

The data from the special register is moved as a numeric or non-numeric move, depending on how the data-name is defined.

Generally you'll want to show the date in a more readable format, perhaps with slashes inserted. Figure 4.15 shows one way to do this. The date is ACCEPTed into a group item (TODAYS-DATE). The month, day, and year components are then MOVEd to fields in another record. The VALUE clause is used to insert slashes into DISPLAY-DATE for a more readable appearance.

Figure 4.15 Handling DATE in Programs

```
01    TODAYS-DATE.
      05    TODAYS YEAR          PIC 99.
      05    TODAYS-MONTH         PIC 99.
      05    TODAYS-DAY           PIC 99.
01    DISPLAY-DATE.
      05    DISPLAY-MONTH        PIC 99.
      05    FILLER               PIC X      VALUE "/".
      05    DISPLAY-DAY          PIC 99.
      05    FILLER               PIC X      VALUE "/".
      05    DISPLAY-YEAR         PIC 99.
. . .

      ACCEPT TODAYS-DATE FROM DATE
      MOVE TODAYS-MONTH TO DISPLAY-MONTH
      MOVE TODAYS-DAY TO DISPLAY-DAY
      MOVE TODAYS-YEAR TO DISPLAY-YEAR
      DISPLAY DISPLAY-DATE.
```

DAY Special Register   The DAY value is stored in 9(5) format. The first two digits are the year of the century, while the last three are the day of the year. This is often called a Julian date.

You can define a data item to receive this date as X(5) or 9(5). If you use X(2), the field would receive only the year of the century. If you use 9(3), the field would receive only the sequential day of the year.

TIME Special Register   The TIME value is stored in 9(8) format, based on a 24-hour clock (2:00 pm is 1400 hours). The first two digits are the hour of the day (00 through 23). The next two are the minute of the hour (00 through 59). The next two are the second of the minute (00 through 59). The last (rightmost) two digits are used in some compilers to show hundredths of seconds; they're set to zero if the system doesn't show hundredths of seconds. The highest value possible for TIME is 23595999, at just .01 second before the stroke of midnight, which is represented as 00000000.

If your compiler doesn't use hundredths of seconds, or if they aren't important to your program, you could describe your data-name to receive TIME as X(6). The last two characters will be truncated.

Example   Suppose at a certain point in a program, you want to display the message "This point reached at " and the current-time.

To create the display, you need these statements:

```
01    TIME-LINE.
      05    FILLER              PIC X(22)
                          VALUE "THIS POINT REACHED AT ".
      05    TIME-OF-DAY    PIC X(6).
      ...

      ACCEPT TIME-OF-DAY FROM TIME.
      DISPLAY TIME-LINE.
```

To display a message such as "This program was run on the *nth* day of the year" you could do this:

```
01  DATE-LINE.
    05  FILLER              PIC X(29)
                    VALUE "THIS PROGRAM WAS RUN ON THE ".
    05  SEQUENCE-DAY   PIC 999.
    05  FILLER              PIC X(19)
                    VALUE " TH DAY OF THE YEAR".
...
        ACCEPT SEQUENCE-DAY FROM DAY.
        DISPLAY DATE-LINE.
```

Alternative Method

Some compilers provide additional special registers called CURRENT-DATE and TIME-OF-DAY. These special registers are formatted differently. CURRENT-DATE is an 8-byte field formatted with slashes, as in mm/dd/yy. TIME-OF-DAY is formatted just like TIME. These names are reserved words; you don't define them. Instead of ACCEPTing the values, you must MOVE them to defined fields. Instead of ACCEPT EXACT-TIME FROM TIME you would code MOVE TIME-OF-DAY TO EXACT-TIME. The effect is the same in both statements. Use the format and names required by your compiler.

Summary You can define special names to allow a program to receive ACCEPT input and/or produce DISPLAY output on nondefault devices. These special mnemonic names are referred to in the Procedure Division statements.

Special registers in the computer contain the current date and time. You can access values from these registers using the ACCEPT statement and the DATE, DAY, or TIME keywords. Some compilers use the MOVE statement with TIME-OF-DAY and CURRENT-DATE instead. The values can then be used in the program.

Comprehension Questions

Use your compiler manual to answer questions 1 through 3.

1. What form of ACCEPT can you use to receive user input in your installation?

   a. None

   b. Basic form (ACCEPT data-name)

   c. Use FROM _____ with SPECIAL-NAMES

2. Which of the following is used to access the date in your installation?

   a. ACCEPT data-name FROM DATE

   b. MOVE CURRENT-DATE TO data-name

   c. Other _____

3. Which of the following is used to access the time in your installation?

   a. ACCEPT data-name FROM TIME

   b. MOVE TIME-OF-DAY TO data-name

   c. Other _____

4. In which division and section would you code a SPECIAL-NAMES paragraph? _____

5. Which of the following statements is/are in the correct format?

   a. `ACCEPT FIRST-NAME UPON TERMINAL.`   c. `DISPLAY TIME.`

   b. `DISPLAY FIRST-NAME UPON TERMINAL.`   d. `ACCEPT DATE.`

6. Name the special register in which each of the following is stored, and show how each value would be stored.

   a. The time one-thirty-six and 40 seconds: Register _____

      Value: _____

   b. The fifty-seventh day of 1986: Register: _____ Value: _____

   c. The fourth of July, 1985: Register: _____

      Value: _____

Answers

===

1–3 Depend on your installation. See your training manager or Reference Manual if you don't know the answers.   **4.** Environment Division (Configuration Section)
5. b. Here's what's wrong with the others: a—Should use FROM rather than UPON. c—You can't DISPLAY a special register value directly. d—You need a data-name to accept the register value FROM.   **6.** a. TIME—01364000 b. DAY—86057 c. DATE—850704 You should use the special register names your compiler accepts.

Application Questions

1. Suppose a program includes these lines:

```
SPECIAL-NAMES.   CONSOLE IS COMPUTER-TERMINAL.
      .
      .
      .
   05   START-SIGNAL        PIC X.
   05   START-MESSAGE       PIC X(26)
            VALUE "PROGRAM SERVICE IS RUNNING".
   05   GET-SIGNAL-MESSAGE  PIC X(19)
            VALUE "PLEASE TYPE Y OR N.".
```

   a. Write a statement to display "PROGRAM SERVICE IS RUNNING" on the device designated as CONSOLE.

   _____

   b. Write statements that will ask the console operator to enter Y or N as START-SIGNAL, and then read in the value.

   _____

   _____

2. You need to show the current time in a message like this:

```
THE EXACT TIME IS:   time
```

   a. Define data items for the message and current time.

   _____

   _____

   b. Write statement(s) to show the message.

   _____

   _____

3. You want to display the current year and the sequence number of the day, like this:

```
YEAR: 19nn DAY: nnn.
```

   a. Define data items for the special register value and the message.

   _____

   _____

   _____

   b. Write statements to show the message.

   _____

   _____

   _____

Answers

1. a. `DISPLAY START-MESSAGE UPON COMPUTER-TERMINAL.`

Some compilers will let you code UPON CONSOLE.

b. `DISPLAY GET-SIGNAL-MESSAGE UPON COMPUTER-TERMINAL.`
`ACCEPT START-SIGNAL FROM COMPUTER-TERMINAL.`

2. a.
```
01   DISPLAY-LINE.
     05   FILLER       PIC X(20)  VALUE "THE EXACT TIME IS: ".
     05   EXACT-TIME   PIC X(8).
```

You could use 9(8) or a subdivided item for the time field.

b. `ACCEPT EXACT-TIME FROM TIME.`
`DISPLAY DISPLAY-LINE.`

You could use MOVE TIME-OF-DAY TO EXACT-TIME if your compiler uses that form.

3. a.
```
01   JULIAN-DATE.
     05   YEAR-OF-CENTURY      PIC XX.
     05   DAY-OF-YEAR          PIC XXX.

01   MESSAGE-LINE.
     05   FILLER               PIC X(8)  VALUE "YEAR: 19".
     05   THIS-YEAR            PIC XX.
     05   FILLER               PIC X(8)  VALUE "  DAY:  ".
     05   THIS-DAY             PIC XXX.
```
b.
```
     ACCEPT JULIAN-DATE FROM DAY.
     MOVE YEAR-OF-CENTURY TO THIS-YEAR.
     MOVE DAY-OF-YEAR TO THIS-DAY.
     DISPLAY MESSAGE-LINE.
```

Chapter Review Questions

In these questions you will write all the parts necessary for a complete COBOL program. The program will access the date from the operating system and format it in two ways for display. Use separate paper for your answer.

The report will contain several lines, as follows:

line 1 THIS IS THE FORMATTED DATE

line 2

line 3 mm/dd/yy

line 4 THE YEAR IS 19yy

Use initialized Data Division entries to format the display.

1. Write the complete first division. Use at least one optional paragraph.

2. Write the second division as required at your installation.

3. The program will need five record descriptions.

    a. Code the division and section headers.

    b. Code a record to hold the first line:

        THIS IS THE FORMATTED DATE

    c. Code a record to be used to display a blank line.

d. Code a record description for fields to contain the date from a special register.

e. Code a record description for the formatted date as needed for line 3.

f. Code a record description to format and display line 4.

4. Now write the Procedure Division. Create the pseudocode first, if you like. Use the names defined in the Data Division.

Answers

Check your answers carefully. Watch spelling, punctuation, and spacing. Your indentation should reflect the A and B areas.

1.
```
IDENTIFICATION DIVISION.
PROGRAM-ID.  CH4REV.
AUTHOR.  RUTH ASHLEY
            TRAINING DEPARTMENT.
```
You could have used a different, valid program-name, as well as other optional paragraphs.

2.
```
ENVIRONMENT DIVISION.
```
You should have included the Configuration Section if your compiler requires it.

3. a.
```
DATA DIVISION
WORKING-STORAGE SECTION.
```

b.
```
01  MESSAGE-LINE        PIC X(30)
                VALUE "THIS IS THE FORMATTED DATE".
```

c.
```
01  SPACE-LINE          PIC X    VALUE SPACE.
```

d.
```
01  EXACT-DATE.
    05  EXACT-YEAR      PIC XX.
    05  EXACT-MONTH     PIC XX.
    05  EXACT-DAY       PIC XX.
```

e.
```
01  FORMATTED-DATE.
    05  FORMATTED-MONTH PIC XX.
    05  FILLER          PIC X    VALUE "/".
    05  FORMATTED-DAY   PIC XX.
    05  FILLER          PIC X    VALUE "/".
    05  FORMATTED-YEAR  PIC XX.
```

f.
```
01  EXPANDED-YEAR.
    05  FILLER          PIC X(14)
                VALUE "THE YEAR IS 19".
    05  FIX-YEAR        PIC XX.
```

4.
```
PROCEDURE DIVISION.
FORMAT-DATES.
    DISPLAY MESSAGE-LINE.
    DISPLAY SPACE-LINE.
    ACCEPT EXACT-DATE FROM DATE.
    MOVE EXACT-MONTH TO FORMATTED-MONTH.
    MOVE EXACT-DAY TO FORMATTED-DAY.
    MOVE EXACT-YEAR TO FORMATTED-YEAR.
    DISPLAY FORMATTED-DATE.
    MOVE EXACT-YEAR TO FIX-YEAR.
    DISPLAY EXPANDED-YEAR.
    STOP RUN.
```

Section Two Exercise

A source program must be in an input medium acceptable to the COBOL compiler. At your installation you might use an online editor, you might send your program off to a data entry group, or you might even use a keypunch or key entry machine yourself.

This course does not teach you how to use your data entry system. You'll have to ask your training manager or an experienced colleague to show you how to enter your programs into the system.

You will need to enter two separate programs to be used later. One is the program you just completed in the Chapter 4 Review. Enter the entire program, giving it a name such as CH4BXXX in which XXX are your initials. Then locate the program you wrote at the end of Lesson 4.4 and enter it into your system; name it CH4AXXX. You'll run these programs at the end of the next section.

Running Programs

Chapter 5

The Compile-Link-Go Process

Writing programs and creating source modules is a large part of programming, but it is by no means all. Programs must still be translated into machine language using a compiler and tested with data to make sure they work.

This chapter reviews the process by which programs are compiled, link edited, and tested.

This chapter consists of three lessons:

Lesson 5.1: The Process
Lesson 5.2: Types of Computer Runs
Lesson 5.3: How to Do It

The Process

The program development process includes these steps:

1. Problem definition
2. Analysis
3. Design
4. Coding
5. Testing
6. Documentation

This book is primarily concerned with the coding and testing phases. So far, in fact, it's been all coding. The coding phase, however, includes compilation; and a program just isn't complete until it's tested. In an actual program development process, you consider testing from the very first step. This chapter discusses the steps involved in compiling and testing a COBOL program.

Objectives By the end of this lesson you'll be familiar with the tasks involved in compilation and testing.

Rationale All programmers compile and test programs as a part of their jobs. Compilation and testing are interrelated. You will understand the details of these processes more clearly, and you'll be better able to deal with them as they are conducted at your installation, if you see the big picture first.

Program Development from the Programmer's Viewpoint

Figure 5.1 shows the process of preparing a program as seen from the programmer's viewpoint. The process has three major steps, each of which involves several smaller steps.

Creating a source module includes writing the program and storing the source code where the system can reach it. This generally means entering the program onto disk, using an online editor. You'll use whatever method your installation is set up for.

Once the source program is in the system, you should **desk check** it. Desk checking means that you thoroughly examine a listing of the source code, looking for errors. Look at typing, spelling, and punctuation as well as the program logic. When you desk check, play the role of the computer. Use some sample data and ask yourself what happens as each statement is executed.

Figure 5.1 Coding and Testing a Program

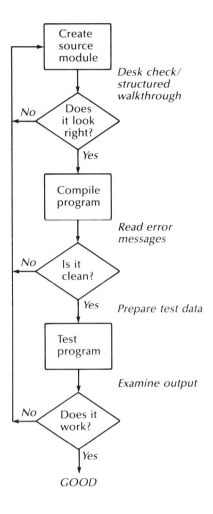

After the desk checking, conduct a **walkthrough**. If your organization doesn't arrange formal walkthroughs at this stage, at least walk through your source code with a fellow programmer. The walkthrough will probably identify more corrections to be made.

Compiling the source program is the next step. Many syntax errors may be caught by the compiler. You need to correct *all* compilation errors and get a clean compilation (with no errors) before going on to the next step. Notice in Figure 5.1 that you go back to the source module creation stage to correct compilation errors.

Testing the program involves running it with controlled test data until you are sure the program works as it is supposed to. This involves creating test data if input is needed, then linking and loading the object module that resulted from the compilation step. Errors discovered during testing are of two major types: those that cause the program to bomb and those that result in invalid output. Whenever an error occurs, you have to decide what caused it, correct the source program, recompile it, and repeat the testing step.

After controlled tests are successful, a program will go on to live tests and perhaps other types of tests. As a programmer, you may not be directly involved in these tests, but you will have to make any corrections they identify.

Program Development from the System's Viewpoint

You will make several computer runs during the compilation and testing process. At first you're just trying to get a clean compilation; this might involve many executions of the COBOL compiler. Then you're ready to test the program. You link it by executing the linker program. Then you execute the new program. Every time you make a change to the source program, it must be recompiled and relinked before it can be tested.

Let's look at the input required and the output produced by a program during compilation and testing.

The Compiler

The COBOL compiler translates COBOL source code into object code. Figure 5.2 shows the various inputs and outputs involved.

Figure 5.2 Inputs/Outputs of the Compiler

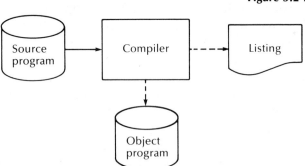

The input to the compiler is the source program—that is, the four COBOL divisions you have learned to code. This may come from cards or from a file you created with your editor. There are two possible outputs: a **compiler listing** and an **object program**. Figure 5.2 uses dashed arrows to indicate that either of these outputs may be suppressed.

The compiler listing may contain many different features, depending on your compiler; you may be able to control the features included in your listing. Even a very basic listing will include error messages. Most systems will also include a copy of the source program in the listing unless you suppress it; the line numbers on the source program may be used in the error messages, or the compiler may just number the lines sequentially for its own reference. Some systems will also list the object program, if any; the object program is the assembly language translation of the source program.

You may also be able to get a name map, a list of each name (data-name or paragraph-name) in the program and its memory address. A cross-reference listing shows each name and all line numbers that refer to it.

Most of these features are used by system consultants to help you track down the source of a tricky error. The only features you need in order to handle compiler error messages at this time are the messages themselves and a listing of the source program.

Most compilers recognize two types of errors: low-level and high-level. **Low-level errors** are errors the compiler tries to fix. They result in warning messages but do not prevent the object program from being produced. For example, if you include a literal in a VALUE clause that is longer than the data item, most compilers will treat it as a low-level error: They will truncate the literal to the picture size and then will issue a message to warn you about what happened. In most cases you'll want to correct these errors yourself and not accept the compiler's corrections.

High-level errors are errors that the compiler can't even try to fix; they are also called **fatal errors** because they prevent the object program from being produced. For example, if you code DISPLAY MESSAGE-LINE and MESSAGE-LINE is not defined in the Data Division, most compilers will issue a fatal error message and suppress the object program.

The object program, if produced, contains the machine language translation of the COBOL code. The compiler probably puts it on a disk, unless you specify otherwise. In most systems an object program is not executable; it must be link edited to produce an executable module.

The Linker

Your system will have a set of special routines for handling I/O and other commonly needed operations. These routines will be stored on disk as object modules. The linker edits them or includes them in your programs as appropriate.

Even the simplest program requires some I/O routines because every different COBOL I/O statement (including ACCEPT and DIS-PLAY) results in a standard routine being edited into the program. Some compilers do the job of editing I/O routines into the object module, but most compilers leave that work for the linker.

The linker copies the I/O routines into the object program, creating an executable module; it fixes all addresses so the whole program works smoothly. It also lets you link together several object modules that have been compiled separately (perhaps because they were written by different members of the programming team) to form a single program.

If your operating system depends on a linker, you must run every object program through the linker to turn it into an executable module or load module.

Figure 5.3 shows the inputs and outputs of a typical linker program. The inputs include the object module, or modules if you're linking more than one together, and the system I/O routines. The outputs are a listing and possibly an executable program.

Figure 5.3 Inputs/Outputs of a Linker

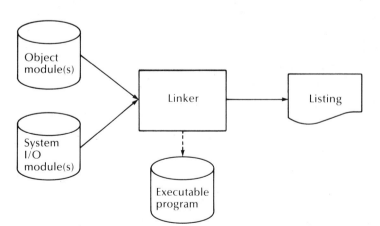

The listing is usually brief. It contains error messages if the linkage editor couldn't find the modules it needed. It might also contain the memory addresses of all the modules it linked together. Some linkers list a message showing the total size of the program. You will probably never use a linker listing until you learn to use assembly language and dumps to debug programs. If you do see link error messages at this stage, see your training manager or a helpful colleague.

The executable program is produced if the linker could find all the modules it needed (which it usually does).

Testing the Program

You test a program by executing it with test data. As you can see from Figure 5.4, the inputs and outputs depend on the program itself. When you test a program, you must provide whatever inputs it demands. The outputs produced will tell you whether it worked or not.

Summary Figure 5.5 summarizes the programmer's and system's viewpoints of the coding and testing phases of program development. The programmer codes the source program and enters it into the system. The source code is desk checked, walked through, and corrected. The programmer then asks the system to compile it. The programmer examines the compiler listing and corrects any errors it identifies. The program is corrected and recompiled until a clean compile is obtained. Then the programmer asks the system to link and, if the link is successful, execute the program. The program is tested, using input data created by the programmer. The programmer examines the output from the test run to determine if the program worked. If not, corrections are made to the source program and the entire process is repeated.

Figure 5.4 Inputs/Outputs of the Executable Program

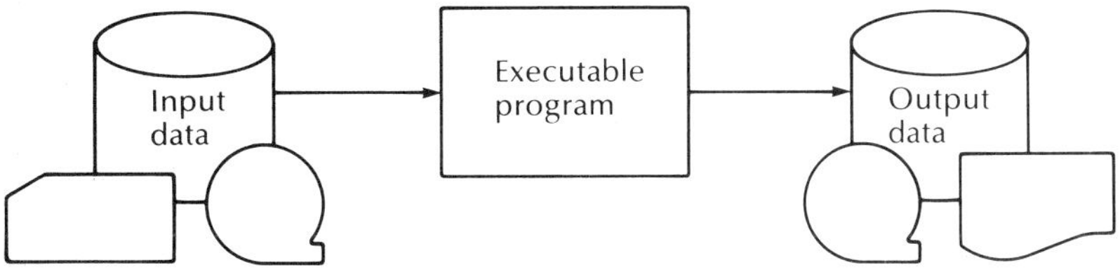

Figure 5.5 Interaction of Programmer and System in Coding and Testing Phases

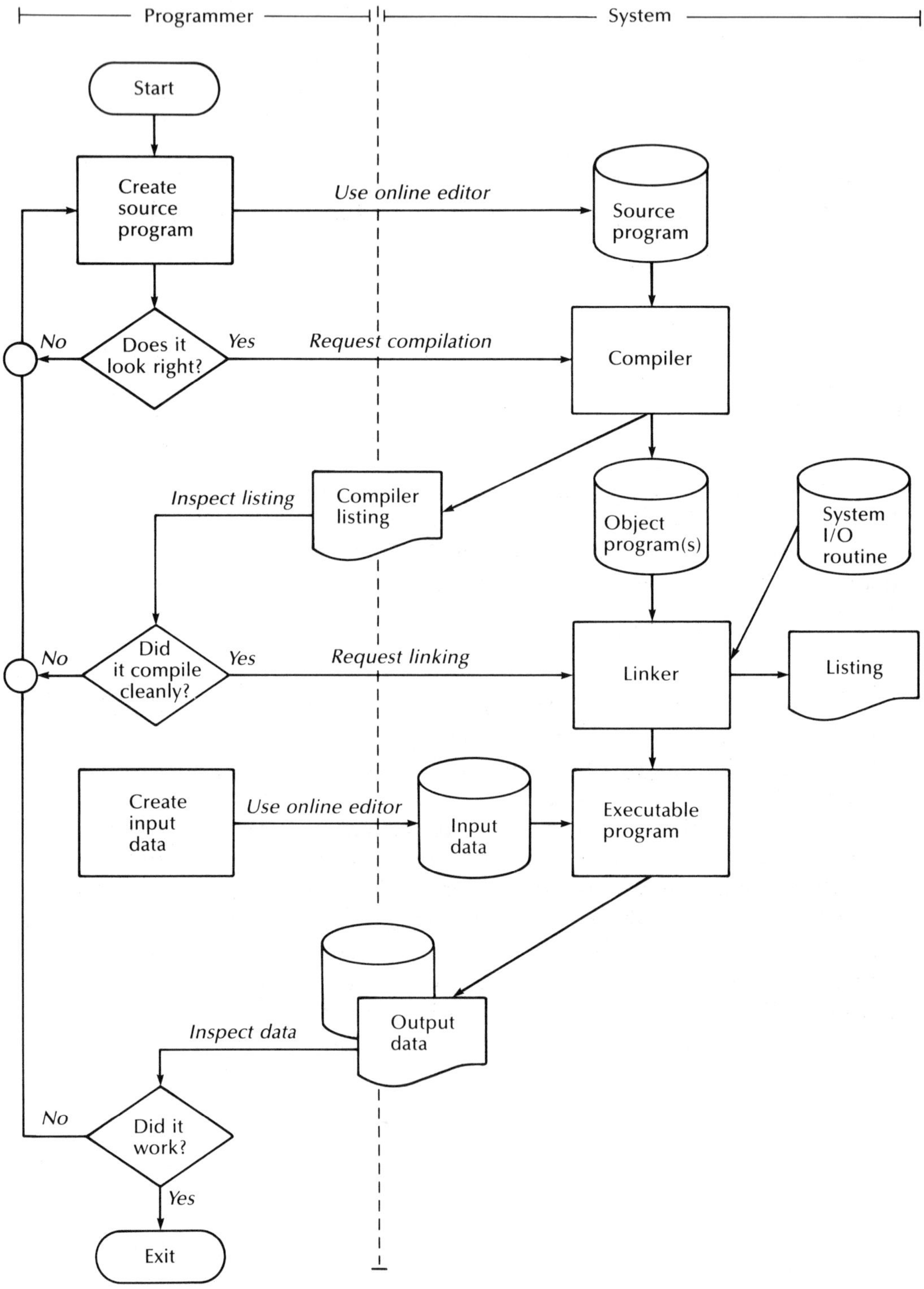

Comprehension Questions

1. Identify the output for each program. *Some outputs are used more than once.*

   _____ A. Linker
   _____ B. Executable program
   _____ C. Compiler

   a. Listing
   b. Object module
   c. Executable program
   d. Test results

2. During which part of program development do you play the role of the computer?

   _____

3. During which part do you go over the source code with fellow programmers?

   _____

4. After compilation, how can you find out what errors the compiler found?

   _____

   _____

5. Match the level of errors with the type of messages issued. *Some types are not used.*

   _____ A. High-level errors
   _____ B. Low-level errors

   a. Warning messages
   b. Fatal error messages
   c. No messages issued

6. True or false? Once a program compiles cleanly, you can make corrections to the object program so you never have to compile the source program again. _____

7. All of the following can be included in the listing for the IBM OS/VS COBOL compiler. (This compiler has other features as well.) Indicate which items you need in order to correct any syntax errors the compiler found.

   a. Warning messages
   b. Fatal error messages
   c. Listing of object program (in assembly language)
   d. Listing of source code
   e. Cross-reference listing

8. True or false? Every different COBOL I/O statement causes a system I/O module to be copied into the executable program. _____

9. Which of the following statements is true?

   a. Most COBOL programmers ignore the linker listings.
   b. COBOL programmers always use the linker listings.

10. Which of the following statements is true?

    a. Most programs will link cleanly the first time.
    b. Most programs will link cleanly the second time, after you fix all the errors from the first attempt.
    c. Most programs need to be linked and corrected several times before they link cleanly.

Answers

1. A - a, c; B - d; C - a, b **2.** Desk checking **3.** Walkthrough **4.** Look in the compiler listing **5.** A - b; B - a; c is not used **6.** False; corrections are made to the source program, which must be recompiled. **7.** a, b, d **8.** True **9.** a **10.** a

Application Questions

1. Put these steps in their proper order.

_____ a. Walkthrough

_____ b. Desk check

_____ c. Compile

2. Suppose you have written a complete source program and entered it into the system, using your online editor. It looks like this:

```
IDENTIFICATION DIVISION.
PROGRAM-ID.  CH5L1.
ENVIROMENT DIVISION.
DATA DIVISION.
WORKING STORAGE SECTION.
01  USER-DATA.
    05  USER-NAME                 PIC X(26).
    05  USER-CODE                 PIC X(4).
01  MESSAGE-LINE-1.
    05  OUT-CODE                  PIC X(4).
    05  FILLER                    PIC X(4)
                                  VALUE SPACES.
    05  OUT-NAME                  PIC X(20).
01  MESSAGE-LINE-2                PIC X(12)
                    VALUE "ENTRY LISTED".
PROCEDURE DIVISION.
PREPARE-COMPLETE-LIST.
    ACCEPTUSER-DATA.
    MOVE USER-CODE TO OUTCODE.
    MOVE USER-NAME TO OUTNAME.
    DISPLAY MESSAGE-LINE-1.
    DISPLAY MESSAGE-LINE-2.
    STOP RUN.
```

Desk check the program for spelling and punctuation errors.

3. We found several errors and corrected them. The program now looks like this:

```
IDENTIFICATION DIVISION.
PROGRAM-ID.  CH5L1.
ENVIRONMENT DIVISION.
DATA DIVISION.
WORKING-STORAGE SECTION.
01  USER-DATA.
    05  USER-NAME                 PIC X(26).
    05  USER-CODE                 PIC X(4).
01  MESSAGE-LINE-1.
    05  OUT-CODE                  PIC X(4).
    05  FILLER                    PIC X(4)
                                  VALUE SPACES.
    05  OUT-NAME                  PIC X(20).
01  MESSAGE-LINE-2                PIC X(12)
                    VALUE "ENTRY LISTED".
PROCEDURE DIVISION.
PREPARE-COMPLETE-LIST.
    ACCEPT USER-DATA.
    MOVE USER-CODE TO OUT-CODE.
    MOVE USER-NAME TO OUT-NAME.
    DISPLAY MESSAGE-LINE-1.
    DISPLAY MESSAGE-LINE-2.
    STOP RUN.
```

Now we want to check the logic.

a. Fill in some sample input data.

USER-NAME   USER-CODE

b. What is contained in USER-DATA when the program begins?

_____

c. Using your input data, what is displayed by the first DISPLAY statement?

_____

d. What is displayed by the second DISPLAY statement?

_____

4. Assume you have now verified the logic. In the on-the-job situation, especially with a longer program, what would you do next?

   a. Structured walkthrough
   b. Compilation
   c. Link
   d. Test

5. Number the following in sequence.

_____ a. Link

_____ b. Compile

_____ c. Test

6. Suppose you get an error message when you compile the program. What do you do next?

   a. Fix the error
   b. Recompile
   c. Link
   d. Test

Answers

1. a. 2 b. 1 c. 3   **2.** Spell ENVIRONMENT correctly; put hyphen in WORKING STORAGE; put space after ACCEPT; put hyphens in OUTCODE and OUTNAME in the Procedure Division.

3. a. Here's an example. You'll probably have different data.

JUDI N. FERNANDEZ	AAAA

b. garbage
c. JUDI N. FERNANDEZ   AAAA
d. ENTRY LISTED

4. a   **5.** a. 2 b. 1 c. 3   **6.** a

Types of Computer Runs

In the previous lesson you saw the various steps in the compilation and testing process. The three different computer programs discussed there (compiler, linker, and executable module) don't have to be run separately. You can ask the computer to execute two, or even all three, of them in a single run. This lesson considers when you might want to run a program separately and when you might want to combine it with others.

Objectives   You'll be able to identify the best type of run to use for a particular situation.

Rationale   When you finish coding a program, you have to decide how you want to compile and test it. There's no great harm done if you decide, for example, to compile-link-and-go when a compile-only run would have been more appropriate — but it's better to use the right job at the right time. Your installation may have guidelines for this; your training manager will let you know.

System resources are valuable. They are expensive if your organization must pay for the computer time and storage space it uses. They also must be shared among many users, and the more users there are, the longer each has to wait. So, submit the jobs you need to get your work done, but avoid asking for unnecessary processing. You will see this philosophy reflected in the material presented in this lesson.

Checking for Syntax

The first time you compile a program, you most likely will find errors. You can save time and resources by executing only the compiler and directing it to suppress creation of the object module. When you suppress the object module, the compiler examines each source program line and issues appropriate error messages, but it doesn't take the time to translate the source program to an object program. The error messages will be exactly the same as if you had not suppressed the object program.

When you run the compiler but suppress the object module, you're doing a **syntax check**. If the first syntax check produces a large number of problems, you might make the next run a syntax check, too. Keep doing syntax checks until only a few errors are identified. Then, after corrections have been made, you might be ready for the object module.

Generating an Object Module

When you think the next run will produce a clean compile, run the compiler without suppressing the object module. If you're like most beginning programmers, you'll probably have to do this a couple of times before you actually get a clean compile. If any serious errors are detected, the object module won't be generated in most systems. You'll get fatal error messages instead.

Testing the Program

Since linking almost never produces errors, most programmers either compile and link or link and test in one run. This means that a link follows a clean compile or that you ask the computer to link the program and then immediately execute it. You're counting on the linking succeeding or there won't be any program to execute. If the linker doesn't produce an executable program, one of two things will happen when the system tries to execute the program. An earlier version of the program will be executed, if there is one, or you'll get a system message saying that the requested program was not found.

When you're in this stage of testing, you're pretty sure that the program will need correcting. Therefore, you usually don't save the executable program. You direct the linker to generate it to be executed just once and not to save it in a permanent disk file.

Compile-Link-and-Go

After the first test run you'll identify errors to be corrected. If you have to make a lot of corrections to the source program, you'll need to repeat the above steps to compile and test it. However, if you have made only a couple of corrections and are pretty sure it will compile the first time, then you might ask the computer to compile, link, and execute the program in one run. The system will run the compiler, save the object program from the compiler and feed it to the linker, and then execute the program produced by the linker. All you have to do is provide any input and wait for the results. The system probably won't save the results permanently; you need special commands to arrange that.

You may have to make many runs to debug a program; most of them will be compile-link-and-go runs.

Saving the Executable Program

Once a program has completed controlled testing and is ready for live testing, you may want to generate a permanent executable program. If you save the executable program on disk (or wherever the system expects to find it), you can execute it repeatedly with different input data without waiting for the compile and link steps.

To save the executable program, run the good object module through the linker, telling the linker to save the output.

Cleaning Up at the End

When you have a fully working program to turn over to the user, you should clean up all your work files. Erase all earlier versions of the source, object, and executable programs, if your system hasn't done this automatically. Save a copy of the current source program, ready for maintenance changes; this is necessary so you or other programmers can clean up or modify the program later. You might move it from the active disk onto a vault disk or tape. You can erase the object module unless it is part of a larger program that is still being developed. You should save the executable module, of course. Exactly where you save it depends on the system, the application, and the user.

You should always save the latest compiler and linker listings, either on disk or on paper. They should go into the program's technical documentation.

Summary When you first start compiling a program, do syntax checks until you're pretty sure the next run will be clean. Then run the compiler without suppressing the object program until you get a clean compile. You can then link-and-go in one run to test the program. If you make only a few corrections to the source program, try a compile-link-and-go. Don't bother saving copies of the executable module until the program is ready for live testing. When the program goes into production, save the final source program, executable program, compiler listing, and linker listing.

Comprehension Questions

1. When you run the compiler but suppress the object module, what is the purpose of the run?

   _____

   _____

2. Why bother suppressing the object module?

   _____

   _____

3. True or false? A syntax check finds exactly the same errors as a regular compiler run. _____

4. Which of the following statements is true?

   a. Most programmers do a link-only run the first time they try to link edit a program.
   b. Most programmers link and test in one run, even the first time.

5. Suppose you submit a link-and-go run, but the linking fails and no executable program is produced. What will happen when the computer tries to execute a nonexistent program?

   a. The computer will be damaged, and you'll lose your job.
   b. The system will execute whatever version of the program it can find.
   c. The system will execute a program with a similar name.
   d. The system will issue an error message such as PROGRAM NOT FOUND.

6. In which type of run might you want to save the executable module?

   a. Compile-link-and-go
   b. Link-and-go
   c. Link only

7. Which type of run will you use most often in developing a program?

   _____

8. When do you save the executable program?

   a. Before the first test run
   b. After controlled testing and before live testing
   c. Only when the program is ready to go into production

9. What type of run do you use to save the executable program?

   _____

10. After a program goes into production, why should you save a copy of the source program on a vault disk or tape?

    _____

Answers

1. To check syntax **2.** To save time and system resources **3.** True **4.** b **5.** b or d, depending on circumstances (this depends on your system) **6.** c **7.** Compile-link-and-go (when you get into more complex programs, you may do dozens of compile-only runs as well) **8.** b **9.** Link only or compile-link **10.** For maintenance; so others can see it; in case executable program is damaged

Application Questions

1. You have just finished coding the first level of your source program—about 200 lines of code. What type of run should you use now?

   a. Compile-link-and-go
   b. Compile with object module
   c. Syntax check
   d. Link and save executable program
   e. Link-and-go (don't save executable program)

2. Your first attempt at compilation produced 10 warning messages and 23 fatal error messages. You have fixed all those errors (you think). What type of run should you use now?

   a. Compile-link-and-go
   b. Compile with object module
   c. Syntax check
   d. Link and save executable program
   e. Link-and-go (don't save executable program)

3. Your next attempt at compilation produced no warning messages and seven fatal error messages. You have fixed all those errors (you think). What type of run should you use now?

   a. Compile-link-and-go
   b. Compile with object module
   c. Syntax check
   d. Link and save executable program
   e. Link-and-go (don't save executable program)

4. Your next attempt at compilation produced two warning messages and no fatal error messages. You have fixed the errors that produced the warning messages. What type of run should you use now?

   a. Compile-link-and-go
   b. Compile with object module
   c. Syntax check
   d. Link and save executable program
   e. Link-and-go (don't save executable program)

5. You have a clean compile and the object program is on disk. Your input test data is ready. What type of run should you use to test the program?

   a. Compile-link-and-go
   b. Compile with object module
   c. Syntax check
   d. Link and save executable program
   e. Link-and-go (don't save executable program)

6. Your first test run bombed. You have located the error (you think) and made the corrections. You recoded two paragraphs, changing about 20 lines. What type of run should you use now?

    a. Compile-link-and-go
    b. Compile with object module
    c. Syntax check
    d. Link and save executable program
    e. Link-and-go (don't save executable program)

7. Your seventh test run resulted in some minor errors in the output. You have fixed the errors, changing two lines. What type of run should you use now?

    a. Compile-link-and-go
    b. Compile with object module
    c. Syntax check
    d. Link and save executable program
    e. Link-and-go (don't save executable program)

8. Your eleventh test run produces the correct output for the controlled test data. You're ready to start testing your program with live data. What type of run should you use now?

    a. Compile-link-and-go
    b. Compile with object module
    c. Syntax check
    d. Link and save executable program
    e. Link-and-go (don't save executable program)

9. Your program is ready to turn over to the user. Which of the following should be saved?

    a. The source code for the working program
    b. The source code for earlier versions of the program
    c. The object code for the working program
    d. The object code for earlier versions of the program
    e. The working executable program
    f. Earlier (imperfect) versions of the executable program
    g. The compiler listing for the working version of the program
    h. Compiler listings for earlier versions of the program
    i. The linker listing for the working version of the program
    j. Linker listings for earlier versions of the program

Answers

    1. c **2.** c **3.** c **4.** b **5.** e **6.** c (or a if you are fairly confident) **7.** a **8.** d
    9. a, e, g, and i

How to Do It

In this lesson you'll see how some installations compile and test COBOL programs. Your installation, in all likelihood, has different commands and/or different names for its procedures. It may have different options or requirements. At the end of this lesson you'll learn how to proceed at your installation.

Objectives   You'll be able to ask the right questions to find out how to compile and test programs that use only ACCEPT and DIS-PLAY statements for I/O.

Rationale   The process of compiling a COBOL program varies somewhat according to the computer system and COBOL compiler being used. You'll have to learn to use the method at your installation. If your installation uses one of the systems discussed here (IBM VSE, MVS SPF, or PDP 11/70 with IAS), pay special attention to that example. Otherwise scan the examples and read the summary before going on to the questions.

IBM VSE

The first example involves an IBM 4341 computer using the VSE operating system. The online editor is called ICCF (Interactive Computing and Control Facility). ICCF lets the programmer enter source program files and data files using a terminal. ICCF also lets the user execute **procedures**. A procedure is a set of commands, stored on disk, that tells the VSE operating system what to do.

At our sample installation, two procedures are used heavily by COBOL programmers. The first one, called COMP, executes the COBOL compiler and, if possible, the linker. The procedure includes all the VSE commands necessary to compile the program, run the link editor if an object module is produced, and save the executable program. The second procedure, called TEST, will execute the program.

The programmer creates the source file and then types a command like this on the terminal (assuming that the new program is named DOMONTHS):

```
COMP DOMONTHS
```

After submitting this command, the programmer has several ways of checking the status of the compile-and-link job. Some commands will check the status of DOMONTHS; other commands will let the programmer see what the computer is working on, what's waiting in line to be worked on, and what output files are waiting to be printed or displayed.

When the DOMONTHS job has finished, the programmer can either look at the listings on the terminal or have them printed. To look at them on the terminal, the programmer enters this command: /LP DOMONTHS. To print them, the programmer enters this command: /RP LST,DOMONTHS.

When the program has compiled and linked correctly, the programmer can test it with the TEST procedure. First the programmer must create a procedure file for the program. This file contains special operating system commands that will cause DOMONTHS to be executed. (The programmer must know how to write such commands for VSE or get a sample set.) If the procedure file is called TRYDOM, the programmer would then enter this command: TEST TRYDOM.

After TRYDOM is finished, the output will be wherever DO-MONTHS put it. DISPLAYed data might be printed or sent to the programmer's terminal, depending on the installation.

The programmer continues to use COMP and TEST until the program has passed all tests and is ready to go.

IBM MVS

The next example uses an IBM S/370 computer with the MVS operating system. The online editor is SPF (System Productivity Facility). SPF offers the programmer a main menu that looks something like Figure 5.6. The programmer chooses option 2 (Edit) to create source program and data files. After the programmer enters the number 2, the primary option menu disappears. SPF asks for the name of the file to be edited, then lets the programmer put data in that file. SPF maintains the file on a disk.

When the source file is ready, the programmer goes back to the primary option menu and chooses option 4 (Foreground). Then SPF displays a foreground selection menu as in Figure 5.7.

The programmer selects option 2 (OS/VS COBOL COMPILER). SPF then asks for the name of the file and causes the compiler to be executed. The system displays a special message on the terminal when the run is finished. The programmer then returns to the main menu and can view the compiler listing by using primary option 1 (Browse). SPF will ask for the name of the file to be browsed; the programmer enters the name of the compiler listing file. SPF displays that file and lets the programmer examine it.

Figure 5.6 SPF Primary Option Menu

```
-------------------- SPF PRIMARY OPTION MENU --------------------
SELECT OPTION ===>
-----------------------------------------------------------------
                                               USERID   - DU01
   0  SPF PARMS  - SPECIFY TERMINAL AND SPF PARAMETERS    TIME     - 05:06
   1  BROWSE     - DISPLAY SOURCE DATA OR OUTPUT LISTINGS TERMINAL - 3277
   2  EDIT       - CREATE OR CHANGE SOURCE DATA           PF KEYS  - 12
   3  UTILITY    - PERFORM SPF UTILITY FUNCTIONS
   4  FOREGROUND - COMPILE, ASSEMBLE, LINK EDIT, OR DEBUG
   5  BACKGROUND - COMPILE, ASSEMBLE, OR LINK EDIT
   6  TSO        - ENTER TSO COMMAND OR CLIST
   7  TUTORIAL   - DISPLAY INFORMATION ABOUT SPF


   X  EXIT       - TERMINATE SPF USING LIST/LOG DEFAULTS
-----------------------------------------------------------------
   PRESS END KEY TO TERMINATE SPF
-----------------------------------------------------------------
```

When the program compiles cleanly, the programmer can return to the foreground selection menu and choose option 6 (Linkage Editor) to link the program. Then the programmer must use primary option 2 (Edit) to create a file of commands that will cause the new program to be executed. The programmer can run this job by entering the command SUBMIT while editing the file.

Figure 5.7 SPF Foreground Selection Menu

```
-------------------- FOREGROUND SELECTION MENU --------------------
SELECT OPTION ===>

     1 - SYSTEM ASSEMBLER

     2 - OS/VS COBOL COMPILER

     3 - FORTRAN IV (G1) COMPILER

     4 - PL/I CHECKOUT COMPILER

     5 - PL/I OPTIMIZING COMPILER

     6 - LINKAGE EDITOR

     7 - COBOL INTERACTIVE DEBUG

     8 - FORTRAN INTERACTIVE DEBUG
```

After the job finishes, the DISPLAYed data will be displayed on the terminal or printed, depending on how the installation is set up. SPF includes options for printing a file that was supposed to be displayed and vice versa.

As you can see, SPF is very oriented toward selection menus. The programmer continues to select options and fill in data until the program is ready to go. Some installations, however, do not permit use of Foreground Processing because it monopolizes system resources immediately. In that case programmers may select Background Processing from the primary option menu for compilation. For testing they must often use the TSO option and execute procedures. In any case, Browse and Edit are used for creating programs and reviewing output.

Digital Equipment Corporation PDP 11/70

This example uses a PDP 11/70 with IAS operating system. The source program can be created using any of the PDP editors. The source program name should have the extension .CBL; for example, if a program is called MALLOW, the source program should be named MALLOW.CBL.

After leaving the editor, this program is compiled. To produce a source listing and error messages, the programmer types this command to IAS:

```
COBOL/LIST:MYLIST MALLOW
```

The source listing, including error messages, will be put into the file MYLIST.LST. The programmer views the listing by typing TYPE MYLIST.LST. Other output from the compiler will be an object program named MALLOW.OBJ and a file named MALLOW.SKL, which contains information that may be used by the link editor.

The command LINK MALLOW links this program. If the link ends successfully, it creates an executable file named MALLOW.TSK. The command RUN MALLOW runs the program. The system will execute MALLOW.TSK.

Summary The methods you use to compile and test programs depend on the system and compiler being used. You have seen three different types. Yours may be similar to one of these.

Comprehension Questions

Suppose your system has an online editor with these commands:

EDIT filename	— will allow you to create or correct a file.
COMP filename [SYNTAX]	— will compile the indicated file; SYNTAX does a syntax check only, suppressing the object module.
LINK filename	— will link edit the indicated files. They are automatically saved.
TEST filename	— will submit the indicated file for execution.
LINKTEST filename [SAVE]	— combines LINK and TEST; the executable module is kept only if SAVE is specified.
CLTEST filename [SAVE]	— combines COMP, LINK, and TEST: SAVE works as in LINKTEST.
VIEW filename	— will display the indicated files on your terminal.
PRINT filename	— will print the indicated file on a printer.

1. You are ready to begin coding your source program, to be stored in a file named CHAP6. Write a command that will allow you to create the file.

   _____

2. Now you have created the source file. Write a command to do a syntax check on it.

   _____

3. Your terminal displays a message saying COMP RUN COMPLETED. Write a command to examine the compiler listing at your terminal. It will be named CHAP6.LIST.

   _____

4. Your syntax check produced only four errors! (Congratulations.) Write a command that will let you correct the source program.

   _____

5. You have corrected the program. Write a command to recompile the program. This time, generate an object module.

   _____

6. Your terminal says COMP RUN COMPLETED. Write a command to examine the compiler listing at your terminal.

_____

7. You got a clean compile. Write a command to link and test the program. (The object module is called CHAP6.OBJ.)

_____

8. Your program accepts and displays data as it runs. As you work with it, you discover some corrections to be made to the source program. Write a command that will allow you to correct the source program.

_____

9. You have made minor corrections to the source program. Write a command to compile-link-and-go.

_____

10. Your program works perfectly! Write a command to generate and save a copy of the executable module. (The object module is called CHAP6.OBJ.)

_____

11. Write a command to print a copy of the compiler listing.

_____

12. Write a command to print a copy of the linker listing; its name is CHAP6.LLIST.

_____

See how easy it is? Your system may be more complex than this, of course. You may also have to make more runs to get a perfect program.

Answers

1. EDIT CHAP6   2. COMP CHAP6 SYNTAX   3. VIEW CHAP6.LIST   4. EDIT CHAP6
5. COMP CHAP6   6. VIEW CHAP6.LIST   7. LINKTEST CHAP6.OBJ
8. EDIT CHAP6   9. CLTEST CHAP6   10. LINK CHAP6.OBJ
11. PRINT CHAP6.LIST   12. PRINT CHAP6.LLIST

Application Questions

Check with your training manager or a knowledgeable programmer at your installation to find the answers to these questions.

1. Suppose you have a file named COBCH6 that contains source code for a COBOL program that uses no file I/O. You want to compile it.

   a. What command will you use to compile the program (syntax only)?

   _____

   b. How will you see the compiler listing?

   _____

2. Suppose your compilation produces two error messages. What do you do next?

   a. Recompile
   b. Correct the source program, then recompile
   c. Test the program

3. Suppose you have a clean compile.

   a. What command will you enter to link and test the program?

   _____

   b. How do you provide input for ACCEPT statements?

   _____

   c. How do you see DISPLAY output?

   _____

Answers

1. a. See your training manager b. See your training manager   2. b.   3. a. See your training manager b. See your training manager c. See your training manager

Chapter Review Questions

Check with your training manager or a helpful colleague to answer these questions.

1. Which of the following run types are recommended at your installation?

   a. Syntax check
   b. Compilation with listing and object
   c. Compile-link-and-go
   d. Run only
   e. Other

   _____

2. How can you compile a program, producing a listing and an object module? Write a brief description of the process you will use at your installation.

   _____

3. How can you see the compiler listing?

   _____

4. After you get a clean compile, how can you run the program?

   _____

5. You have two source programs from Chapter 4 stored in your system. If it is convenient, submit your first program (CH4AXXX from Lesson 4.4) for compilation now. If not, you'll do it in the exercise at the end of Part 3. You'll learn to interpret the listing in the next chapter.

Answers

1. This depends on your system. Use the most recommended runs.   **2.** This depends on your system. You may have a command, an SPF menu, or some other method.   **3.** This depends on your system. You may get an actual printout, or you may enter a command to access the listing file at the terminal.   **4.** This depends on your system.   **5.** You have successfully submitted a program for compilation. Hold on to the compiler listing. Don't worry yet about what it contains.

Chapter 6

Compilation and Testing

Every COBOL source program must be compiled in the process of creating an executable program. Most compiler programs have several options you can control, as well as specific formats for the resulting listings.

In this chapter you'll learn what some common compiler options are and see how they affect the listing. You'll also see a variety of messages that compilers may issue. These messages help you to correct your source program and try again.

Since you won't use any input data in your early programs, you won't have to be concerned with test plans at this time.

This chapter consists of three lessons:

Lesson 6.1: The Compiler Listing
Lesson 6.2: Correcting Compiler Errors
Lesson 6.3: Testing Programs

The Compiler Listing

Most compilers have two major options: you can specify whether an object module and/or a listing are produced. This lesson assumes you will accept the default status for these two options. That is, you will not explicitly state whether these two outputs are produced. Most compilers are set up to produce both outputs by default.

This lesson will show you some other options your compiler may have that affect the content of the compiler listing. This discussion reproduces parts of a typical compiler listing produced by an IBM VSE system. The listing produced by your compiler will probably be somewhat different.

Objectives You'll be able to recognize the parts of a typical compiler listing.

Rationale As a programmer, you'll look at thousands of compiler listings. You need to know what information to ignore, what to use, and how to interpret it.

The Basic Contents

The very basic compiler listing contains at least two components: the source code and messages. Every compiler listing must have these components to be of any use to the programmer.

The source listing and the messages are usually all you need to identify and correct errors at the compilation stage, especially with very short programs. Other parts of the compiler listing are used in advanced debugging only.

Source Listing Figure 6.1 shows the source listing from a compilation run. This program was coded without line numbers. The numbers on the left are provided by the compiler and are used in error messages. Our compilation procedure adds the first working-storage entry, which you see on line 6. (It helps the operator and management identify leftover listings.)

Those strange-looking top lines document the COBOL compiler options in effect for this compilation run. Don't worry about them now. Several of them will be discussed in this lesson.

Figure 6.1 Source Listing

```
        1   IBM DOS/VS COBOL                           REL 3.0
CBL   OPT,CLIST,SXREF,FLAGE,SUBMAP,LIB,NOTRUNC,NOZWB,VERB,APOST
CBL   LANGLEV(1)
00001              IDENTIFICATION DIVISION.
00002              PROGRAM-ID.  COB1E4.
00003              ENVIRONMENT DIVISION.
00004              DATA DIVISION.
00005              WORKING-STORAGE SECTION.
00006              77  FILLER PIC X(32) VALUE 'COB1E4 830715 100145 DUOT'.
00007              01  MESSAGES.
00008                  05  MESSAGE-LINE-1          PIC X(22)
00009                                      VALUE 'THIS IS THE FIRST LINE'.
00010                  05  MESSAGE-LINE-2          PIC X(23)
00011                                      VALUE 'THIS IS THE SECOND LINE'.
00012                  05  MESSAGE-LINE-3          PIC   X(11)
00013                                      VALUE 'END PROGRAM'.
00014                  05  MESSAGE-LINE-SPACE      PIC X       VALUE SPACE.
00015
00016              PROCEDURE-DIVISION.
00017              SHOW-EFFECTS.
00018                  DISPLAY MESSAGE-LINE-1.
00019                  DISPLAY MESSAGE-LINE-SPACE.
00020                  DISPLAY MESSAGE-LINE-2.
00021                  DISPLAY MESSAGE-LINE-SPACE.
00022                  DISPLAY MESSAGE-LINE-3.
00023                  STOP RUN.
```

Error Messages   Figure 6.2 shows the error messages produced when the source program in Figure 6.1 was compiled. Notice the heading "CARD". That refers to the line number in the source listing. ("Card" is still used in messages and conversation, even if the system hasn't seen a punch card in years!) The error messages here refer to line 16.

Each error message is preceded by a message ID code in this listing. If necessary, you can look up the ID code in the compiler manual to find a longer explanation of the problem. In most cases, however, the text of the message itself tells all you need to know. In the figure, the message states that PROCEDURE-DIVISION is an invalid word. If you look at line 16 in the source listing, you'll see that a hyphen was inadvertently included in the division header. This error gave rise to all the messages. Note that the error was fatal.

The next lesson includes a variety of compiler messages.

Figure 6.2 Error Messages

```
      6       COB1E4      10.02.03      07/15/85

CARD   ERROR MESSAGE

00016  ILA1004I-E    INVALID WORD PROCEDURE-DIVISION . SKIPPING TO NEXT RECOGNIZABLE WORD.
       ILA1130I-E    PROCEDURE DIVISION. HEADER MISSING. WORDS IN PROCEDURE STATEMENTS ARE INVALID.


      7       COB1E4      10.02.03      07/15/85

ILA0004I- OUTPUT OPTIONS SUPPRESSED DUT TO ERROR SEVERITY
END OF COMPILATION
```

Other Compiler Listing Sections

Most compilers can include additional information in listings by default or on request. The options available depend on the compiler. Your installation will have selected a standard set to include by default.

List of Defined Data Items   Figure 6.3 shows how our compiler provides a list of defined items. You can see the level numbers and source-names just as in the source listing. Under DEFINITION you can see the length of each item, where C stands for character. The INTERNL NAME is one used internally by the compiler. It may appear in messages instead of the source-name.

In advanced debugging of a large program, this table can be useful in reviewing the defined fields.

Memory Map and Statistics   Figure 6.4 shows the memory map and statistics our compiler provides. You won't have to use this information until you are more experienced. Your compiler, too, will probably tell you more than you want to know about what it did.

Figure 6.3 List of Defined Data Items

```
2       COB1E4        10.02.03      07/15/85

INTRNL NAME    LVL SOURCE NAME        BASE  DISPL  INTRNL NAME  DEFINITION  USAGE  R O O M
DNM=1-016      77  FILLER             BL=1  000    DNM=1-016    DS 32C      DISP
DNM=1-032      01  MESSAGES           BL=1  020    DNM=1-032    DS 0CL57    GROUP
DNM=1-053      02  MESSAGE-LINE-1     BL=1  020    DNM=1-053    DS 22C      DISP
DNM=1-077      02  MESSAGE-LINE-2     BL=1  036    DNM=1-077    DS 23C      DISP
DNM=1-101      02  MESSAGE-LINE-3     BL=1  04D    DNM=1-101    DS 11C      DISP
DNM=1-125      02  MESSAGE-LINE-SPACE BL=1  058    DNM=1-125    DS 1C       DISP
```

Figure 6.4 Memory Map and Statistics

```
3            COB1E4       10.02.03      07/15/85

                    MEMORY MAP

                 TGT                 00160

              SAVE AREA              00160
              SWITCH                 001A8
              TALLY                  001AC
              SORT SAVE              001B0
              ENTRY-SAVE             001B4
              SORT CORE SIZE         001B8
              NSTD-REELS             001BC
              SORT RET               001BE
              WORKING CELLS          001C0
              SORT FILE SIZE         002F0
              SORT MODE SIZE         002F4
              PGT-VN TBL             002F8
              TGT-VN TBL             002FC
              SORTAB ADDRESS         00300
              LENGTH OF VN TBL       00304
              LNGTH OF SORTAB        00306
              PGM ID                 00308
              A(INIT1)               00310
              UPS1 SWITCHES          00314
              DEBUG TABLE PTR        0031C
              CURRENT PRIORITY       00320
              TA LENGTH              00321
              PRBL1 CELL PTR         00324
              UNUSED                 00328
              COUNT TABLE ADDRESS    0032C
              VSAM SAVE AREA ADDRESS 00330
              UNUSED                 00334
              COUNT CHAIN ADDRESS    0033C
              UNUSED                 00340
              DBG R14SAVE            00354
              UNUSED                 00358
              UNUSED                 0035C
              DBG R11SAVE            00360
              PCS LIT PTR            00364
              DBG INF PTR            00368
              OVERFLOW CELLS         00378
              BL CELLS               00378
              DTFADR CELLS           0037C
              FIB CELLS              0037C
              TEMP STORAGE           00380
              TEMP STORAGE-2         00380
              TEMP STORAGE-3         00380
              TEMP STORAGE-4         00380
              BLL CELLS              00380
              VLC CELLS              00384
              SBL CELLS              00384
              INDEX CELLS            00384


4            COB1E4       10.02.03      07/15/85

              SUBADR CELLS           00384
              ONCTL CELLS            00384
              PFMCTL CELLS           00384
              PFMSAV CELLS           00834
              VN CELLS               00384
              SAVE AREA =2           00384
              SAVE AREA =3           00384
              XSASW CELLS            00384
              XSA CELLS              00384
              PARAM CELLS            00384
              RPTSAV AREA            00384
              CHECKPT CTR            00384
              IOPTR CELLS            00384
              DEBUG TABLE            00384

                 PGT                 00388

              DEBUG LINKAGE AREA     00388
              OVERFLOW CELLS         00388
              VIRTUAL CELLS          0038C
              PROCEDURE NAME CELLS   0039C
              GENERATED NAME CELLS   0039C
              SUBDTF ADDRESS CELLS   0039C
              VNI CELLS              0039C
              LITERALS               003A0
              DISPLAY LITERALS       003A0
              PROCEDURE BLOCK CELLS  003A0

      REGISTER ASSIGNMENT

  WORKING-STORAGE STARTS AT LOCATION 00100 FOR A LENGTH OF 00060.

      PROCEDURE BLOCK ASSIGNMENT

       PBL = REG 11

       PBL =1   STARTS AT LOCATION 0003A4  STATEMENT 0
       PBL =2   STARTS AT LOCATION 0003A8  STATEMENT 0

  *STATISTICS*        SOURCE RECORDS =        DATA ITEMS =      6    PROC DIV SZ =
  *STATISTICS*        PARTITION SIZE = 262024 LINE COUNT =     56    BUFFER SIZE =    2048
  *OPTIONS IN EFFECT*  PMAP RELOC ADR =  NONE SPACING    =      1    FLOW        =    NONE
  *OPTIONS IN EFFECT*   NOLISTX     APOST    SYM   NOCATALR     LIST      LINK    NOSTXIT    LIB
  *OPTIONS IN EFFECT*    CLIST      FLAGE   NOZWB  NOSUPMAP     XREF      ERRS    SXREF      OPT
  *OPTIONS IN EFFECT*   NOSTATE    NOTRUNC   SEQ   NOSYMOMP    NODECK     VERB    NCSYNTAX   NOLVL
  *OPTIONS IN EFFECT*   LANGLVL(1) NOCOUNT   ADV            NOVERBSUM  NOVERBREF
  *LISTER OPTIONS*        NONE
```

Cross-Reference Listings Figure 6.5 shows two cross-reference data item listings, one from a program with more data items than the program in Figure 6.1. Each data-name is listed here, followed by the number of the line on which it was defined. Then the number of each line that refers to the item is listed. This information won't be helpful until you get involved in advanced debugging, but it may be included in listings just the same. Notice that the first listing shows no references to the data items. Remember that the Procedure Division header wasn't recognized, so the references in the Procedure Division aren't considered valid.

Figure 6.6 shows a cross-reference procedure-name listing. This lists paragraph-names (as PROCEDURE-NAMES) and shows where each is defined (by its appearance in area A) and where each reference to it is made. No cross-reference procedure listing was produced for the source program in Figure 6.1, since the Procedure Division header was invalid. As with other compiler listing information, this data will not be needed until you debug advanced programs.

Other Listing Information The compiler listing may also include control statements and messages relating to the successful (or unsuccessful) completion of the compilation. If an object module was produced, the listing may indicate what happened to it.

Many compiler runs include the link step. The output will then include the link listing too. The contents of the link listing are sel-

Figure 6.5 Cross-Reference Data Item Listings

```
    5        COB1E4          10.02.03        07/15/85

                                    CROSS-REFERENCE DICTIONARY

DATA NAMES                    DEFN    REFERENCE

MESSAGE-LINE-SPACE            000014
MESSAGE-LINE-1                000008
MESSAGE-LINE-2                000010
MESSAGE-LINE-3                000012
MESSAGES                      000007

    7        COB154          17.24.59        02/22/85

                                    CROSS-REFERENCE DICTIONARY

DATA NAMES                    DEFN    REFERENCE

DATE-FIELD                    000017  000038
EMPLOYEE-CATEGORY             000010  000051  000057
EMPLOYEE-DATA                 000005  000032  000044
EMPLOYEE-HOURS                000012  000042  000069  000073  000077  000081
EMPLOYEE-NAME                 000008  000046
EMPLOYEE-NUMBER               000006  000033
FOOTING-LINE                  000025  000035
HEADING-LINE                  000013  000039
OUT-CATEGORY                  000024  000058  000060  000064  000068  000072  000076  000080
OUT-HOURS                     000022  000061  000065  000069  000073  000077  000081
OUT-LINE                      000018  000048
OUT-NAME                      000020  000046
```

Figure 6.6 Cross-Reference Procedure Listing

```
   8       COB154          17.24.59        02/22/85

PROCEDURE NAMES                  DEFN     REFERENCE

CASE-PREPARE-LINE                000050   000047
CASE-PREPARE-LINE-EXIT           000083   000047   000062   000066   000070   000074   000078   000082
CASE1-HANDLE-EXECUTIVES          000063   000051
CASE2-HANDLE-MANAGERS            000067   000051
CASE3-HANDLE-CLERICAL-STAFF      000071   000051
CASE4-HANDLE-SHOP-FOLKS          000075   000051
CASE5-HANDLE-ROAD-CREW           000079   000051
DO-HEADING                       000037   000031
HANDLE-EMPLOYEE                  000045   000043
PREPARE-EMPLOYMENT-REPORT        000030
PROCESS-DATA                     000041   000033
```

dom useful to novice programmers. If anything goes wrong in linkage, you'll probably have to get the help of an in-house troubleshooter.

Selecting Compiler Options

As indicated earlier, the format of your compiler listing depends on the options in effect. How you specify the options, and what you can specify, depends on the compiler. Most installations have a basic procedure for using the compiler, which sets the options they consider most useful.

The listing shows what options are in effect. The sample listing reflects IBM's FCOBOL compiler run on an IBM 4331 computer with the VSE operating system. Two lines preceding the source listing in Figure 6.1 specify the nondefault options used here. Near the bottom of Figure 6.4 is a complete listing of the options in effect, including default ones.

You can find out what options are available for your compiler by checking the documentation or asking a colleague. In most cases you'll get along fine with the standard options at your installation. As long as you have a numbered source listing and the messages, you'll be able to identify errors.

Summary In this lesson you examined a typical compiler listing. The most useful parts of this listing are the source listing and the error messages. Most compilation problems can be solved using only these two sections. Other sections are generally used only in debugging more advanced programs.

You may be able to specify options to control what is included in your compiler listings. Check your compiler documentation or ask a colleague.

Comprehension Questions

1. In which of the following do you find error messages?

   a. Source module
   b. Object module
   c. Compiler listing

2. Which section of a compiler listing shows every line that uses a particular data item?

   a. Memory map
   b. Cross-reference listing
   c. Statistics
   d. Error messages

3. Which section of a compiler listing shows what statement the compiler considers to be CARD 00030?

   a. Source listing
   b. Memory map
   c. Cross-reference listing
   d. Statistics
   e. Error messages

4. Which two sections of a compiler listing are sufficient to identify most compile-stage errors?

   a. Source listing
   b. Memory map
   c. Cross-reference listing
   d. Statistics
   e. Error messages

5. What compiler option would you request to produce a listing of all paragraphs and where each is referenced?

   a. Source listing
   b. Object module
   c. Cross-reference listing
   d. Link

Answers

   1. c   **2.** b   **3.** a   **4.** a, e   **5.** c

Application Questions

For this exercise, locate a compiler listing from your installation. This can be a clean compile or it can include errors. Be sure to get a listing produced by the standard compile procedure used by COBOL programmers.

1. Find out what command invoked the compiler run.

_____

2. Is there a source listing? _____

3. Is there a cross-reference listing:

a. for data-names? _____

b. for paragraph-names? _____

4. Is there a listing of errors? _____

Answers

These depend on your installation. Compiler listings produced by your compiler will be similar in format.

Correcting Compiler Errors

You will use messages produced by a compilation run to identify syntax errors in your source program. In this lesson, you'll see an assortment of error messages with corresponding source code. Although the messages are worded differently by different compilers, the general intent of the message will be clear in most cases. Since message numbers and exact wording of compiler messages vary so much, the figures will include only the line number and text of messages produced.

Objective   You'll be able to specify corrections for a wide variety of compilation errors.

Rationale   While a clean first compile would be great, it seldom occurs, especially with longer programs. Every programmer has to deal with compilation error messages, correct the source code, and try again.

Compiler Messages

The following section will walk through a number of messages and show how to correct the errors. Your compiler may issue several levels of message, such as warnings and error messages. All messages should be handled before you rerun a program. The source program must be corrected and recompiled until a clean compile (one with no errors) is achieved.

Data Definition Problems   Figure 6.7 shows several lines of source code and a message produced by the compiler.

Figure 6.7 Compiler Listing Excerpts

Source code
```
00007      05  MESSAGE-LINE              PIC X(10)
00008              VALUE "THIS IS THE INITIALIZED VALUE".
00009      PROCEDURE DIVISION.
```

Line	Message
00007	VALUE CLAUSE LITERAL TOO LONG. TRUNCATED TO PICTURE SIZE.

The message explains the problem and tells what the compiler did about it. In this case, the problem is that the literal in the VALUE clause is too long. When you look at the referenced line, you see that the value was defined as PIC X(10). The literal (which is coded on the subsequent line) is clearly longer than ten characters. The compiler "TRUNCATED" the value "TO PICTURE SIZE"; this means the value assigned to MESSAGE-LINE is "THIS IS TH" rather than the coded value.

Errors of this type can be corrected in either of two ways. You can change the picture so the coded value will fit, or you can shorten the literal to match the coded picture. Which you do depends on the program specifications. In this case, use a picture of X(29) or longer.

Figure 6.8 shows a related problem. Here the message for line 8 says the literal was not continued appropriately. If you look at line 00008, you'll see that the ending quote was omitted. The compiler reacts to this by assuming the literal ends on the "LAST CARD", or the last line of the program. This assumption gives rise to the next message. If the literal extends to the last card, then it is too long; so it is truncated to 30 characters (the picture size). This includes part of the division header.

Figure 6.8 Compiler Listing Excerpts

Source code

```
00007      05   MESSAGE-LINE                    PIC X(30)
00008                          VALUE 'THIS IS THE INITIALIZED VALUE.
00009      PROCEDURE DIVISION.
```

Line   **Message**

```
00008      NONNUMERIC LIT NOT CONTINUED WITH HYPHEN AND QUOTE.
           END LITERAL ON LAST CARD.
00007      VALUE CLAUSE LITERAL TOO LONG.  TRUNCATED TO PICTURE SIZE.
```

Figure 6.9 Compiler Listing Excerpts

Source code

```
00078      MOVE CURRENT-DATE TO DATE-FIELD
```

Line   **Message**

```
00078      DATE-FIELD NOT DEFINED.  DISCARDED.
```

You would correct both these errors by inserting an ending quote for the literal. Notice in this case that one error caused two error messages. Sometimes you'll get dozens of messages from a single error.

Figure 6.9 shows another type of data definition problem. Here the message tells you that data item DATE-FIELD was not defined. The referenced line is from the Procedure Division. The compiler reacts by discarding the statement involved.

Upon reading this message you should check the Data Division for the definition of DATE-FIELD. In all likelihood it was omitted or spelled differently. The definition should be added or corrected.

Figure 6.10 shows a similar problem. You can see that the name in the Data Division is spelled differently from the name in the Procedure Division. You most likely would correct this error by changing USR-NAME on line 0013 to USER-NAME.

Figure 6.10 Compiler Listing Excerpts

Source code

```
00006      WORKING-STORAGE SECTION.
00007      01  USER-DATA.
00008          05  USER-NAME              PIC X(26).
00009          05  USER-CODE              PIC X(4).
               .
               .
               .
00013          MOVE USR-NAME TO OUT-NAME.
```

Line   Message

```
00013      USR-NAME NOT DEFINED.   TEST DISCARDED.
```

Procedure Division Problems   Figure 6.11 shows the effect of omitting a trailing quote in the Procedure Division. The compiler makes the same assumption as it did in the Data Division (Figure 6.8); that is, it assumes that the literal ends on the program's last line. As before, the appropriate correction is to insert the quotation mark.

Figure 6.12 shows the effect of omitting the Procedure Division header. The paragraph name is not valid in the Data Division, so the compiler skips ahead to the next recognizable word. It soon realizes that the Procedure Division header is missing, so all the words are invalid. You would eliminate these messages by inserting the header.

Figure 6.11 Compiler Listing Excerpts

Source code

```
00015      DISPLAY 'ALL ITEMS LISTED.
00016      STOP RUN.
```

Line   Message

```
00015      NONNUMERIC LIT NOT CONTINUED WITH HYPHEN AND QUOTE.
           END LITERAL ON LAST CARD.
```

Figure 6.12 Compiler Listing Excerpts

Source code

```
00023          05   OUT-NAME                    PIC X(20).
00024
00025          PREPARE-USER-REPORT.
00026              ACCEPT USER-INPUT.
```

Line   **Message**

```
00025      INVALID WORD PREPARE-USER-REPORT.
               SKIPPING TO NEXT RECOGNIZABLE WORD.
           PROCEDURE DIVISION.  HEADER MISSING.
               WORDS IN PROCEDURE STATEMENTS ARE INVALID.
```

Other Message Types   Here are some more messages, all of which are self-explanatory.

```
(1) ID DIVISION HEADER MISSING OR MISPLACED.  ASSUMED PRESENT.
(2) ' STOP-RUN ' NOT DEFINED.  DELETING TILL LEGAL ELEMENT FOUND.
(3) PICTURE CONFIGURATION ILLEGAL.  PICTURE CHANGED TO 9.
```

You will be able to correct most compilation errors after reading the messages and examining the lines. However, your corrections may generate more errors or may allow the compiler to discover things it didn't see before, so don't be surprised if you don't get a clean compilation the second time either.

Compiler Flexibility in Standard COBOL Format

Compilers differ in what they allow. Most compilers allow some small variations from standard COBOL. For example, some compilers will let you code all level numbers in area B. Some will not insist on a space following a period or comma.

This book uses code that meets the COBOL standard. If your compiler allows you more flexibility, you may use it. Doing so will make your program less compatible with other systems, however.

Summary   Any syntax errors or inconsistencies in a COBOL program generate messages on compilation. Sometimes one error results in several messages. Sometimes, also, the compiler doesn't recognize the real error but instead sees an inconsistency later on. You must examine the messages and the source lines and try to determine what errors were made. You then correct the source program and recompile it.

Comprehension Questions

1. Suppose you receive a compilation listing that includes this message:

```
00006      PICTURE CONFIGURATION ILLEGAL.  PICTURE CHANGED TO 9.
```

What do you do next?

   a. Recompile the program.
   b. Change the picture in line 6 to 9, then recompile the program.
   c. Examine the picture in line 6 and correct it, then recompile the program.
   d. Examine the picture in line 6 and correct it, then test the program.
   e. Test the program.

2. Suppose a compilation listing includes this message:

```
00026              DISPLAY FOOTING-LINE.
                 .
                 .
                 .
00026        'FOOTING-LINE' NOT DEFINED.  DISCARDED.
```

What could be the problem?

   a. You may have spelled the item differently in the Data Division.
   b. You may have defined FOOTING-LINE as a record rather than an elementary item.
   c. You may not have assigned an initial value to FOOTING-LINE.

3. Suppose a compilation listing includes this message:

```
00026          DISPLAY FOOTING-LINE.
             .
             .
             .
00026     'FOOTING-LINE' NOT DEFINED.  DISCARDED.
```

What did the compiler do here?

   a. Discarded the source program
   b. Discarded the DISPLAY statement
   c. Discarded the value of FOOTING-LINE

Answers

   1. c   **2.** a   **3.** b

Application Questions

1. Source code

```
00005      WORKING-STORAGE SECTION.
00007      01  USER-DATA.
00008          05  USER-NAME             PIC (26)X.
00009          05  USER-CODE             PIC XXXX.
```

Line	Message
00008	PICTURE CONFIGURATION ILLEGAL. PICTURE CHANGED TO 9.

How would you correct this error?

_____

2. Source code

```
00014          MOVE ERROR-MESSAGE MESSAGE-LINE.
00015          DISPLAY MESSAGE-LINE.
00016          DISPLAY BLANK-LINE.
00017          MOVE TYPE-ERROR TO ENDING-LINE.
00018          DISPLAY ENDING-LINE.
00019          STOP-RUN.
```

Line	Message
00014	TO MISSING OR MISPLACED IN MOVE STATEMENT. ASSUMED IN REQUIRED POSITION.
00019	' STOP-RUN ' NOT DEFINED. DELETING TILL LEGAL ELEMENT FOUND.

How would you correct this program?

_____

_____

3. Source code

```
00007    01   USER-DATA.
00008         05USER-NAME                      PIC X(26).
00009         05USER-CODE                      PIC X(14).
...

00018    PROCEDURE DIVISION.
00019    PRACTICE-DISPLAY.
00020         ACCEPT USER-DATA.
00021         MOVE USER-NAME USER-NAME-OUT.
00022         MOVE USER-CODE TO USER-CODE-OUT.
00023         DISPLAY MESSAGE-LINE.
00024         DISPLAY SPACE-LINE.
00025         STOP RUN.
```

Line	Message
00008	INVALID WORD 05USER-NAME . SKIPPING TO NEXT RECOGNIZABLE WORD.
00007	ELEMENTARY ITEMS NOT INTERNAL FLOATING-POINT MUST HAVE PICTURE. PICTURE ASSUMED9.
00021	' USER-NAME ' NOT DEFINED. TEST DISCARDED.
00022	' USER-CODE ' NOT DEFINED. DISCARDED.

How would you correct these errors?

_____

_____

_____

4. Source code

```
00001    IDENTIFICATION DIVISION.
00002    PROGRAM-ID.
00003        C1ERR.
00004    ENVIRONMENT DIVISION.
00005    DATA DIVISION.
00006    WORKING-STORAGE SECTION.
00007    01   DISPLAY-LINES.
00008         05   DOUBLE-LINE     PIC X(25)    VALUE ALL "=".
00009         05   SPACE-LINE      PIC X        VALUE SPACE.
00010         05   HELLO-LINE      PIC X(23)
00011                              VALUE "        HELLO         ".
00012    PROCEDURE DIVISION.
00013    PRACTICE-DISPLAY.
00014         DISPLAY DOUBLE-LINE.
00015         DISPLAY SPACE-LINE.
00016         DISPLAY HELLO-LINE.
00017         DISPLAY SPACE-LINE.
00018         DISPLAY DOUBLE-LINE.
00019         STOP RUN.
```

Line	Message
00001	ID DIVISION HEADER MISSING OR MISPLACED. ASSUMED PRESENT.
00001	INVALID WORD DENTIFICATION. SKIPPING TO NEXT RECOGNIZABLE WORD.
00002	PROGRAM-ID MISSING OR MISPLACED. IF PROGRAM-ID DOES NOT IMMEDIATELY FOLLOW IDENTIFICATION DIVISION, IT WILL BE IGNORED.
	DATA DIVISION. HEADER MISSING. WORDS IN DATA STATEMENTS ARE INVALID.
	PROCEDURE DIVISION. HEADER MISSING. WORDS IN PROCEDURE STATEMENT ARE INVALID.

What caused *all* of these messages?

_____

_____

_____

5. If you submitted your program for compilation at the end of the last chapter, take time now to check your compiler listing. If any errors were identified, make corrections to your source program and recompile the program.

Answers

1. Change picture to X(26).   2. Insert TO in MOVE statement. Replace hyphen in STOP-RUN with a space.   3. Insert spaces after level 05.   4. Column 7 was used for the left column; it should be column 8. (Notice that the second message refers to the word "DENTIFICATION".).   5. You should have a clean compilation by now. See your training manager or a colleague if you have problems. If you haven't submitted your program for compilation yet, don't worry. You'll get to it shortly.

Testing Programs

Introduction to Computer Programming covered many testing concepts. You learned to write a test plan and to consider various error possibilities. In this lesson you'll apply those concepts to simple, no-input programs of the type you have learned to code and compile. You won't have to design test data since these programs use no external input.

Objectives   You'll be able to specify expected output for a simple program. You'll also find out how to test a program that accesses the date and uses DISPLAY statements.

Rationale   You'll be concerned about testing for every program you write. This lesson will help you get ready to test your own programs.

Incorrect Output

A test plan for programs that use no input from outside the program is quite simple: you just sketch the output you expect. Suppose, for example, you have written a program to display your company name in a box. The expected output from the program would be the company name in a box, as shown in Figure 6.13.

After the program compiles, you run it. If the output doesn't look like the sketch, you modify your program, recompile it, and run it again until it does.

If your program accesses the date or time, you have another source of potential errors. Suppose you are testing a program that includes this definition:

```
01   JULIAN-DATE.
     05   JULIAN-DAY      PIC XXX.
     05   JULIAN-YEAR     PIC XX.
```

Figure 6.13 Expected Output

```
|------------------------|
|                        |
|      DUOTECH, INC      |
|                        |
|------------------------|
```

The program compiles and runs fine, but (on January 21, 1986) it displays this message:

```
DAY 860    YEAR 21
```

By examining the output you can see that the date field is not subdivided correctly. (The year is first in all system date fields.)

Incorrect output generally shows you what is wrong with a program. Common sense (and careful thinking) tells you how to fix your program.

Program Bomb

All programs may bomb, but the very simple ones you are running now aren't likely to. The only hangups you may find involve accessing the system date and time fields and sending data for display. If your program bombs, check with your training manager or a helpful programmer.

Summary   You must know what to expect from a program before you know if it works. Specify the expected output, then modify the source program as needed to produce the output. If a bomb occurs and you can't figure out why, get help.

Comprehension Questions

1. Which of the following is true?

    a. Before testing a program you need a clean compilation run.

    b. You can begin testing a program before identifying all compilation errors.

2. Suppose a program is supposed to show the time like this:

`06:47`

A test run shows this:

`47:06`

What sort of error would you suspect?

    1. a   **2.** An error in subdividing TIME fields

Application Questions

Here is a copy of the program you may already have compiled:

```
IDENTIFICATION DIVISION.
PROGRAM-ID.
    FIRST.
ENVIRONMENT DIVISION.
DATA DIVISION.
WORKING-STORAGE SECTION.
01   DISPLAY-LINES.
     05   ASTERISK-LINE       PIC X(25)   VALUE ALL "*".
     05   SPACE-LINE          PIC X       VALUE SPACE.
     05   NAME-LINE           PIC X(23)
                              VALUE "MY NAME IS RUTH ASHLEY.".
PROCEDURE DIVISION.
PRACTICE-DISPLAY.
     DISPLAY ASTERISK-LINE.
     DISPLAY SPACE-LINE.
     DISPLAY NAME-LINE.
     DISPLAY SPACE-LINE.
     DISPLAY ASTERISK-LINE.
     STOP RUN.
```

1. Sketch the expected output.

2. If you have computer access, test your program now. If you have any problems, see your training manager or an experienced colleague. Continue to correct and test the program until it produces the expected output.

3. Figure 6.14 repeats the program you wrote at the end of Chapter 4. Sketch the output expected from running the program on May 18, 1989.

Figure 6.14 Program to Be Tested

```
IDENTIFICATION DIVISION.
PROGRAM-ID.  CH4REV.
AUTHOR.  RUTH ASHLEY
         TRAINING DEPARTMENT.
ENVIRONMENT DIVISION.
DATA DIVISION.
WORKING-STORAGE SECTION.
01   MESSAGE-LINE            PIC X(30)
               VALUE "THIS IS THE FORMATTED DATE".
01   SPACE-LINE              PIC X        VALUE SPACE.

01   EXACT-DATE.
     05   EXACT-YEAR         PIC XX.
     05   EXACT-MONTH        PIC XX.
     05   EXACT-DAY          PIC XX.
01   FORMATTED-DATE.
     05   FORMATTED-MONTH    PIC XX.
     05   FILLER             PIC X        VALUE "/".
     05   FORMATTED-DAY      PIC XX.
     05   FILLER             PIC X        VALUE "/".
     05   FORMATTED-YEAR     PIC XX.

01   EXPANDED-YEAR.
     05   FILLER             PIC X(14)
               VALUE "THE YEAR IS 19".
     05   FIX-YEAR           PIC XX.

PROCEDURE DIVISION.
FORMAT-DATES.
     DISPLAY MESSAGE-LINE.
     DISPLAY SPACE-LINE.
     ACCEPT EXACT-DATE FROM DATE.
     MOVE EXACT-MONTH TO FORMATTED-MONTH.
     MOVE EXACT-DAY TO FORMATTED-DAY.
     MOVE EXACT-YEAR TO FORMATTED-YEAR.
     DISPLAY FORMATTED-DATE.
     MOVE EXACT-YEAR TO FIX-YEAR.
     DISPLAY EXPANDED-YEAR.
     DISPLAY SPACE-LINE.
     STOP RUN.
```

Answers

1. You should see your output in this format:

```
***********************

MY NAME IS RUTH ASHLEY

***********************
```

2. If you note any errors, correct them and retest your program.

3. You should see your output in this format:

```
THIS IS THE FORMATTED DATE

05/18/89
THE YEAR IS 1989
```

Chapter Review Questions

1. Suppose you receive these messages from a compilation:

Source code

```
00027   01  FOOTING-LINE.
00028       05  FILLER              PIC X(5)    VALUE SPACES.
00029       05  FILLER              PIC X(35)
00030                               VALUE 'END OF EMPLOYEE DATA REPORT'.
00031
00032   PROCEDURE DIVISION.
00033   PREPARE-EMPLOYMENT-REPORT.
00034       PERFORM DO-HEADING.
00035       ACCEPT EMPLOYEE-DATA.
00036       MOVE EMPLOYEE-DATA OUTPUT-LINE.
00037       DISPLAY OUTPUT-LINE.
00038       DISPLAY FOOTING.
00039       STOP RUN.
```

Line	Message
00036	TO MISSING OR MISPLACED IN MOVE STATEMENT. ASSUMED IN REQUIRED POSITION.
00038	FOOTING IS ILLEGALLY USED IN DISPLAY STATEMENT. DISCARDED.
00038	DISPLAY STATEMENT INCOMPLETE. STATEMENT DISCARDED.

What two corrections would you make?

_____

_____

2. Suppose you compile a program and get the result shown in Figure 6.15.

Figure 6.15 Result of Compilation

Source code

```
23              01   EXPANDED-TIME.
24                   05   FILLER                              PIC X(12)
25                                      VALUE "THE TIME IS ".
26                   05   FIX-MINUTE                          PIC XX.
27                   05   FILLER                              PIC X(15)
28                                      VALUE " MINUTES AFTER ".
29                   05   FIX-HOUR                            PIC XX.
30                   05   FILLER                              PIC X(9)
31                                      VALUE " O'CLOCK.".
32                   PROCEDURE DIVISION.
33                   FORMAT-TIMES.
34                       DISPLAY MESSAGE-LINE.
35                       DISPLAY SPACE-LINE.
36                       ACCEPT EXACT-TIME FROM TIME.
37                       MOVE EXACT-HOUR TO FORMATTED-HOUR.
38                       MOVE EXACT-MINUTE TO FORMATTED-MINUTE.
39                       MOVE EXACT-SECOND TO FORMATTED-SECOND.
40                       DISPLAY FORMATTED-TIME.
41                       MOVE EXACT-MINUTE FIX-MINUTE.
42                       MOVE EXACT-HOUR TO FIX-HOURS.
43                       DISPLAY EXPANDED-TIME.
44                       DISPLAY SPACE-LINE.
45                       STOP-RUN.
```

Line   **Message**

```
0041:     TO MISSING OR MISPLACED IN MOVE STATEMENT.
          ASSUMED IN REQUIRED POSITION
0042:     'FIX-HOURS' NOT DEFINED.   DISCARDED.
0045:     'STOP-RUN' NOT DEFINED.
          DELETING TILL LEGAL ELEMENT FOUND.
```

What corrections would you make?

_____

_____

_____

3. You have made the corrections and the program (see Figure 6.16) now compiles correctly. The expected output looks like this:

```
THIS IS THE FORMATTED TIME

10:00:00
THE TIME IS 00 MINUTES AFTER 10 O'CLOCK
```

The actual output looks like this:

```
THIS IS THE FORMATTED TIME

100000  10 00 00
THE TIME IS 00 MINUTES AFTER 10 O'CLOCK
```

What correction(s) would you make to the program?

_____

_____

_____

Figure 6.16 Corrected and Compiled Program

```
IDENTIFICATION DIVISION.
PROGRAM-ID.  ERRORS.
AUTHOR.  RUTH ASHLEY
         TRAINING DEPARTMENT.
ENVIRONMENT DIVISION.
DATA DIVISION.
WORKING-STORAGE SECTION.
01   MESSAGE-LINE                        PIC X(30)
              VALUE "THIS IS THE FORMATTED TIME".
01   SPACE-LINE                          PIC X        VALUE SPACE.

01   EXACT-TIME.
     05   EXACT-HOUR                      PIC XX.
     05   EXACT-MINUTE                    PIC XX.
     05   EXACT-SECOND                    PIC XX.
     05   FORMATTED-TIME                  PIC X(8).
     05   FORMATTED-HOUR                  PIC XX.
     05   FILLER                          PIC X        VALUE ":".
     05   FORMATTED-MINUTE                PIC XX.
     05   FILLER                          PIC X        VALUE ":".
     05   FORMATTED-SECOND                PIC XX.

01   EXPANDED-TIME.
     05   FILLER                          PIC X(12)
                         VALUE "THE TIME IS ".
     05   FIX-MINUTE                      PIC XX.
     05   FILLER                          PIC X(15)
                         VALUE " MINUTES AFTER ".
     05   FIX-HOUR                        PIC XX.
     05   FILLER                          PIC X(9)
                         VALUE " O'CLOCK.".
PROCEDURE DIVISION.
FORMAT-TIMES.
     DISPLAY MESSAGE-LINE.
     DISPLAY SPACE-LINE.
     ACCEPT EXACT-TIME FROM TIME.
     MOVE EXACT-HOUR TO FORMATTED-HOUR.
     MOVE EXACT-MINUTE TO FORMATTED-MINUTE.
     MOVE EXACT-SECOND TO FORMATTED-SECOND.
     DISPLAY EXACT-TIME.
     MOVE EXACT-MINUTE TO FIX-MINUTE.
     MOVE EXACT-HOUR TO FIX-HOUR.
     DISPLAY EXPANDED-TIME.
     DISPLAY SPACE-LINE.
     STOP RUN.
```

Answers

1. Insert TO in MOVE statement. Change FOOTING to FOOTING-LINE in the DISPLAY statement.   **2.** Insert TO in MOVE statement. Change FIX-HOURS to FIX-HOUR. Remove hyphen in STOP-RUN.   **3.** Put FORMATTED-TIME at level 01 instead of 05, and remove its PICTURE clause. Use DISPLAY FORMATTED-TIME instead of DISPLAY EXACT-TIME.

Section Three Exercises

1. If you have not yet compiled and tested the program from Lesson 4.4, do so now. Use these steps.

   a. Desk check the source code. It should be in your system already.
   b. Compile, using the standard compilation command or procedure at your installation.
   c. Make needed corrections and recompile until no errors are found.
   d. Test the program. You specified its expected output in the Application Questions for Lesson 6.3.
   e. If your program does not run correctly, see your training manager or an experienced colleague.

2. Now that you have compiled and tested one very simple program, you are ready to try another. You should already have the program from the end of Chapter 4 (reproduced in Figure 6.14) stored on disk as a source program.

   a. Desk check the program and correct any errors you find.
   b. Compile it. Make corrections and recompile until there are no errors and you have an object module.
   c. You specified expected output as part of the Application Questions in Lesson 6.3. Test the program now.
   d. Continue testing and correcting until you get the desired output.

   If you have problems in any part of this exercise, take the time to solve them now. See your training manager or an experienced colleague. The skills you are practicing here will be needed throughout your programming career.

   If your system has slow turnaround, feel free to start the next chapter while waiting. Whenever a run completes, return to this exercise.

Using Unit Record Files

Chapter 7

Describing Unit Record Files

So far in this book you have learned to write and run programs that use no files. As you know, that is not a typical business application. In this chapter you'll learn to describe the basic file form, the unit record file.

Most COBOL programs use at least one unit record file, because print data is usually handled as such a file. Card-image input can also be handled as a unit record file.

This chapter consists of three lessons:

Lesson 7.1: Unit Record Files
Lesson 7.2: Environment Division Coding
Lesson 7.3: Data Division Coding

Unit Record Files

Virtually every COBOL program uses print data for some of its output. So far, you have been printing data by DISPLAYing it. But it's much more common, and efficient, to put the data in a unit record print file. Certain frequently used input files are also best treated as unit record files. In this lesson you'll learn what distinguishes a unit record file from other types of files.

Objectives   By the end of this lesson you'll know what unit record files are and why they are used in so many COBOL programs.

Rationale   Before you can learn the details of coding unit record file handling procedures, you must know when and how you'll use such files. This lesson will give you the needed background.

What Are Unit Record Files?

Every file contains records of data. A unit record file is one where each unit of the physical medium, such as a single punch card or a printed line, is one record. The physical characteristics of the medium dictate the characteristics of the record—and the file.

The file on punched cards is a traditional unit record file. Each card represents an 80-character record. When cards are used as input, each record (each card) is physically separate from the others; they cannot be blocked. When cards are used as output, each card is punched independently.

Most installations today do not use cards. They use **card-image** files stored on disk somewhere in the computer system. Those, too, are unit record files. The data in them looks just as if it came from a card file. The card-image file generally has records of 80 characters or less; however, since they aren't really on cards, the records can actually be any length. In many respects the system treats unit record files as if they were on cards.

When you compile a COBOL program, your source code is used as unit record input to the compiler program. An object program produced by a COBOL compiler may be a card-image file in the form of punch output. This can then be used later as unit record input to a linker program.

The other traditional unit record file is the printer file. Each print line is one record and is limited by the physical characteristics of the printer. The records cannot be blocked. Records (or lines) are sent to a printer file one at a time. Many systems send print files to a disk instead of sending them directly to the printer. The data can then be viewed at a terminal and/or printed out later, as the user desires. The listing produced by the COBOL compiler is prepared as a unit record file.

Advantages of Unit Record Files

The system can process data in files much more efficiently than it can process records via ACCEPT and DISPLAY statements. When a file is involved, the system sets up areas in memory called buffers, as shown in Figure 7.1. Triple buffers are shown, but the system might use fewer or more buffers than that. The system feeds records from the input file into the input buffer until the buffer is full. It does this automatically, without waiting for separate input statements.

Each READ statement pulls a record from the buffer into the input area. A memory-to-memory transfer is much, much faster than a file-to-memory transfer, so the program doesn't have to wait as long for the READ statement to be processed. This makes the program run faster.

The same thing happens on the output side. A WRITE statement transfers the record from the output area to the output buffer. The system transfers the record to the file later on.

A second major advantage of unit record files over ACCEPT and DISPLAY data is that you have more options for the file media. You

Figure 7.1 Buffering Records to Speed Up I/O Processing

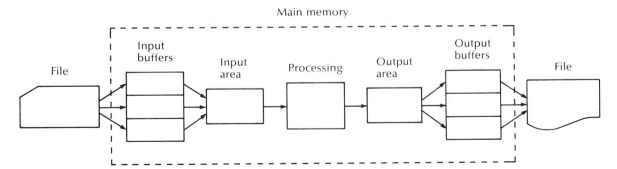

can place a unit record file on almost any batch I/O device, whereas ACCEPT and DISPLAY are limited to a few devices.

With unit record files you can have more than one file on the same device. Figure 7.2 diagrams a program that uses two print files. If the print records were displayed instead of printed, both types of records would be mixed into the same printout; but if two unit record print files are used, most systems will keep the two types of records separate (on disk) and print first one file and then the other.

Because of their advantages, unit record files are used in preference to ACCEPT and DISPLAY files for batch data. ACCEPT and DISPLAY files are used for very low-volume data (for example, a single-record input file) and for online data in some COBOL systems that have no better means of handling terminal I/O.

Characteristics of Unit Record Files

Unit record files have much in common with all files, but they also have some specific differences.

Records in a unit record file are organized **sequentially**. This means that the system must read each record in turn or write each in turn. It can't read backwards in an input card-image file to check a previous value, for example, and it can't back up and redo a line that has already been printed. In these features unit record files are similar to other sequential files.

The major differences between unit record files and other sequential files are in permanence and storage format. At one time card files were stored in drawers or boxes. When a program read a card, the system kept the information only long enough to process it. The permanent storage was external to the system. This was also true on

Figure 7.2 An Example of a Program with Two Print Files

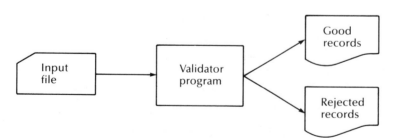

the output side. After a record was printed or punched, the internal data was not kept. The output cards or paper were stored externally.

Although cards aren't used much anymore, the concept is the same. A unit record input file may be entered into the system only long enough to be used. The next time you run the program, you must re-enter the unit record file. Similarly, unit record output stays in the system only long enough to be printed or displayed; then it is eliminated internally. However, card-image unit record files may be stored on disk as editor-created input files or program-created output files in many systems. These files may be stored until you delete them. They are stored differently from standard sequential disk files, however.

Summary   Unit record files are commonly used to provide card-image input to programs and to receive output in the form of printed data or punched data. The records are treated as independent units within a sequentially organized file. Unit record files are not stored in the same manner as other files.

Review Questions

1. Which of the following is an example of a unit record input file?

   a. A set of records permanently stored on disk as a standard sequential file
   b. A printed report
   c. A set of card-image records
   d. Data to be ACCEPTed by a program

2. Which of the following is an example of a unit record output file?

   a. A set of records stored on disk as a standard sequential file
   b. A printed report
   c. A set of card-image records
   d. Data to be DISPLAYed by a program

3. Which of the following are features of a unit record input file?

   a. Records are handled in groups.
   b. Records are read in strict sequential order.
   c. The file is permanently stored within the system.
   d. The file may be on a printer.

4. Which of the following are features of a unit record output file?

   a. Records are handled in groups.
   b. Records are read in strict sequential order.
   c. A card-image file generated by the program may be stored on disk.
   d. The file may be on a printer.

5. A program will access about 100 records from the system's logical input device. Is it more efficient to use a unit record file or ACCEPT statements?

   _____

6. A program will print about 500 lines of data. Is it more efficient to use a unit record file or DISPLAY statements?

   _____

1. c   **2.** b, c (punch output is card-image format)   **3.** b   **4.** c, d   **5.** Unit record file   **6.** Unit record file

Environment Division Coding

Every file you use in a program must be defined. In the Environment Division you tell the system where to find the file. In the Data Division you tell the system how data in the file is structured. This lesson considers the Environment Division coding needed to define unit record files. You'll need to find out how your compiler requires certain information to be provided, but the framework is always the same.

Objective   You will be able to code all required Environment Division entries for defining unit record input and output files.

Rationale   The system must know what devices are needed to run the program. You specify the type of file in the Environment Division, and the system uses this information to determine what equipment is needed.

File-Names

A program may be stored in a file, and it may use several files as well. We're concerned with the files it uses here; these may be of similar or different types. Each file must have a name that the program will use to refer to it in the Procedure Division.

You must tell the system what physical file the program needs. This can be done in the Environment Division or the Data Division, depending on the compiler. You may also have to use special control language commands to identify files. When a file is stored on tape or disk, you give it a name that is put in the tape label or the disk directory and is used by the system to access the file. For the purposes of this discussion, that name is called the **physical name**.

Some COBOL systems require you to use the file's physical name in the program. Thus, if the file is named JULYINV, you would SELECT JULYINV, OPEN INPUT JULYINV, READ JULYINV, CLOSE JULYINV, and so forth.

Most COBOL systems, however, allow you to use a **logical name** in the COBOL program. The logical name is created and used only within the program and usually refers to the file's function within the program. Figure 7.3 illustrates how the system gets from the logical name to the physical name. Whenever you want to run the program, you must tell the system what physical name to use for each logical name.

Figure 7.3 Using Logical and Physical Names

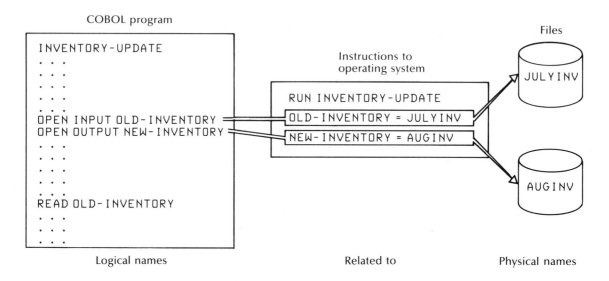

This system has distinct advantages. It means you can write generalized programs that can be used with more than one set of files. For example, you could run the INVENTORY-UPDATE program from Figure 7.3 using AUGINV as the input file and SEPTINV as the output file without making any changes to the Procedure Division of the program. However, you might have to change the Environment Division if the connection of logical name to physical name is made there.

This course assumes that you can use logical file-names. Therefore, you can create meaningful file-names that may not be the files' physical names.

You define a file-name in the Environment Division, describe it further in the Data Division, and refer to it in the Procedure Division. The name is formed according to the same rules as data-names.

Environment Division Structures

Figure 7.4 shows an expanded structure of the Environment Division. As you know, the Configuration Section can be omitted in many compilers. If used, however, it must immediately follow the division header.

The Input-Output Section is used to specify entries related to files that are used for input and/or output. A unit record file must be used for either input or output; however, it can't be used for both in the same program. The FILE-CONTROL paragraph-name must follow the Input-Output Section header. Both these names are coded beginning in area A.

Figure 7.4 Environment Division Structure

Format:
```
ENVIRONMENT DIVISION.
[CONFIGURATION SECTION.
[SOURCE-COMPUTER.  [source-computer-entry.]]
[OBJECT-COMPUTER.  [object-computer-entry.]]
[SPECIAL-NAMES.  [compiler-name IS mnemonic-name.]]]
[INPUT-OUTPUT SECTION.
[FILE-CONTROL.
      file-related-entries...]]
```

Examples:
```
ENVIRONMENT DIVISION.

ENVIRONMENT DIVISION.
INPUT-OUTPUT SECTION.
FILE-CONTROL.
    SELECT STUDENT-DATA-FILE
        ASSIGN TO ...
```

Notes:
1. Some compilers allow the Configuration Section to be omitted.
2. The Input-Output Section is used to describe any files.
3. Entries are system specific.
4. Include a separate file-related entry for each file.

File Related Entries

Each file you use in a program must be identified in the FILE-CONTROL paragraph of the Environment Division. Figure 7-5 shows the format you will use to make the entry for each file.

SELECT Clause   Each file has one and only one SELECT clause. It specifies the name used in the COBOL program Procedure Division to refer to the file — the logical name. Any later statement or entry format that requires a file-name refers to this name. Here are several examples:

```
SELECT PRINTED-REPORT . . .
SELECT INVENTORY-FILE-1984 . . .
SELECT PERSONNEL-DATA . . .
```

ASSIGN Clause   The ASSIGN clause always immediately follows the SELECT clause; it is used to relate the file-name to a particular device in the system. In many COBOLs the ASSIGN clause provides the physical file-name.

The word TO in the ASSIGN clause is optional, as you can see from the format. Since its use makes the function of the clause clearer, however, you might as well include it.

Figure 7.5 FILE-CONTROL Paragraph Entries

Format:
```
{SELECT file-name
     ASSIGN TO system-name
     [ORGANIZATION IS SEQUENTIAL].}...
```

Examples:
```
SELECT INPUT-FILE
    ASSIGN TO INDATA6.

SELECT OUTPUT-FILE
    ASSIGN TO PRINTER.
```

Notes:
1. Each file requires one SELECT/ASSIGN entry.
2. System-name is compiler-dependent.
3. ORGANIZATION clause is optional. Some compilers require ORGANIZATION IS LINE SEQUENTIAL for unit record files.

The entry in the ASSIGN clause is called a system-name; it is very system- or compiler-dependent. Each compiler has a specific format or set of options you use for constructing a valid system-name. Figure 7.6 shows you several of these. Your compiler manual will have instructions for forming system-names for your system.

You should use a system-name in a format acceptable to your compiler. If you need an external-name, as with IBM OS compilers, use a unique word of seven letters or less. (The external-name is the physical name in most systems.)

ORGANIZATION Clause The ORGANIZATION clause specifies how a file is organized. Unit record files are always sequential. If this clause is omitted, the value SEQUENTIAL is assumed. Thus, the entry below has the same effect with or without the ORGANIZATION clause.

```
SELECT STUDENT-FILE
    ASSIGN TO UR-S-INLINES
    ORGANIZATION IS SEQUENTIAL.
```

Some nonstandard compilers require a different form of the ORGANIZATION clause for unit record disk files. Here's an example:

```
SELECT EMPLOYEE-DATA-FILE
    ASSIGN TO DISK
    ORGANIZATION IS LINE SEQUENTIAL.
```

Figure 7.6 System Name Examples

IBM OS/MVS Systems: UR-S-name or external-name

> UR means unit record; S means sequential; external-name is the physical file-name.

IBM VSE Systems: UR-device-S

> UR means unit record; S means sequential; the device may be the model number of a reader or printer.

Univac 1100 Series Systems: device [external name]

> device can be PRINTER or CARD-READER, to access those devices; external-name is the physical file-name needed if unit record file is on disk.

Microcomputer Systems:

> DISK and PRINTER are common system-names in compilers for microcomputers; some require the physical name here as well.

Here the additional key word LINE means the file is a unit record rather than a standard sequential file. In this case the file is not a true unit record file, although it acts like one. If you use an ANS compiler, the word LINE will be invalid in the ORGANIZATION clause.

Don't include the ORGANIZATION clause unless required by your compiler or preferred by your installation.

Summary of FILE-CONTROL Clauses The SELECT and ASSIGN clauses must be included for each file a program uses. You'll need an ORGANIZATION clause only for certain nonstandard compilers. The SELECT clause specifies the file-name as used in the program. The ASSIGN clause specifies a compiler-dependent system-name that identifies the hardware required.

Example

Here's an example of a complete Environment Division for a program that uses unit record card-image input and produces print output. The system-names used here are meaningful to the compiler, though not to us.

```
ENVIRONMENT DIVISION.
INPUT-OUTPUT SECTION.
FILE-CONTROL.
    SELECT MAILING-LIST-FILE
        ASSIGN TO SYS006.
    SELECT PHONE-REPORT
        ASSIGN TO SYS008.
```

The SELECT entries can be in any sequence. Many experienced programmers prefer to code them in the sequence in which the files are referenced in the program. The indentation is optional. You could code the SELECT and ASSIGN clauses for one file on the same line, if there's room. For clarity, however, it's better to code one clause per line. The indentation helps to group the entries that pertain to a single file.

Notice that a period is required at the end of the entry describing one file. Notice the hyphens also; to the compiler, FILE CONTROL is not the same as FILE-CONTROL.

Summary Each file used by a program for either input or output must have a defining entry in the FILE-CONTROL paragraph of the Input-Output Section of the Environment Division. You must include one and only one SELECT clause and ASSIGN clause for each file.

Comprehension Questions

1. Suppose a program uses two files. How many of each of these would you code?

   _____ a. Input-Output Section header   _____ c. SELECT entry

   _____ b. FILE-CONTROL paragraph name   _____ d. ASSIGN clause

2. Which Input-Output Section clause specifies the file-name as used in the rest of the program?

   a. SELECT
   b. ASSIGN
   c. ORGANIZATION

3. Which Input-Output Section clause relates the file-name to a device in the system?

   a. SELECT
   b. ASSIGN
   c. ORGANIZATION

4. Which Input-Output Section clause is compiler-dependent?

   a. SELECT
   b. ASSIGN
   c. ORGANIZATION

5. What value does the ORGANIZATION clause assume if you omit it?

   _____

6. This coding includes several errors. What are they?

```
ENVIRONMENT DIVISION.
FILE CONTROL.
    SELECT INPUT-FILE.
        ASSIGN TO UR-S-INCARDS.
    SELECT OUT-PRINT.
        ASSIGN TO UR-S-OUTLIST.
```

   _____

7. What errors are included in this coding?

```
ENVIROMENT DIVISION.
FILE-CONTROL.
    SELECT SALES-FILE.
        ASSIGN TO DISK.
    SELECT REPORT-SALES
        ASSIGN TO PRINTER.
IDENTIFICATION DIVISION.
```

   _____

Answers

1. a. 1 b. 1 c. 2 d. 2   2. a   3. b   4. b; c is required by some compilers for unit record files on disk.   5. SEQUENTIAL   6. The Input-Output Section header is missing. The hyphen in FILE-CONTROL is missing. There are extra periods before ASSIGN clauses.   7. ENVIRONMENT is spelled wrong. Identification Division must precede Environment Division. An extra period is in the first SELECT entry.

Application Questions

1. Find out the form of ASSIGN clause your installation uses for:

   a. A unit record input file _____

   b. A print output file _____

2. Code the section header and paragraph-name needed in the Environment Division to define files to be used in a program.

   _____

   _____

3. Code an entry to specify that the program will use a file called LIST-DATA.

   _____

4. Code a clause to specify that the program file identified in question 3 is to be created on the printer. Use your installation's requirements.

   _____

5. Suppose a program uses file TIME-CARD-FILE as unit record input and produces HOUR-LISTING as a printed report. Code the complete Environment Division. (Omit the Configuration Section.)

Answers

1. Check with an experienced programmer or use your reference manual.

2. `INPUT-OUTPUT SECTION.`
   `FILE-CONTROL.`

3. `SELECT LIST-DATA`

4. `ASSIGN TO system-name.`
   You should use the system-name your compiler requires. You could omit TO.

5. `ENVIRONMENT DIVISION.`
   `INPUT-OUTPUT SECTION.`
   `FILE-CONTROL.`
   `    SELECT TIME-CARD-FILE`
   `        ASSIGN TO system-name.`
   `    SELECT HOUR-LISTING`
   `        ASSIGN TO system-name.`

   Check your coding carefully. Be sure you used an appropriate system-name for your system. Be sure you included hyphens and periods as in the coding here.

Data Division Coding

The Environment Division entries for a file specify the file name as used in the program and relate it to a device in the system. However, the program needs additional information before it can process the file. In the Data Division you provide more information about the file and what it contains.

In this lesson you'll learn how to code the entries to complete the file description. Each file has data stored in records; you describe the layout of the record associated with each file in the File Section. You'll also learn to code more complex records than you have used so far.

Objectives You'll be able to code the Date Division entries to describe unit record files and associated data records.

Rationale The system must know how to process a file and how much space to allocate for an input or output area to store the data record. This information must be provided in the Data Division to supplement the Environment Division entries before a program can use files in the Procedure Division.

Concepts of Data Division Entries

In the Data Division you name the file as in the SELECT clause and give the system some information about its structure. Then you describe the record or records associated with the file.

File Labels Most files used by COBOL programs are stored on disk or tape. Internal labels are also stored on the medium; the system processes them to be sure it has the right file and to check how data is stored. Unit record files, however, have no labels, since they aren't permanently stored. In the Data Division, you have to inform the system whether a file has labels.

Space Allocation Each file needs to have memory area allocated to it so that a record can be stored after it is read (input) or before it is written (output). When you define a record associated with a file, a space the size of that record becomes the buffer for that file.

215

If a file contains records in several different formats, you can associate several record descriptions with the file, but no extra I/O areas or buffers are allocated per file. The program has to determine the record format.

Data Division Structure

Figure 7.7 shows the structure of the Data Division. When a program uses both sections, the File Section must precede the Working-Storage Section. You will need one file description entry and at least one record description entry for each file in the program.

FD (File Description)   Figure 7.8 shows the format of the file description entry. It includes the FD clause, which identifies the file, and the LABEL clause, which specifies the status of file labels.

Figure 7.7 Data Division Structure

Format:
```
DATA DIVISION.
[FILE-SECTION.
{FD file-description-entry
{01  record-description-entry}...}...]
[WORKING-STORAGE SECTION.
[77  level-description-entry]...
[record-description-entry]...]
```

Example:
```
DATA DIVISION.
FILE SECTION.
FD   STUDENT-DATA-FILE
     LABEL RECORDS ARE OMITTED.
01   STUDENT-DATA.
     05   STUDENT-NAME        PIC X(20).
     05   REST-OF-RECORD      PIC X(50).
FD   LISTING-FILE
     LABEL RECORDS ARE OMITTED.
01   LINE-OF-PRINT           PIC X(80).
WORKING-STORAGE SECTION.
01   END-SIGNAL             PIC X       VALUE "Y".
```

Notes:
1. When both are used, the File Section precedes the Working-Storage Section.
2. One file description entry is required for each file SELECTed in the Environment Division.
3. At least one record description entry is required for each file description entry.

Figure 7.8 The FD Entry Format

Format:

```
DATA DIVISION.
FILE SECTION.
FD  file-name
     LABEL {RECORD  [IS] }{OMITTED }
           {RECORDS [ARE]}{STANDARD}
```

Examples:

```
FD  INPUT-FILE
     LABEL RECORDS ARE OMITTED.
```

Notes:

1. FD must appear in area A.
2. The remainder of each file description entry is contained in area B.
3. The file-name is the same as in the SELECT clause.
4. You can use RECORD IS or RECORDS ARE; we use RECORDS ARE, since our standard file has two labels, but the singular form works as well.
5. Use OMITTED for unit record files.
6. Use STANDARD for most other files.

FD appears in area A; it identifies the beginning of the entry for the named file. You use the same file-name as in the SELECT clause; that is the name the Procedure Division will use to refer to the file.

Every file description must have a LABEL clause; it must include OMITTED for unit record files. Any of these LABEL clauses would be valid:

```
LABEL RECORD OMITTED
LABEL RECORDS OMITTED
LABEL RECORD IS OMITTED
LABEL RECORDS ARE OMITTED
```

The format shown in the last example is used in this course, but you can use a different format if you like. Each clause in the FD entry may be on a separate line, as you see in Figure 7.8.

Notice that a period follows the LABEL clause to terminate the file description entry in Figure 7.8. A common mistake is to put a period after the file-name, as you do with a group-name in a record description entry.

Record Description Entry A record description entry follows the FD entry for each file. This record is described beginning with level 01, just like records described in the Working-Storage Section.

The first example in Figure 7.7 describes a 70-character record; the input area established for the file will be 70 bytes long. Each time a record is read from the file, its data will be placed in this area, overlaying any previous values that were stored there. If the file contains records in several formats, another record description could immediately follow the first one.

The second record description entry in Figure 7.6 defines an output area. In this case the record is not subdivided. This area is used to hold a record of data to be sent to the printer.

Remember that any data associated with a file must be contained in a record. Level 77 (independent data items) can be used only in the Working-Storage Section.

The record description entry is the same in the File Section as in the Working-Storage Section, with one exception: You can't use a VALUE clause to initialize fields in the File Section. If you try it, you'll get error messages on compilation.

Summary of FD Entries Each file you name in a SELECT clause requires a corresponding FD entry in the File Section of the Data Division. Each unit record file requires LABEL RECORDS ARE OMITTED. The record description that follows a file description entry determines the size of the I/O area for that file.

More Complex Record Descriptions

So far, we have been using record descriptions with two levels. Actually, records can contain up to 49 levels. This section will show you how to code more complex record descriptions. They can be used in either the File Section or the Working-Storage Section; the only difference between the two is that you can't use the VALUE clause to initialize data items in the File Section.

Here is a sample data record of the type you've been using, with its coding.

STUDENT-DATA			
NUMBER	NAME	ADDRESS	LEVEL
1 9	10 34	35 74	75 76

```
01  STUDENT-DATA.
    05  STUDENT-NUMBER      PIC 9(9).
    05  STUDENT-NAME        PIC X(25).
    05  STUDENT-ADDRESS     PIC X(40).
    05  STUDENT-LEVEL       PIC XX.
```

Of course, you could use different names, as long as they adhere to the standard name-forming rules. You also could use different levels where we use 05; any level between 02 and 49 is valid. Each entry shown with a PICTURE clause is an elementary item; it is not subdivided. STUDENT-DATA is the record name; as such, it has level 01. Since STUDENT-DATA is subdivided, it is a group item and has no picture. Its length is the total length of the elementary items it contains—76 bytes in this example.

Three-Level Record Hierarchy   You may want to refer to specific parts of some fields in this record. You can subdivide them in the record description. Here's one possibility:

STUDENT-DATA								
	NAME			ADDRESS				
NUMBER	LAST	FIRST	MID	STREET	CITY	STATE	ZIP	LEVEL
1 9	10 22	23 33	34	35 54	55 67	68 69	70 74	75 76

The name field here is subdivided into three fields and the address into four fields. Now STUDENT-NAME is a group item that contains three elementary items, and STUDENT-ADDRESS is a group item that contains four elementary items. In the record description, remember, only elementary items have pictures. Here's how the record is coded:

```
01   STUDENT-DATA.
     05   STUDENT-NUMBER            PIC X(9).
     05   STUDENT-NAME.
          10   STUDENT-LAST-NAME    PIC X(13).
          10   STUDENT-FIRST-NAME   PIC X(11).
          10   STUDENT-MIDDLE-INITIAL PIC X.
     05   STUDENT-ADDRESS.
          10   STUDENT-STREET       PIC X(20).
          10   STUDENT-CITY         PIC X(13).
          10   STUDENT-STATE        PIC XX.
          10   STUDENT-ZIP          PIC X(5).
     05   STUDENT-LEVEL             PIC XX.
```

Level 10 is used here for the third level; actually, you can use any number higher than the level number of the previous level, up to 49. With a three-level record, you could use 01, 02, 03 (or 1, 2, 3) or 01, 03, 05 or even 01, 10, 20. The important point is that all items that are subdivisions of the same group item must have the same level number, and that number must be greater than that of the group item. Most programmers use a specific numbering scheme so that all items at the same level will have the same number. This makes the record description much easier to read and understand.

The indentation you see in the example is for the purpose of clarity. We have deliberately aligned the picture clauses for the same reason. We recommend that you do the same.

The data name STUDENT-NAME still refers to the same 25 bytes in the record as before, but now you can use other names to refer to different parts of STUDENT-NAME. There is no need to subdivide a field unless you need to refer to the subdivided parts.

Higher Levels in a Record Hierarchy   Fields in a record can be subdivided as often as necessary. Suppose you need to access the street number as a separate item; it will always be in the first five positions of the street field. You would recode STUDENT-ADDRESS like this:

```
05   STUDENT-ADDRESS.
     10   STUDENT-STREET.
          15   STUDENT-STREET-NUMBER      PIC X(5).
          15   STUDENT-STREET-NAME        PIC X(15).
     10   STUDENT-CITY                    PIC X(13).
     10   STUDENT-STATE                   PIC XX.
     10   STUDENT-ZIP                     PIC X(5).
```

STUDENT-ADDRESS still refers to the entire 40 bytes. STUDENT-STREET still refers to the first 20 bytes of STUDENT-ADDRESS. Now, however, additional names have been provided for further subdivisions. The definition for STUDENT-STREET-NAME is necessary to make STUDENT-STREET the correct size but it could be called FILLER if the program doesn't refer to this field.

Summary   File Description entries for unit record files in the File Section of the Data Division include the file-name and the LABEL clause. Each file description entry is followed by a record definition that specifies the data format to be associated with that file. Record descriptions can be subdivided as necessary to fully describe the I/O area. PICTURE clauses are associated only with elementary items; group items at any level never have a PICTURE clause. You can refer to either group names or elementary names (or both) in the Procedure Division.

Comprehension Questions

1. Suppose a program uses two files. How many of each of these must you code?

   _____a. FD entries

   _____b. LABEL clauses

   _____c. SELECT entries

   _____d. Record description entries

   _____e. File sections

2. The name used in the Procedure Division to refer to a file is named in two other clauses. Name the clause in each of these divisions.

   a. Environment Division _____

   b. Data Division _____

3. Under what circumstances do you include a LABEL clause in the Data Division entries for a unit record file?

   a. Never
   b. When labels are omitted
   c. When labels are standard
   d. Always

4. Which of the following is a correct Data Division entry for a unit record file?

   ```
   a. FD   LABEL RECORDS ARE OMITTED.
           INPUT-FILE.
   b. FD   INPUT-FILE.
           LABEL RECORDS ARE OMITTED.
   c. FD   INPUT-FILE
           LABEL RECORDS ARE OMITTED.
   d. FD   INPUT-FILE
           LABEL RECORDS ARE STANDARD.
   ```

5. Under what circumstances do you code a record description in the File Section?

   a. Never
   b. At least once for each file
   c. Only once for each file
   d. Only when a file requires an I/O area

6. Here's coding from a program:

```
DATA DIVISION.
FILE SECTION.
FD  ARTIFACT-FILE
    LABEL RECORDS ARE OMITTED.
01  ARTIFACT-DESCRIPTION.
    05  ARTIFACT-NAME            PIC X(15).
    05  ARTIFACT-FACTS.
        10  ARTIFACT-AGE         PIC 99.
        10  ARTIFACT-SOURCE      PIC X(10).
        10  ARTIFACT-STORAGE     PIC X(10).
        10  ARTIFACT-HISTORY     PIC X(20).
    05  ARTIFACT-LOCATION.
        10  ARTIFACT-ROOM        PIC XXX.
        10  ARTIFACT-SHELF       PIC XXX.
        10  ARTIFACT-BIN         PIC XXX.
    05  ARTIFACT-EXPLANATION     PIC X(12).
```

a. What is the file-name? _____

b. What is the record-name? _____

c. What size is the I/O area? _____

d. How many group items are defined (including the record itself)? ____

e. How many elementary items are defined? _____

Suppose a record contains this data in the first 66 bytes (b̸ indicates a blank):

STATUETTE-BRASS42EGYPTIANb̸b̸ARID+60DFb̸LOCb̸BYMORANTZ,1928b̸b̸127A31060

What is the value of each of these:

f. ARTIFACT-LOCATION _____

g. ARTIFACT-SHELF _____

h. ARTIFACT-SOURCE _____

i. ARTIFACT-NAME _____

Application Questions

1. What section of the Data Division do you use to describe files and their associated records?

   _____

2. If a Data Division includes the File Section and the Working-Storage Section, which must appear first?

   _____

3. Which of the following can be coded in a record description entry in the File Section?

   a. Level 01
   b. Level 05
   c. Level 77
   d. PICTURE clause to show data format
   e. VALUE clause for initialization

4. Code the complete file description entry for the unit record file defined like this in the Environment Division:

```
FILE-CONTROL.
    SELECT LIST-DATA
        ASSIGN TO UR-S-LISTOUT.
```

   _____

   _____

5. Code the lines needed to set up a 90-character output area for file LIST-DATA; it does not need subdivision. Create your own record name for it.

   _____

6. You coded this Environment Division in the previous lesson:

```
ENVIRONMENT DIVISION.
INPUT-OUTPUT SECTION.
FILE-CONTROL.
    SELECT TIME-CARD-FILE
        ASSIGN TO system-name.
    SELECT HOUR-LISTING
        ASSIGN TO system-name.
```

   Now code the Data Division entries to describe the files and their I/O areas. The input record has this format:

		Days						
Code	Ending Date	MON	TUE	WED	THU	FRI	Name	
1 9	10 17	18 19	20 21	22 23	24 25	26 27	28 40	

   Describe the output record as 80-byte punch output.

Answers

    1. File Section   **2.** File Section   **3.** a, b, d

    4.
```
FD   LIST-DATA
     LABEL RECORDS ARE OMITTED.
```

    5.
```
01   LIST-OUT                    PIC X(90).
```

    6. Here's one solution. You probably used different names.
```
DATA DIVISION.
FILE SECTION.
FD   TIME-CARD-FILE
     LABEL RECORDS ARE OMITTED.
01   TIME-CARD-DATA.
     05   TIME-CODE              PIC X(9).
     05   TIME-DATE              PIC X(8).
     05   TIME-DAYS
          10   TIME-MON          PIC XX.
          10   TIME-TUE          PIC XX.
          10   TIME-WED          PIC XX.
          10   TIME-THU          PIC XX.
          10   TIME-FRI          PIC XX.
     05   TIME-NAME              PIC X(13).
FD   HOUR-LISTING
     LABEL RECORDS ARE OMITTED.
01   HOURS-OUT                   PIC X(80).
```

Chapter Review Questions

In this chapter review, you'll write entries for a program that uses unit record input and print output. Here's the program structure:

Here's the input format:

Customer record						
	Name			Balance	Limit	Other data (not used)
Number	First	Initial	Last			
1　　　7	8　　　20	21	22　　　33	34　　　39	40　　　45	46　　　78

Each output line will have this format:

Listing record					
Blanks	Number	Blanks	Last　name	Blanks	Balance
1　　4	5　　11	12　　15	16　　　27	28　　31	32　　37

1. Code the complete Environment Division.

2. Code the beginning of the Data Division, up through the file description entry for the input file.

3. Code the record description entry for the input file. Use character data for all fields.

4. Now code the Data Division entries for the output file. Use character data for all fields.

Answers

```
1. ENVIRONMENT DIVISION.
   INPUT-OUTPUT SECTION.
   FILE-CONTROL.
       SELECT CUSTOMER-FILE
           ASSIGN TO system-name.
       SELECT CUSTOMER-LIST
           ASSIGN TO system-name.

2. DATA DIVISION.
   FILE SECTION.
   FD  CUSTOMER-FILE
       LABEL RECORDS ARE OMITTED.

3. 01   CUSTOMER-RECORD.
        05   CUSTOMER-NUMBER            PIC X(7).
        05   CUSTOMER-NAME.
             10   CUSTOMER-FIRST-NAME   PIC X(13).
             10   CUSTOMER-INITIAL      PIC X.
             10   CUSTOMER-LAST-NAME    PIC X(12).
        05   CUSTOMER-BALANCE           PIC X(6).
        05   CUSTOMER-LIMIT             PIC X(6).
        05   FILLER                     PIC X(33).
```

You could have used 9 to describe the BALANCE and LIMIT fields.

```
4. FD   CUSTOMER-LIST
        LABEL RECORDS ARE OMITTED.
   01   LISTING-RECORD.
        05   FILLER                     PIC X(4).
        05   LISTING-NUMBER             PIC X(7).
        05   FILLER                     PIC X(4).
        05   LISTING-LAST-NAME          PIC X(12).
        05   FILLER                     PIC X(4).
        05   LISTING-BALANCE            PIC X(6).
```

You could have used 9 to describe the BALANCE field. You could have defined LISTING-RECORD PIC X(37) and formatted the record in working storage. Be sure you didn't use VALUE in the File Section.

Chapter 8

Handling Unit Record Files

Unit record files can be used for either input or output. Most unit record output files are printer files. They are formatted for reading by human readers rather than by a computer. Many of these files will be read at a terminal rather than printed on paper, but the principles are the same for both types of output devices. Most unit record input files are created under an online editor, although some are still on cards. Output unit record files are sometimes sent to cards or an editor file as well.

This chapter consists of four lessons:

Lesson 8.1:   Unit Record File I/O Statements
Lesson 8.2:   Processing Unit Record Data
Lesson 8.3:   Handling Printer Files
Lesson 8.4:   Other Unit Record Output

Lesson **8.1**

Unit Record File I/O Statements

In processing unit record input and output, the program gets one record, does the necessary processing, then gets the next, and so on, until all the records have been processed.

Each file must be prepared for use with an OPEN statement. A READ statement accesses one record from an input file. When the system recognizes the end of the file, it must be told what to do next. COBOL includes a special clause to define end-of-file processing. A WRITE statement is used to send one record to an output file. Finally, a CLOSE statement is used to terminate each file.

Objectives   You'll be able to code the Procedure Division statements required for processing unit record files.

Rationale   You'll be using unit record files in most of the programs you write, both in this course and on the job. Therefore, you need to know how to process them.

File Preparation and Termination

In the Procedure Division all files must be opened before they are processed and closed before the program terminates. The OPEN and CLOSE statements are used for all files, including unit record files.

You tell the system in an OPEN statement that a file will be used. The system then makes the I/O area you defined available for use. In the case of an output file, that means you can now move data to the output area so it can be sent to the file. In the case of an input file, you can now read a record. If you do not OPEN a file, you cannot access the file or refer to fields in its associated I/O area.

Each file should be terminated with a CLOSE statement before the program ends. This allows for a normal ending to the file. Some compilers will warn you if you fail to include an OPEN and CLOSE statement for each file.

The OPEN Statement   Figure 8.1 shows the format of the OPEN statement. Each file a program will use must be named in an OPEN statement before any other statement refers to it. The I/O area

Figure 8.1 OPEN Statement Format

Format:

```
OPEN {{INPUT } {file-name}... }...
      OUTPUT
```

Examples:
```
OPEN OUTPUT LISTING-FILE.
OPEN OUTPUT STUDENT-OUT, SUMMARY-REPORT.
OPEN INPUT STUDENT-DATA-FILE
     OUTPUT LISTING-FILE REJECTS-FILE.
```

Notes:
1. Each file must be OPENed before it is used.
2. Use the OUTPUT option for printer files.
3. Name as many files for INPUT or OUTPUT as needed.
4. You can use a separate OPEN statement for each file or one OPEN for all files in a program.

defined with the file is not available to the program until after an OPEN statement is executed. Either INPUT or OUTPUT must be specified for each file. Printer files require the word OUTPUT since the printer is always an output device.

As you can see in the figure, you can name many files in one OPEN statement. You can open both input and output files with the same statement, although the same file can't be specified as both INPUT and OUTPUT. Either the input or the output files can be listed first. Each of the following will successfully open both files:

```
OPEN INPUT STUDENT-DATA-FILE
     OUTPUT STUDENT-LISTING-FILE.

OPEN OUTPUT STUDENT-LISTING-FILE
     INPUT STUDENT-DATA-FILE.
```

Any file-names you list following the word INPUT, up to the word OUTPUT or a period, are opened for input purposes. Any files listed following OUTPUT are opened for output purposes. As soon as a file is OPENed, the I/O area defined in the FD is made available to the program. The contents of an I/O area are garbage immediately after the OPEN is executed. You READ records into the input area or MOVE data into the output area.

The CLOSE Statement   Figure 8.2 shows the format of the CLOSE statement. Each file a program uses should be named in a CLOSE statement before the program terminates. Once the CLOSE statement is executed, the fields in the I/O area are no longer available. You can't refer to them later in the program.

Figure 8.2 CLOSE Statement Format

Format:
```
CLOSE {file-name}...
```

Examples:
```
CLOSE LISTING-FILE.
CLOSE STUDENT-OUT, SUMMARY-REPORT.
```

Notes:
1. Each file should be CLOSEd before the program ends.
2. You can use a separate CLOSE statement for each file or one statement for all files in a program.

Notice that you don't specify INPUT or OUTPUT in the CLOSE statement. You can list as many files as necessary.

Summary of OPEN and CLOSE   Suppose a program will produce a printer file defined in the Data Division like this:

```
FD  PART-LIST
    LABEL RECORDS ARE OMITTED.
01  PART-RECORD.
    05  FILLER          PIC X.
    05  PART-IDENT      PIC X(6).
    05  FILLER          PIC X(61).
```

The file would be opened with this statement:

```
OPEN OUTPUT PART-LIST.
```

After processing is completed, this statement is executed:

```
CLOSE PART-LIST.
```

Accessing Records

Records from an input file are accessed one at a time with a READ statement. When each READ statement is executed, one record is read from the file and copied into the defined input area. If the system identifies the end of the file while attempting to execute a READ statement, the end-of-file processing is executed.

READ Statement Format   Figure 8.3 shows the READ statement format. In the READ statement you name the file to be accessed, just as in OPEN and CLOSE statements.

Figure 8.3 READ Statement Format

Format:

```
READ file-name [INTO data-name]
    AT END imperative-statement.
```

Examples:

```
READ STUDENT-DATA-FILE
    AT END MOVE "Y" TO END-OF-FILE-SWITCH.

READ NEW-INPUT INTO DETAIL-RECORD
    AT END PERFORM HANDLE-END-OF-INPUT.
```

Notes:

1. A record is read from the named file and placed in the defined input area.
2. The data-name in the INTO option can be any item except a record-name associated with the file.
3. If the INTO option is used, a group move copies the record to data-name; it is in both places.
4. The AT END clause is activated when a READ is executed after the last record in the file is read; no data is read if AT END is activated.

When the READ statement is executed, the system attempts to read a record from the input file, placing the data in the input area. Let's assume for a minute that a record is successfully obtained. The data is moved into the input area associated with that file and left justified in the input area.

Some systems treat this just like a group move and truncate or pad with spaces on the right if the actual record length does not match the length of the input area. Other systems leave extra space in the input area unchanged. You won't have to worry about this if you define the input area to be the same length as the input records, which you should.

After the record has been read, you can access the data in the record by the names you assigned to the input area in the Data Division. Here's an example:

```
FD  TRANSACTION-DATA
    LABEL RECORDS ARE OMITTED.
01  TRANSACTION-RECORD.
    05  TRANSACTION-ACCOUNT-ID       PIC X(10).
    05  TRANSACTION-TYPE             PIC X.
    05  TRANSACTION-AMOUNT           PIC X(7).
    05  FILLER                       PIC X(62).
    .
    .
    .
    READ TRANSACTION-DATA
        AT END MOVE "Y" TO TRANSACTION-EOF-FLAG.
```

The READ statement causes a record to be read into TRANSACTION-RECORD. You can refer to the whole record by using the name TRANSACTION-RECORD. You can refer to the first ten bytes by the name TRANSACTION-ACCOUNT-ID; for example, you could say DISPLAY TRANSACTION-ACCOUNT-ID. You can refer to the eleventh byte by the name TRANSACTION-TYPE; for example, you can say MOVE TRANSACTION-TYPE TO OUT-TRANSACTION. You can refer to bytes 12 through 18 as TRANSACTION-AMOUNT. You can't refer to bytes 19 through 80 because they do not have a usable name.

INTO Option   A READ statement causes a record to be read into the input area defined for the file. From there, you can move the data to other program areas. The INTO option causes such a move to take place immediately; the record is then available to the program in two places.

Suppose the program includes these definitions:

```
FD  CUSTOMER-FILE
    LABEL RECORDS ARE OMITTED.
01  CUSTOMER-DATA.
    05  CUSTOMER-NUMBER            PIC 9(6).
    05  FILLER                     PIC X(84).
...
01  WORKING-CUSTOMER-DATA.
    05  CUSTOMER-ID                PIC 9(6).
    05  W-CUSTOMER-NAME            PIC X(30).
    05  W-CUSTOMER-ADDRESS         PIC X(30).
    05  W-CUSTOMER-LIMIT           PIC 9(5).
    05  W-CUSTOMER-HISTORY         PIC X(19).
```

You can use this statement to read a record from the file and move the data to the working-storage record.

```
READ CUSTOMER-FILE INTO WORKING-CUSTOMER-DATA
    AT END MOVE "Y" TO END-OF-CUSTOMER-FILE.
```

This is equivalent to these statements:

```
READ CUSTOMER-FILE
    AT END MOVE "Y" TO END-OF-CUSTOMER-FILE.
MOVE CUSTOMER-DATA TO WORKING-CUSTOMER-DATA.
```

End-of-File Processing   The AT END clause is a required part of every READ statement that accesses a sequential file, including unit record input. When the system tries to read beyond the last record in a file, it encounters an end-of-file signal. This activates the AT END clause. Notice that the last record doesn't do it; the READ attempt after the last record activates the AT END clause. At that time, whatever is placed in the input area is undefined; you cannot rely on the last record read still being present. If the file doesn't contain any records, AT END is activated at the first READ statement.

The AT END clause can contain one or more imperative statements. As you may remember, an imperative statement is any COBOL statement that is not conditional in nature. Of the statements you have learned so far, OPEN, CLOSE, ACCEPT, DISPLAY, MOVE, and STOP RUN are imperative. READ...AT END is conditional and cannot be included in an AT END clause. These statements are acceptable:

```
READ INPUT-FILE
    AT END MOVE "Y" TO EOF-FLAG.

READ INPUT-DATA
    AT END
        CLOSE INPUT-DATA OUTPUT-DATA
        STOP RUN.
```

The usual action taken in an AT END clause is setting an end-of-file flag. This flag is used in processing to control the primary read loop. You'll learn to handle that in the next lesson.

Placing Data in the File

A program sends data to a file one record at a time. For sequential output files you use the WRITE statement. Figure 8.4 shows the format of the WRITE statement.

Figure 8.4 WRITE Statement Format

Format:
```
WRITE record-name [FROM data-name]
```

Examples:
```
WRITE STUDENT-LINE.
WRITE STUDENT-LINE FROM STUDENT-LIST-HEADINGS.
```

Notes:
1. Record-name must be a record associated with the file in the File Section.
2. Data-name may be any item (record, group, or elementary) defined in the Data Division.
3. When you use FROM, a group move occurs from data-name to record-name, then the record is written to the associated file.

WRITE Statement Effect   Notice in the figure that you specify a **record-name** in the WRITE statement. (This is different from READ, OPEN, and CLOSE, in which you specify the file-name.) The record must define an output area for the file. When a WRITE statement is executed, the data currently in the named record is sent to the file associated with that record. For example:

```
WRITE PART-RECORD.
```

This record was defined as the output record for the PART-LIST file. When the above statement is executed, whatever data is in PART-RECORD will be sent to PART-LIST, where it will be printed as a separate line.

When a file is opened, the content of the I/O area is undefined. This means you must place a value there before it contains valid data; for a printer file, you must be sure the data is printable. For the PART-LIST file defined previously, you could do this:

```
MOVE SPACES TO PART-RECORD.
WRITE PART-RECORD.
```

The effect here is to fill the entire PART-RECORD with spaces and print a blank line.

FROM Option   We have been using the basic WRITE statement. Figure 8.4 also shows an optional clause for the WRITE statement. If you use WRITE record-name FROM data-name, it is equivalent to this coding:

```
MOVE data-name TO record-name.
WRITE record-name.
```

The MOVE is done as an alphanumeric move, so every byte in the data-name field is copied to the record-name field, from left to right. You will learn later that we use the FROM option heavily.

Summary   In this lesson, you have learned to code the four statements essential for handling unit record files: OPEN, CLOSE, READ, and WRITE. OPEN and CLOSE are required for all files, READ accesses a record from a file opened as INPUT, while WRITE is used to send data to files opened as OUTPUT. The INTO option of the READ statement copies the input record into another area. The AT END clause in the READ statement is activated after the last record in the file has been read. The FROM option of the WRITE statement can be used to move data to the output area for printing.

Comprehension Questions

Suppose a print file is defined like this:

```
FD   CUSTOMER-LIST
     LABEL RECORDS ARE OMITTED.
01   CUSTOMER-LINE                    PIC X(80).
```

1. Which of the following is correctly coded?

   a. `OPEN CUSTOMER-LIST.`
   b. `OPEN CUSTOMER-LIST OUTPUT.`
   c. `OPEN OUTPUT CUSTOMER-LIST.`
   d. `OPEN CUSTOMER-LINE.`
   e. `OPEN CUSTOMER-LINE OUTPUT.`
   f. `OPEN OUTPUT CUSTOMER-LINE.`

2. Which of the following is correctly coded?

   a. `CLOSE CUSTOMER-LIST.`
   b. `CLOSE CUSTOMER-LIST OUTPUT.`
   c. `CLOSE OUTPUT CUSTOMER-LIST.`
   d. `CLOSE CUSTOMER-LINE.`
   e. `CLOSE CUSTOMER-LINE OUTPUT.`
   f. `CLOSE OUTPUT CUSTOMER-LINE.`

3. Under what circumstances must a program OPEN a file it is going to use?

   a. Always
   b. If it will contain a large number of records
   c. Never

4. Under what circumstances must a program CLOSE a file that it used?

   a. Always
   b. If it will contain a large number of records
   c. Never

5. Which of the following is correctly coded?

   a. `WRITE CUSTOMER-LIST.`
   b. `WRITE CUSTOMER-LINE.`
   c. `WRITE CUSTOMER-LIST FROM CUSTOMER-LINE.`
   d. `WRITE CUSTOMER-LINE FROM CUSTOMER-LIST.`

6. At what point is the output area first available for use by the program?

   a. When the Procedure Division begins
   b. As soon as the OPEN statement is executed
   c. When the first WRITE statement is executed
   d. After the CLOSE statement is executed

7. What is contained in CUSTOMER-LINE just after the file is opened?

   a. Nothing
   b. Spaces
   c. Zeros
   d. Undefined garbage

8. Which of the following could be specified in the FROM option?

    a. The file-name
    b. The name of the record associated with the print file
    c. The name of some record defined in working storage
    d. A figurative constant

9. Which of the following can place values in the output area?

    a. A MOVE statement
    b. The FROM option
    c. The VALUE clause

10. What statement accesses a record from an input file?

    a. OPEN
    b. READ
    c. WRITE
    d. CLOSE

11. What clause is used in a READ statement to detect the end of the file?

_____

12. Which statement below causes a record to be available in two places?

```
a. READ CUSTOMER-FILE
       AT END MOVE "Y" TO END-OF-FILE.
b. READ CUSTOMER-FILE FROM CUSTOMER-DATA
       AT END MOVE "Y" TO END-OF-FILE.
c. READ CUSTOMER-FILE INTO CUSTOMER-DATA
       AT END MOVE "Y" TO END-OF-FILE.
```

Answers

    1. c   **2.** a   **3.** a   **4.** a   **5.** b; d is incorrect because the FROM option here specifies a file-name, but a data-name is needed.   **6.** b   **7.** d   **8.** c   **9.** a, b; the VALUE clause can't initialize fields in the File section.   **10.** b   **11.** AT END   **12.** c

Application Questions

A program will read records from an input unit record file and list them on the printer. Here are some definitions.

```
DATA DIVISION.
FILE SECTION.
FD  TIME-CARD-FILE
    LABEL RECORDS ARE OMITTED.
01  TIME-CARD-DATA.
    05  TIME-CODE                 PIC X(9).
    05  TIME-DATE                 PIC X(8).
    05  TIME-DAYS
        10  TIME-MON              PIC XX.
        10  TIME-TUE              PIC XX.
        10  TIME-WED              PIC XX.
        10  TIME-THU              PIC XX.
        10  TIME-FRI              PIC XX.
    05  TIME-NAME                 PIC X(13).
FD  HOUR-LISTING
    LABEL RECORDS ARE OMITTED.
01  HOURS-OUT                     PIC X(80).
WORKING-STORAGE SECTION.
01  END-OF-TIME-FLAG              PIC X     VALUE "N".
```

1. Write a statement to prepare both files for use.

2. Write input statements to accomplish the following:

a. Place one input record in TIME-CARD-DATA. At the end of the file, move "Y" to END-OF-TIME-FLAG.

b. Place one input record directly in the output area. Use the same end-of-file processing.

3. Assume a program includes the statement you wrote in question 2a. Write the statement(s) needed to print the record.

4. Write a statement to close both files.

1. OPEN INPUT TIME-CARD-FILE
     OUTPUT HOUR-LISTING.
Be sure you specified the file names and used INPUT and OUTPUT correctly.

2. a. READ TIME-CARD-FILE
       AT END MOVE "Y" TO END-OF-TIME-FLAG.
   Be sure you specified the file-name.

   b. READ TIME-CARD-FILE INTO HOURS-OUT
        AT END MOVE "Y" TO END-OF-TIME-FLAG.
    Be sure you specified the input file-name and the output record-name.

3. WRITE HOURS-OUT FROM TIME-CARD-DATA.
  or
MOVE TIME-CARD-DATA TO HOURS-OUT.
WRITE HOURS-OUT.
Be sure you specified the output record name, *not* the output file-name.

4. CLOSE TIME-CARD-FILE HOUR-LISTING.
Be sure you specified both file-names.

Repeating Code in a Program

So far you have learned to code several statements, including file I/O statements. When the statements are coded in sequence, they are executed in sequence, one after the other. Once you start using files, you need to modify sequential processing so that all records in a file can be processed. You will need to use a repetition structure.

Objective When you have finished this lesson, you'll be able to code PERFORM statements to execute paragraphs once or a number of times until a specified condition is true.

Rationale In a program, you will frequently need to repeat a section of code. You may want to repeat headings at the top of each page, for example, or process each input record in the same way. The PERFORM statement allows you to do this.

Basic PERFORM Statement

The basic PERFORM statement is used to execute a segment of code just once; then control returns to the statement following the PERFORM statement. The basic PERFORM statement is not used for repetition structures. Figure 8.5 shows how this statement works.

Figure 8.5 Flow of Control in Basic PERFORM

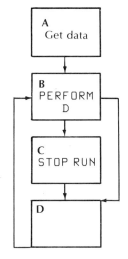

Figure 8.6 Basic PERFORM Statement Format

Format:

```
PERFORM paragraph-name-1 [{THRU      } paragraph-name-2]
                          {THROUGH   }
```

Examples:

```
PERFORM GET-INPUT-DATA.
PERFORM PROCESS-EACH-EMPLOYEE.
PERFORM HANDLE-TAXES THRU HANDLE-TAXES-EXIT.
```

Notes:

1. The paragraph specified as paragraph-name-1 is executed following the PERFORM statement.
2. If THRU paragraph-name-2 is specified, all paragraphs from paragraph-name-1 through the last line of paragraph-name-2 are executed after the PERFORM statement.
3. After the last line of paragraph-name-1 (or paragraph-name-2) is executed, control returns to the next statement after PERFORM.

When you specify PERFORM paragraph-name, that paragraph is executed immediately. Then control returns to the statement after the PERFORM statement. Figure 8.6 shows the basic PERFORM format.

Suppose you have written a program that needs to read a record at various points. You could code the READ statement as a separate paragraph:

```
READ-ONE-RECORD.
    READ AUTO-PART-FILE
        AT END MOVE "Y" TO END-OF-PARTS.
```

Then each time you want to read a record from AUTO-PART-FILE you use PERFORM READ-ONE-RECORD. The paragraph READ-ONE-RECORD is executed, then control returns to the statement after the PERFORM statement.

The THRU option is used to specify the last in a series of paragraphs to be executed before control returns to the statement following PERFORM. You won't need it just yet.

Using the PERFORM Statement to Create a Loop

Another format of the PERFORM statement can be used to set up a loop that will be executed repeatedly until a condition becomes true. For example, a program generally processes input until there isn't any more. Most COBOL programs set up the main processing loop with a PERFORM statement.

Figure 8.7 DO UNTIL Logic

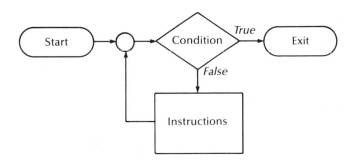

Logic of the COBOL Repetition Structure As you know, the logic of a repetition structure can be expressed as DO WHILE or DO UNTIL. COBOL uses DO UNTIL logic as shown in Figure 8.7.

Notice that the condition must be expressed so that the block of code is executed when the condition is false. The instructions are executed UNTIL the condition becomes true. If it is true at the beginning, the instructions are not executed at all.

Here's an example of pseudocode for this logic structure:

```
get one record
DO UNTIL end of data
    process data
    get one record
ENDO
```

PERFORM...UNTIL Format Figure 8.8 shows this format of the PER-FORM statement. Notice that we use PERFORM...UNTIL as the key words. This sets up the COBOL logic for the DO UNTIL structure of pseudocode. You specify the name of the paragraph that contains the block of code you want executed. (You can use the THRU option to cause a set of paragraphs to be executed.) You also specify a condition. As soon as the PERFORM...UNTIL statement is

Figure 8.8 PERFORM . . . UNTIL Format

Format:
```
PERFORM paragraph-name-1 [THRU paragraph-name-2]
     UNTIL condition
```

Examples:
```
PERFORM GET-INPUT-DATA
    UNTIL VALID-DATA = "YES".
PERFORM PROCESS-EACH-EMPLOYEE
    UNTIL END-OF-FILE-INDICATOR = "Y".
```

Notes:
1. You may use THRU paragraph-name-2 if necessary.
2. Any valid condition can be used; you'll learn the relation condition in this lesson.

executed, the condition is tested. In the first example in Figure 8.8, the system checks to see if a field named VALID-DATA has the value YES. If it does, the named paragraph isn't executed and control falls through to the next statement. If the condition isn't true (if VALID-DATA contains anything other than YES), the named paragraph is executed once. Then the condition is tested again.

Figure 8.9 shows the PERFORM ... UNTIL logic. You can see that the specified paragraph is executed repeatedly until the condition becomes true. You can also see that it is wise to ensure that something that happens in the specified paragraph can affect the condition in some way; otherwise, a closed loop would be created.

Specifying the Condition   The simplest form of COBOL condition is the **relation condition**. In this condition, two values are related to each other; if the relation is true, the condition is true. Figure 8.10 shows the relations you can specify in a relation condition. The operator words and symbols are equivalent; you can use whichever are more comfortable for you.

Each condition takes this format:

$$\begin{Bmatrix} \text{literal} \\ \text{data-name} \\ \text{expression} \end{Bmatrix} \quad \text{operator} \quad \begin{Bmatrix} \text{literal} \\ \text{data-name} \\ \text{expression} \end{Bmatrix}$$

You can compare two data-names, but you can't compare two literals. Notice that you can also code expressions (such as TAX + 2 or INTEREST / 2); you'll learn how to use them later. Here are some examples of valid relation conditions:

```
QUANTITY-ON-HAND > MINIMUM-QUANTITY
PRICE-TO-PUBLIC IS GREATER THAN BASIC-PRICE
PRICE-TO-PUBLIC GREATER BASIC-PRICE
END-OF-FILE-FLAG = "Y"
```

Figure 8.9 Logic of PERFORM...UNTIL

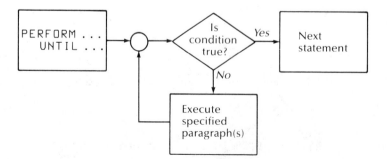

Figure 8-10 Relation Condition Operators

Operator	Symbol	Example
IS EQUAL TO	=	A = B
IS NOT EQUAL TO	NOT =	A NOT = B
IS GREATER THAN	>	A > B
IS NOT GREATER THAN	NOT >	A NOT > B
IS LESS THAN	<	A < B
IS NOT LESS THAN	NOT <	A NOT < B

Notes:

1. A space is needed before and after each operator or symbol in many compilers.
2. Either field may be replaced by a literal, but not both.
3. In comparing alphanumeric values in EBCDIC, digits are greater than letters and Z is greater than A. In ASCII, letters are greater than digits.

Notice in Figure 8.10 that only one key word or symbol is required to code any positive operator. The word NOT makes the operator negative. In most cases, you'll want to code positive conditions; they're easier for other people to understand. Optional words can be used or not, as you wish.

You'll learn to code more condition types in a later book. You'll find that the relation condition can be used for most simple applications.

Condition Examples Suppose you want to cause a paragraph named GET-VALUES to be executed repeatedly until the value of AGE is set to zero. You could code this statement:

```
PERFORM GET-VALUES
    UNTIL AGE = 0.
```

Here are some sample COBOL conditions for several situations. We used words as operators here, but you could use the symbols instead.

A field named EMPLOYEE-NUMBER is equal to or lower than TEMPORARY-RANGE.

```
EMPLOYEE-NUMBER NOT GREATER THAN TEMPORARY-RANGE
```

A field named TOTAL-HOURS is larger than OVERTIME-INDICATOR.

```
TOTAL-HOURS GREATER THAN OVERTIME-INDICATOR
```

A field named PART-NUMBER is the same as a field named PART-SALE.

```
PART-NUMBER EQUAL TO PART-SALE
```

A field named PART-NUMBER is larger or smaller than PART-SALE.

```
PART-NUMBER NOT EQUAL TO PART-SALE
```

As indicated in Figure 8.10, the result of alphanumeric comparisons depends on whether your system uses EBCDIC, ASCII, or some other character code. In any system, Z is greater than A, and the character space (" ") is less than A. This means that a standard alphabetic sequence like the one below is in ascending order.

```
ART
ARTHUR
BART
BELL
```

In an EBCDIC sequence, values beginning with digits would follow the letters in ascending sequence. In an ASCII sequence, values beginning with digits precede those beginning with letters. Lowercase letters are generally "less than" uppercase letters in EBCDIC, but "greater than" uppercase letters in ASCII.

In any alphanumeric comparison, the items being compared are assumed to be the same length; the shorter item is padded with spaces on the right to make this true. The result of comparing "ABC" to "A" is the same as comparing "ABC" to "A "; "ABC" is greater. Numeric comparisons are done algebraically, so that 2.0 is greater than 1.56. The system knows where decimal places are, so you don't have to worry about them.

Using PERFORM...UNTIL in a Program

Figure 8.11 shows a sample Data Division. Notice that the Working-Storage Section defines a field to be used to indicate the end of the input file. It is initialized to "N". The AT END clause will set it to "Y" when the file is empty.

Figure 8.12 shows the program structure and the COBOL Procedure Division coding. This basic structure is used in most COBOL programs.

The Procedure Division uses a simple PERFORM to execute the READ statement paragraph (READ-ONE-RECORD). A program is

Figure 8.11 Sample Data Division

```
DATA DIVISION.
FILE SECTION.
FD  DATE-FILE
    LABEL RECORDS ARE OMITTED.
01  DATE-RECORD.
    05  INPUT-DATE              PIC X(4).
    05  INPUT-NAME              PIC X(26).
    05  FILLER                  PIC X(50).
FD  DATE-LISTING
    LABEL RECORDS ARE OMITTED.
01  DATE-LISTING-RECORD         PIC X(80).
WORKING-STORAGE SECTION.
01  END-OF-FILE-FLAG            PIC X       VALUE "N".
```

better structured if only one READ statement is coded per file. Since this program reads records at two points, the READ statement is placed in a separate paragraph and performed as needed. Notice that the AT END clause sets END-OF-FILE-FLAG to "Y".

The PERFORM...UNTIL statement sets up the main processing loop. The PROCESS-RECORDS paragraph will be executed once for

Figure 8.12 Procedure Division Coding

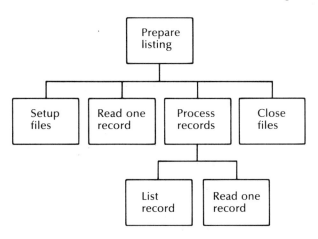

```
PREPARE-LISTING.
    OPEN INPUT DATE-FILE
        OUTPUT DATE-LISTING.
    PERFORM READ-ONE-RECORD.
    PERFORM PROCESS-RECORDS
        UNTIL END-OF-FILE-FLAG = "Y".
    CLOSE DATE-FILE DATE-LISTING.
    STOP RUN.
PROCESS-RECORDS.
    WRITE DATE-LISTING-RECORD FROM DATE-RECORD.
    PERFORM READ-ONE-RECORD.
READ-ONE-RECORD.
    READ DATE-FILE
        AT END MOVE "Y" TO END-OF-FILE-FLAG.
```

each record in the input file. When the READ statement sets the END-OF-FILE-FLAG, the condition will be true, so control will fall through.

The result of this program is an unformatted listing of the input file.

Notice the coding details in this program. Paragraph-names are spelled exactly the same way in the PERFORM statement as when coded as paragraph-names (beginning in area A). The program reads one record from the input file before entering the PROCESS-RECORDS repetition structure to avoid a bomb if there are no records in the file.

Summary   A basic PERFORM statement executes a subordinate routine just once; no loop is established. The PERFORM...UNTIL statement establishes a loop that is executed until the specified condition becomes true. In pseudocode this logic is represented by the DO UNTIL structure.

One type of condition you can use in PERFORM...UNTIL statements is the relation condition, which tests the relationship of two values. Six relational operators are available. The PERFORM...UNTIL statement is used to set up the main processing loop in most programs that use sequential files.

Comprehension Questions

The first three comprehension questions are based on this coding:

```
PREPARE-INFORMATION.
    DISPLAY MESSAGE-LINE-1.
    PERFORM GET-RECORD.
    PERFORM SET-UP-DISPLAY
        UNTIL END-OF-FILE = "Y".
    DISPLAY DATA-MESSAGE.
    STOP RUN.
SET-UP-DISPLAY.
    DISPLAY USER-NAME.
    PERFORM GET-RECORD.
GET-RECORD.
    READ USER-FILE
        AT END MOVE "Y" TO END-OF-FILE.
```

1. What is the effect of the first PERFORM statement in the program?

   a. It causes DATA-MESSAGE to be displayed.
   b. It causes SET-UP-DISPLAY to be executed under certain conditions.
   c. It causes GET-RECORD to be executed once.

2. What statement is executed immediately **after** PERFORM SET-UP-DISPLAY (assuming END-OF-FILE = "N")?

   a. DISPLAY DATA-MESSAGE.
   b. STOP RUN.
   c. DISPLAY USER-NAME.
   d. MOVE USER-CODE TO CODE-OUT.

3. What causes the PERFORM...UNTIL statement to stop executing SET-UP-DISPLAY?

   a. GET-RECORD.
   b. STOP RUN.
   c. The value of END-OF-FILE is set to "N".
   d. The value of END-OF-FILE is set to "Y".

4. Consider this statement:

   ```
   PERFORM GET-VALID-INPUT
       UNTIL INPUT-FLAG = "Y".
   ```

   a. What is the condition?

   _____

   b. What paragraph will be executed if INPUT-FLAG = "N"?

   _____

   c. Which of the following values of INPUT-FLAG will allow the paragraph to be executed again?

A. "A"	D. 0
B. "N"	E. SPACES
C. "Y"	F. "y"

5. Code relation conditions for the following. Be sure to code valid numeric and nonnumeric literals.

   a. Test whether USER-NAME contains all blanks.

   _____

   b. Test whether INCOME is higher than UPPER-MIDDLE-LINE.

   _____

   c. Test whether INPUT-EOF contains Y.

   _____

   d. Test whether PASSWORD-ENTERED is SPECIAL-PASSWORD.

   _____

   e. Test whether the value of the name entered (USER- NAME) is in the last half of the alphabet.

   _____

Answers

1. c 2. c 3. d

4. a. `INPUT-FLAG = "Y"`
   b. `GET-VALID-INPUT`
   c. A, B, D, E, F

5. a. `USER-NAME = SPACES` or `USER-NAME EQUAL SPACES` or
      `USER-NAME = " "`
      (Be sure you include a space on each side of any relation symbol.)
   b. `INCOME > UPPER-MIDDLE-LINE` or `INCOME IS GREATER THAN`
      `UPPER-MIDDLE-LINE`
   c. `INPUT-EOF = "Y"` or `INPUT-EOF IS EQUAL TO "Y"`
   d. `PASSWORD-ENTERED = SPECIAL-PASSWORD` or
      `PASSWORD-ENTERED IS EQUAL TO SPECIAL-PASSWORD`
   e. `USER-NAME GREATER THAN "N"` or
      `USER-NAME > N`
      (You could use USER-NAME > "MZZZ" as well. This isn't exactly equivalent, but it is close enough.)

Application Questions

1. Suppose you want to display the message stored in DATA-MESSAGE followed by ACCEPT SOME-THING at several points in a program.

   a. Code a paragraph containing the statements to be executed.

   _____

   _____

   _____

   b. Code a statement to execute that paragraph.

   _____

2. Code a statement to execute paragraph PROCESS-RECORDS until the data item NO-MORE-INPUT contains the letter Y.

   _____

   _____

3. Here is the pseudocode for a program that lists PART-FILE on PART-LIST. Actual data-names are in capital letters.

```
0 - Prepare complete list
        set up files
        get a record from PART-FILE
        IF  end-of-file
        THEN
            set END-OF-PART-FILE to "Y"
        ENDIF
        DO UNTIL END-OF-PART-FILE = "Y"
            prepare list lines (1)
        ENDO
        display END-MESSAGE
        STOP
1 - Prepare list lines
        copy PART-LIST-DATA to PART-LIST-RECORD
        print PART-LIST-RECORD
        get a record from PART-FILE
        IF  end-of-file
        THEN
            set END-OF-PART-FILE to "Y"
        ENDIF
```

   Code the complete Procedure Division for a COBOL program to accomplish these functions.

Answers

1. a. `SAMPLE-PARAGRAPH.`
      `DISPLAY DATA-MESSAGE.`
      `ACCEPT SOME-THING.`
   b. `PERFORM SAMPLE-PARAGRAPH.`

   Be sure you used the same paragraph-name in both answers.

2. `PERFORM PROCESS-RECORDS`
       `UNTIL NO-MORE-INPUT = "Y".`

3. Here is one solution:

```
PROCEDURE DIVISION.
PREPARE-COMPLETE-LIST.
    OPEN INPUT PART-FILE
        OUTPUT PART-LIST.
    PERFORM READ-RECORD.
    PERFORM PREPARE-LIST-LINES
        UNTIL END-OF-PART-FILE = "Y".
    DISPLAY END-MESSAGE.
    CLOSE PART-FILE PART-LIST.
    STOP RUN.
PREPARE-LIST-LINES.
    WRITE PART-LIST-RECORD FROM PART-LIST-DATA.
    PERFORM READ-RECORD.
READ-RECORD.
    READ PART-FILE
        AT END MOVE "Y" TO END-OF-PART-FILE.
```

Check your coding carefully, paying special attention to your PERFORM statements. They should be nearly identical to ours in content and format.

Handling a Printer File

Printer files are often called reports. They are prepared to make a record of data or calculations processed by the computer in a form that people can read. You must consider the layout of each line to be printed. The report will need page headings and perhaps column headings. You may need to control the number of lines to be printed per page.

This lesson deals only with the basics of printer files. You'll learn to code the basic Procedure Division statements for handling such files and to use records from working storage to print headings. Later you'll learn to handle paging and other vertical spacing in printed reports.

Objectives You'll be able to write the statements necessary to create a basic printer file in a program.

Rationale Since printer files are used in the vast majority of COBOL programs, the ability to code statements producing such files is essential.

Printer File Considerations

Record Length A printer file has a built-in limitation on record length; the longest line that can be printed on your system's printer is the largest possible record. A printer is said to be able to handle 150, 132, 121, or 80 characters; this means that it can handle a file with a record length up to that value.

First Position Reserved Some compilers reserve the first byte of the output area for a special code called a carriage-control code. This one-byte field is used to control vertical spacing on the report. We are not going to deal with that now. Instead, we'll add one to the record length and leave the first position blank. If your compiler uses the carriage control byte, the blank will cause single spacing. (Single spacing is the default in most systems.) If your compiler doesn't use the carriage-control byte, everything will be indented one space, but that shouldn't be a big problem, as long as your data doesn't reach the last available column.

Line Layout Output can be structured in accordance with program specifications. Suppose the program specifications request a report of student numbers and names from input records in this format:

```
01   STUDENT-DATA.
     05   STUDENT-NUMBER      PIC X(9).
     05   STUDENT-NAME        PIC X(25).
     05   STUDENT-ADDRESS     PIC X(40).
     05   STUDENT-LEVEL       PIC XX.
```

Here are several possibilities for formatting a line of typical output:

```
(1)   123456789FERNANDEZ     JUDI         N

(2)   123456789    FERNANDEZ    JUDI         N

(3)   STUDENT ID   NAME
      123456789    FERNANDEZ    JUDI         N
```

Notice that the first example is hard to read because the number and name fields are not separated by spaces. In the second example, extra spaces are used to separate the fields. The third example has column headings added to enhance the readability even more.

Many programming assignments specify what layout to use. In others you have to design a readable layout yourself. Keep readability in mind, since the entire purpose of the report is for someone to read it.

Printer File Layout

One way of formatting a line for the printer is to subdivide the output area, as shown in Figure 8.13. Notice the reserved carriage-control byte and the use of FILLER to insert appropriate spacing. Since the VALUE clause can't be used in the File Section, CARRIAGE-CONTROL-BYTE and FILLER have to be initialized to blanks in the Procedure Division. You do this by moving SPACES to the entire record, since you can't address the FILLER item directly.

Figure 8.13 Detailing the Output Area

```
FD   STUDENT-LISTING
     LABEL RECORDS ARE OMITTED.
01   STUDENT-LINE.
     05   CARRIAGE-CONTROL-BYTE      PIC X.
     05   STUDENT-DATA-OUT.
          10   STUDENT-NUMBER-OUT    PIC X(9).
          10   FILLER                PIC XXX.
          10   STUDENT-NAME-OUT      PIC X(25).
```

Figure 8.14 Defining Printer Lines in Working Storage

```
    .
    .
    .
FD  STUDENT-LISTING
    LABEL RECORDS ARE OMITTED.
01  STUDENT-LINE              PIC X(50).
WORKING-STORAGE SECTION.
    .
    .
    .
01  STUDENT-LIST-HEADING.
    05  FILLER               PIC X  VALUE SPACE.
    05  FILLER               PIC X(10)
                             VALUE "STUDENT ID".
    05  FILLER               PIC X  VALUE SPACE.
    05  FILLER               PIC X(4)
                             VALUE "NAME".

01  STUDENT-DATA-OUT.
    05  FILLER               PIC X  VALUE SPACE.
    05  STUDENT-NUMBER-OUT    PIC X(9).
    05  FILLER               PIC XX VALUE SPACE.
    05  STUDENT-NAME-OUT      PIC X(25).
```

Figure 8.14 shows a more common way of handling print data. Here the output area (STUDENT-LINE) is defined as a single field, rather than being subdivided into smaller fields. In the Working-Storage Section, two separate records are set up for line formatting.

STUDENT-LIST-HEADING creates a heading line. The words "STUDENT ID" and "NAME" are set up as headings. The rest of the line is filled with spaces. STUDENT-DATA-OUT sets up a data line (also called a **detail line**) for the report. The detail line contains the student's number in columns 2 through 10 and name in columns 13 through 37. FILLER initialized to spaces is used to create the correct spacing in the line.

Figure 8.15 illustrates how lines are printed using the definitions in Figure 8.14. To print a line, the line is moved from the working-storage record to the output area (using either MOVE or WRITE FROM). Then STUDENT-LINE is printed.

If you need a dozen differently formatted lines in a file, you can define them all in working storage. Then, to print each line, you put any needed values in the line, move the entire record to the output area, and send the data to the file. You can use separate MOVE statements or the FROM option of the WRITE statement.

Figure 8.15 Printing Records from Working Storage

Since you can initialize data with the VALUE clause in the Working-Storage Section but not in the File Section, it makes sense to set up lines that contain constant data in working storage. Most print records contain constant data for spacing; heading records also contain constant heading data.

Example Suppose you need to print a report in the format shown in Figure 8.16. You need three different types of lines: one report heading line, one column heading line, and a detail line. The detail line will be repeated once with details about each auto part to be included in the report.

The output file is described like this:

```
FD  AUTO-PART-LISTING
    LABEL RECORDS ARE OMITTED.
01  LISTING-LINE                    PIC X(52).
```

Now you need a separate working storage description for each type of line. Here's the heading line:

```
01  REPORT-HEADING.
    05   CARRIAGE-CONTROL-BYTE-1     PIC X
                                     VALUE SPACE.
    05   FILLER                      PIC X(20)
                                     VALUE SPACES.
    05   FILLER                      PIC X(20)
                    VALUE "REPORT OF AUTO PARTS".
    05   FILLER                      PIC XX
                                     VALUE SPACE.
    05   TODAYS-DATE.
         10   TODAYS-MONTH           PIC XX.
         10   FILLER                 PIC X
                                     VALUE "/".
         10   TODAYS-DAY             PIC XX.
         10   FILLER                 PIC X
                                     VALUE "/".
         10   TODAYS-YEAR            PIC XX.
    05   FILLER                      PIC X(8)
                                     VALUE SPACES.
```

Notice a few things about this record description. It reserves a carriage-control byte in case the printer uses it, and initializes it to a space. It used FILLER for other fields that contain constant data such

Figure 8.16 Desired Report Format

```
  .
  .        REPORT OF AUTO PARTS   mm/dd/yy
  .
  .     NUMBER     NAME                       QUANTITY
  .
  .     XXXXX      XXXXXXXXXXXXXXXXXXXXXXXX    9999
  .
```

as blanks or slashes. The date field is subdivided with slashes inserted. This means the program can't ACCEPT TODAYS-DATE FROM DATE. If it does, the six DATE characters will be placed in the first six of the eight positions of TODAYS-DATE. If the date were January 2, 1985, TODAYS-DATE would contain 850102b̶b̶. Both slashes would be gone! The program needs another date field to be used for receiving the date from the system. Spaces are included at the end of the record to fill out the entire line. This isn't essential, however, as MOVE REPORT-HEADING TO LISTING-LINE will pad the receiving field with spaces.

Here's how to code the column heading line:

```
01   COLUMN-HEADING.
     05   CARRIAGE-CONTROL-BYTE-2     PIC X
                                      VALUE SPACE.
     05   FILLER                      PIC X(10)
                                      VALUE "NUMBER".
     05   FILLER                      PIC X(31)
                                      VALUE "NAME".
     05   FILLER                      PIC X(8)
                                      VALUE "QUANTITY".
```

Notice here that we took advantage of automatic padding to space out the three headings. Each VALUE clause will initialize the associated positions beginning on the left and pad with spaces until the field is filled. You may code separate FILLER items for intervening spaces if you prefer.

Finally, here's sample coding for the detail line:

```
01   PART-INFORMATION.
     05   CARRIAGE-CONTROL-BYTE-3     PIC X
                                      VALUE SPACE.
     05   PART-NUMBER-OUT             PIC X(5).
     05   FILLER                      PIC X(5)
                                      VALUE SPACES.
     05   PART-NAME-OUT               PIC X(30).
     05   FILLER                      PIC X(5)
                                      VALUE SPACES.
     05   PART-QUANTITY-OUT           PIC 9(4).
```

Here we initialized the space fields that separate the columns. We provided no initial values for the data fields because appropriate values will be moved to these fields before the data is moved to the output area for printing.

Complete Program

Now let's see how a COBOL program prints the report. Figure 8.17 shows the program. Notice that the basic Procedure Division structure remains the same. Each input record is read and written to the output file.

Figure 8.17 Sample Program

```
IDENTIFICATION DIVISION.
PROGRAM-ID.
     AUTOPART.
ENVIRONMENT DIVISION.
INPUT-OUTPUT SECTION.
FILE-CONTROL.
     SELECT AUTO-PARTS
          ASSIGN TO ....
     SELECT AUTO-PART-LISTING
          ASSIGN TO ....
DATA DIVISION.
FILE SECTION.
FD   AUTO-PARTS
     LABEL RECORDS ARE OMITTED.
01   AUTO-PART-DATA.
     05   PART-NUMBER                PIC X(5).
     05   PART-NAME                  PIC X(10).
     05   PART-DESCRIPTION           PIC X(26).
     05   PART-SOURCE                PIC X(6).
     05   PART-QUANTITY              PIC 9(3).
     05   PART-LOCATION              PIC X(10).
FD   AUTO-PART-LISTING
     LABEL RECORDS ARE OMITTED.
01   LISTING-LINE                    PIC X(52).
WORKING-STORAGE SECTION.
01   END-OF-PART-FILE                PIC X       VALUE "N".
01   DATE-FIELD.
     05   THIS-YEAR                  PIC XX.
     05   THIS-MONTH                 PIC XX.
     05   THIS-DAY                   PIC XX.
01   REPORT-HEADING.
     05   CARRIAGE-CONTROL-BYTE-1    PIC X
                                     VALUE SPACE.
     05   FILLER                     PIC X(10)
                                     VALUE SPACES.
     05   FILLER                     PIC X(20)
                          VALUE "REPORT OF AUTO PARTS".
     05   FILLER                     PIC XX
                                     VALUE SPACE.
     05   TODAYS-DATE.
          10   TODAYS-MONTH          PIC XX.
          10   FILLER                PIC X     VALUE "/".
          10   TODAYS-DAY            PIC XX.
          10   FILLER                PIC X     VALUE "/".
          10   TODAYS-YEAR           PIC XX.
     05   FILLER                     PIC X(8)
                                     VALUE SPACES.
01   COLUMN-HEADING.
     05   CARRIAGE-CONTROL-BYTE-2    PIC X     VALUE SPACE.
     05   FILLER                     PIC X(10)
                                     VALUE "NUMBER".
     05   FILLER                     PIC X(31)
                                     VALUE "NAME".
     05   FILLER                     PIC X(8)
                                     VALUE "QUANTITY".
01   PART-INFORMATION.
     05   CARRIAGE-CONTROL-BYTE-3    PIC X     VALUE SPACE.
     05   PART-NUMBER-OUT            PIC X(5).
     05   FILLER                     PIC X(5)
                                     VALUE SPACES.
     05   PART-NAME-OUT              PIC X(30).
     05   FILLER                     PIC X(5)
                                     VALUE SPACES.
     05   PART-QUANTITY-OUT          PIC 9(4).
```

Continued

```
PROCEDURE DIVISION.
PREPARE-PART-LISTING.
    OPEN INPUT AUTO-PARTS
        OUTPUT AUTO-PART-LISTING.
    PERFORM PREPARE-HEADINGS.
    PERFORM READ-RECORD.
    PERFORM LIST-PARTS
        UNTIL END-OF-PART-FILE = "Y".
    CLOSE AUTO-PARTS AUTO-PART-LISTING.
    STOP RUN.
PREPARE-HEADINGS.
    ACCEPT DATE-FIELD FROM DATE.
    MOVE THIS-YEAR TO TODAYS-YEAR.
    MOVE THIS-MONTH TO TODAYS-MONTH.
    MOVE THIS-DAY TO TODAYS-DAY.
    WRITE LISTING-LINE FROM REPORT-HEADING.
    WRITE LISTING-LINE FROM COLUMN-HEADING.
LIST-PARTS.
    MOVE PART-NUMBER TO PART-NUMBER-OUT.
    MOVE PART-NAME TO PART-NAME-OUT.
    MOVE PART-QUANTITY TO PART-QUANTITY-OUT.
    WRITE LISTING-LINE FROM PART-INFORMATION.
    READ-RECORD.
        READ AUTO-PARTS
            AT END MOVE "Y" TO END-OF-PART-FILE.
```

This program includes a separate PREPARE-HEADINGS routine to access and format the date, then print the report and column headings. This coding could technically have been done in line. Since it is a separate function, however, it is appropriately placed in a separate paragraph.

Examine the coding in Figure 8.17 carefully. Make sure you understand it. You'll code similar routines many times.

Summary   This lesson focused on considerations useful in printing reports. The record length is limited by the size of printer carriage. The first byte of each record may be used to control vertical spacing; a blank usually results in single spacing. Since print records usually involve initialized fields for spacing and headings, and the VALUE clause can't be used in the File Section, you'll usually define an undivided output record in the File Section and create detailed print records in the Working-Storage Section. Before such a record is printed, it is moved from working storage to the output area.

Comprehension Questions

1. Assume that your printer can print up to 132 characters per line. The first byte of each print record is used as a carriage-control byte. Which of the following length records could you associate with the file?

   a. 40 bytes
   b. 120 bytes
   c. 132 bytes
   d. 154 bytes

2. In which of the following can you use the VALUE clause to initialize data?

   a. Environment Division
   b. File Section
   c. Working-Storage Section
   d. Procedure Division

3. What is the effect of having a space as the first character in the output record if the printer . . .

   a. Uses a carriage-control byte? _____

   b. Does not use a carriage-control byte?

   _____

4. What do you insert between data fields to cause a report to have columns?

   _____

Answers

1. a, b, c   2. c   3. a. single spacing b. prints a blank (indents one position)
4. spaces

Application Questions

Suppose you will be writing a program to read records of data (ITEM-RECORD) from ITEM-FILE in this format:

Item		Price		Department		Origin		Other	
1	20	21	25	26	35	36	39	40	80

and produce a printed report like this:

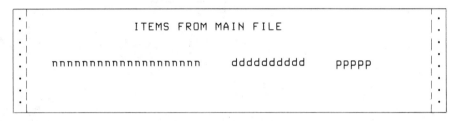

n = item name   d = department   p = price

The report file is to be called SOURCE-REPORT in the program.

1. Code the Environment Division entries for both files.

2. Code the output file description entry for the Data Division.

3. The report will contain a heading line plus a detail line. In which section will you define the output area?

    a. Input-Output Section
    b. File Section
    c. Working-Storage Section

4. Since the report will contain a heading line plus a detail line, in which section will you set up and initialize the format of these lines?

    a. Input-Output Section
    b. File Section
    c. Working-Storage Section

5. Code an output area description for the File Section.

6. Code a working-storage definition for the heading line.

7. Code a working-storage definition for the detail line.

8. a. Code the File Section entries for the input file. Define the input area as a single field.

    b. Define a record with subdivisions for use in working storage. (You'll READ ITEM-FILE INTO this record.)

Answers

1. ```
ENVIRONMENT DIVISION.
  INPUT-OUTPUT SECTION.
  FILE-CONTROL.
      SELECT SOURCE-REPORT
          ASSIGN TO system-name.
      SELECT ITEM-FILE
          ASSIGN TO system-name.
```

2. ```
FILE SECTION.
FD  SOURCE-REPORT
      LABEL RECORDS ARE OMITTED.
```

3. b. Output areas are always defined in the File Section.

4. c. You could set them up in the File Section, but you couldn't initialize them there.

5. ```
01 SOURCE-LINE   PIC X(50).
```
   You should have used at least 38 character positions. The exact number is not critical.

6. ```
01  HEADING-LINE.
    05  HEADING-CONTROL  PIC X       VALUE SPACE.
    05  FILLER           PIC X(10)   VALUE SPACES.
    05  FILLER           PIC X(22)
                      VALUE "ITEMS FROM MAIN FILE".
```
   You could have used different spacing. Be sure you attempted to center the heading.

7. ```
01 DETAIL-LINE.
    05 DETAIL-CONTROL   PIC X   VALUE SPACE.
    05 FILLER   PIC X(4)   VALUE SPACES.
    05 ITEM-OUT   PIC X(20).
    05 FILLER   PIC X(4)   VALUE SPACES.
    05 DEPARTMENT-OUT   PIC X(10).
    05 FILLER   PIC X(4)   VALUE SPACES.
    05 PRICE-OUT   PIC X(5).
```
   The exact spacing isn't important, but be sure you included at least one space before each field for separation. The length of this record should not be greater than the length of the output area.

8. a.
   ```
   FD ITEM-FILE
         LABEL RECORDS ARE OMITTED.
   01 ITEM-RECORD   PIC X(80).
   ```
   b.
   ```
   01 ITEM-DETAILS.
       05 ITEM-NAME   PIC X(20).
       05 ITEM-PRICE   PIC X(5).
       05 ITEM-DEPARTMENT   PIC X(10).
       05 ITEM-SOURCE   PIC X(4).
       05 ITEM-OTHER   PIC X(41).
   ```
   You could use different names.
   ```

Handling Other Output Unit Record Files

Occasionally you may need to code a program that requires punch output to be used as input to another program. Occasionally, too, you may want to create unit record output to be accessed under your editor. These output files are very similar to a printer file that uses only detail lines.

Objective   You will be able to code the entries required for creating output unit record files.

Rationale   You won't have to do this very often. Since the procedure is very much like creating print files, however, we are covering it here.

Why Create Nonprint Unit Record Output?

Occasionally system designers will see a need to create punch output. The resulting output seldom is actually punched on cards, but whether it is on cards or on disk, the primary purpose of punch output is to be used as input to another program. Today most designers would ask you to create a disk file instead. Many compilers create an object module in punch format, then use it as input to the next stage in the process. Once upon a time, object modules were physically punched onto decks of cards.

At times you may create unit record output to be saved and used later as input to other programs.

Defining Output Unit Record Files

These files are defined much like printer files. The only real difference is in the Environment Division. The system-name the compiler requires for a punch file or one to be stored on disk will be different from what it accepts for print files. We'll code it like this for punch files:

```
ENVIRONMENT DIVISION.
INPUT-OUTPUT SECTION.
FILE-CONTROL.
    SELECT PUNCH-OUTPUT
        ASSIGN TO PUNCH.
```

This is *not* a valid system-name for most compilers. Since systems vary widely in this area, however, we'll use this name as a generic punch name.

In the Data Division, a punch file is described just like a print file, but the output area should be exactly 80 bytes long; it is a card-image file. Here's an example:

```
DATA DIVISION.
FILE SECTION.
FD  PUNCH-OUTPUT
    LABEL RECORDS ARE OMITTED.
01  CARD-IMAGE       PIC X(80).
```

You can subdivide the record as needed to refer to individual fields.

Creating Unit Record Output

Procedure Division handling of all unit record output files is much the same. In a sense, nonprint files are easier to handle because they seldom require any headings or special spacing.

Here's a Procedure Division that creates a punch file from input records.

```
PROCEDURE DIVISION.
MAIN-PARAGRAPH.
    OPEN INPUT STUDENT-FILE
         OUTPUT PUNCH-OUTPUT.
    PERFORM GET-INPUT.
    PERFORM MAKE-PUNCH-FILE
         UNTIL END-OF-INPUT = "Y".
    CLOSE PUNCH-OUTPUT STUDENT-FILE.
    STOP RUN.
MAKE-PUNCH-FILE.
    WRITE CARD-IMAGE FROM STUDENT-RECORD.
    PERFORM GET-INPUT.
GET-INPUT.
    READ STUDENT-FILE
         AT END MOVE "Y" TO END-OF-INPUT.
```

Notice that the OPEN, CLOSE, and READ statements name the files, while the WRITE statement names the record, just as with other files.

Summary   In this lesson you have seen that unit record output files are created much like print files. You code a record length of 80 bytes and use the system-name required by your system.

Comprehension Questions

1. In what division is the major coding difference between print and punch files?

_____

2. What record length do you code for punch files?

_____

3. What option do you use on the OPEN statement for a punch file?

_____

4. What statement do you use to send a record to a punch file?

_____

Answers

1. Environment   **2.** 80 bytes   **3.** OUTPUT   **4.** WRITE

Application Questions

You need to convert this input into a punch format output file named PUNCHOUT.

```
input data:

01   ITEM-DATA.
     05   ITEM-NAME         PIC X(20).
     05   ITEM-PRICE        PIC X(5).
     05   ITEM-DEPARTMENT   PIC X(10).
     05   ITEM-SOURCE       PIC XXXX.
```

1. Code the Environment Division entry for the punch file.

2. Code the Data Division entries for the file. Describe the output area as a single field.

3. Code a statement to open the file.

4. The input is received with this statement:

```
ACCEPT ITEM-DATA.
```

Code the statement(s) needed to add one record to the output file.

5. Code a statement to close the file.

Answers

```
1. INPUT-OUTPUT SECTION.
   FILE-CONTROL.
       SELECT PUNCHOUT
           ASSIGN TO system-name.
2. FILE SECTION.
   FD  PUNCHOUT
       LABEL RECORDS ARE OMITTED.
   01  PUNCH-DATA            PIC X(80).
3. OPEN OUTPUT PUNCHOUT.
4. WRITE PUNCH-DATA FROM ITEM-DATA.
       or
   MOVE ITEM-DATA TO PUNCH-DATA.
   WRITE PUNCH-DATA.
   (Be sure you used the same record-name as in question 2.)
5. CLOSE PUNCHOUT.
```

Chapter Review Questions

In this chapter review you'll write file-related entries for a program that creates a print output file from data records in a unit record input file. The output file will contain a double-spaced list of all names in the input data. Here are the file record formats.

Input: CUSTOMER-FILE

Customer record		
Customer number	Customer name	Rest of record
1 7	8 33	34 78

Output: LIST-FILE

```
.┌─────────────────────────────────────────────┐.
.│  CUSTOMER LISTING                             │.
.│                                               │.
.│  Customer  name                               │.
.│                                               │.
.│  Customer  name                               │.
.│     .                                         │.
.│     .                                         │.
.│     .                                         │.
.└─────────────────────────────────────────────┘.
```

Code the missing pieces in the program below. Be sure to be consistent in creating and referencing names.

```
IDENTIFICATION DIVISION.
PROGRAM-ID. CH8REV.
ENVIRONMENT DIVISION.
```

1.
```
┌──────────────────────────────────────────────┐
│                                                │
│                                                │
│                                                │
│                                                │
│                                                │
│                                                │
│                                                │
│                                                │
└──────────────────────────────────────────────┘
```

```
DATA DIVISION.
```

2.
```
┌──────────────────────────────────────────────┐
│                                                │
│                                                │
│                                                │
│                                                │
│                                                │
│                                                │
│                                                │
│                                                │
│                                                │
└──────────────────────────────────────────────┘
```

```
WORKING-STORAGE SECTION.
01   END-OF-INPUT          PIC X         VALUE "N".
01   REPORT-TITLE.
     05   FILLER           PIC X(10)    VALUE SPACES.
     05   FILLER           PIC X(16)
                           VALUE "CUSTOMER LISTING".
     05   FILLER           PIC X(10)    VALUE SPACES.
01   REPORT-LINE.
     05   FILLER           PIC X(10)    VALUE SPACES.
     05   CUSTOMER-NAME-OUT PIC X(26).

PROCEDURE DIVISION.
PRODUCE-LISTING.
```

3.


```
     PERFORM PRINT-HEADING.
     PERFORM READ-RECORD.
     PERFORM PRINT-LINE
          UNTIL END-OF-INPUT = "Y".
```

4.


```
     STOP RUN.
PRINT-HEADING.
```

5.


```
PRINT-LINE.
```

6.

7. `READ-RECORD.`

```
┌────────────────────────────────────────────────────────────┐
│                                                              │
│                                                              │
│                                                              │
│                                                              │
│                                                              │
└────────────────────────────────────────────────────────────┘
```

Answers

You will compile and test this program at the end of the next chapter. Enter it into a source file so you will be ready.

```
        IDENTIFICATION DIVISION.
        PROGRAM-ID.  CH8REV.
        ENVIRONMENT DIVISION.
```

1.
```
        INPUT-OUTPUT SECTION.
        FILE-CONTROL.
            SELECT CUSTOMER-FILE
                ASSIGN TO system-name.
            SELECT LIST-FILE
                ASSIGN TO system-name.
```

```
        DATA DIVISION.
```

2.
```
        FILE SECTION.
        FD  CUSTOMER-FILE
            LABEL RECORDS ARE OMITTED.
        01  CUSTOMER-RECORD.
            05  FILLER                PIC X(7).
            05  CUSTOMER-NAME         PIC X(26).
            05  FILLER                PIC X(45).
        FD  LIST-FILE
            LABEL RECORDS ARE OMITTED.
        01  LIST-RECORD               PIC X(36).
```

```
        WORKING-STORAGE SECTION.
        01  END-OF-INPUT              PIC X         VALUE "N".
        01  REPORT-TITLE.
            05  FILLER                PIC X(10)    VALUE SPACES.
            05  FILLER                PIC X(16)
                                      VALUE "CUSTOMER LISTING".
            05  FILLER                PIC X(10)    VALUE SPACES.
        01  REPORT-LINE.
            05  FILLER                PIC X(10)    VALUE SPACES.
            05  CUSTOMER-NAME-OUT     PIC X(26).

        PROCEDURE DIVISION.
        PRODUCE-LISTING.
```

3.

```
        OPEN INPUT CUSTOMER-FILE
             OUTPUT LIST-FILE.

        PERFORM PRINT-HEADING.
        PERFORM READ-RECORD.
        PERFORM PRINT-LINE
            UNTIL END-OF-INPUT = "Y".
```

4.

```
        CLOSE CUSTOMER-FILE LIST-FILE.

        STOP RUN.
    PRINT-HEADING.
```

5.

```
        WRITE LIST-RECORD FROM REPORT-TITLE.
        MOVE SPACES TO LIST-RECORD.
        WRITE LIST-RECORD.

    PRINT-LINE.
```

6.

```
        MOVE CUSTOMER-NAME TO CUSTOMER-NAME-OUT.
        WRITE LIST-RECORD FROM REPORT-LINE.
        MOVE SPACES TO LIST-RECORD.
        WRITE LIST-RECORD.
        PERFORM READ-RECORD.
```

7.   READ-RECORD.

```
        READ CUSTOMER-FILE
            AT END MOVE "Y" TO END-OF-INPUT.
```

Notes:
1. Be sure you selected both files. Use system-names appropriate for your compiler.
2. Be sure you coded FD and a record description for each file. Your output record must be at least 36 characters long.
3. You could code two separate OPEN statements if you prefer. Be sure you specified INPUT and OUTPUT appropriately.
4. You could code two separate CLOSE statements.
5. Be sure you specified the output record name here. You could have used a MOVE statement instead of the FROM option. The line of spaces creates double spacing.
6. You could have used another MOVE statement instead of the FROM option.
7. Be sure you specified the file-name and set the end-of-file flag.

Compiling and Testing Programs with Files

Virtually every program you write from now on, in this course and on the job, will involve at least one unit record file. In this chapter you'll learn what is required to compile and test such programs. Once you can handle simple unit record input and print a basic report, you will be well prepared for learning more complex programming skills.

This chapter consists of two lessons:

Lesson 9.1   Compiling Programs with Unit Record Files
Lesson 9.2   Testing Programs with Unit Record Files

Compiling Programs with Unit Record Files

Compiling programs that use files is basically the same as compiling programs that don't use files. The file-related entries are, of course, checked for format and completeness. Testing, too, is done similarly. In many systems, however, you need to tell the computer where to find or put files.

Objective   You will be able to interpret file-related compiler messages and correct errors to get a clean compile.

Rationale   You will have to compile all programs you write; most of these will involve unit record files. Therefore, you need to know how to compile programs with unit record files.

Compiling Programs with Files

Compilation of a program that uses files is basically the same as other compilations. The same errors generate the same messages. File-related entries allow more possibilities for errors, however. In this section we'll look at the types of messages you may get for errors in file-related entries.

As you know, the compiler uses the source program as an input unit record file. It doesn't access any files referred to by the source program or produce any source program output. An object module and a listing are the only compiler output. You don't provide test data for compilation; the compile step doesn't even check to see if the files exist. It simply ensures that your program defines files correctly and refers to them consistently.

The compiler listing contains the same parts as a listing from a file-free program. Most of the messages you'll receive will refer to specific lines, just as before. You'll be able to look at the line referenced to make sure you coded the Input-Output Section, FILE-CONTROL paragraph, and File Section entries correctly.

Figure 9.1 shows a complete, correct program that uses two files. This was compiled on an IBM VSE system, which requires single quotes for literals. One error at a time was put into the program to create the messages you'll see in the following discussion. Let's look first at messages that result from file definition errors.

Figure 9.1 Correct Source Program

```
IDENTIFICATION DIVISION.
PROGRAM-ID.  COB1FILE.
ENVIRONMENT DIVISION.
INPUT-OUTPUT SECTION.
FILE-CONTROL.
    SELECT USER-FILE
        ASSIGN TO ...
    SELECT OUT-FILE
        ASSIGN TO ...
DATA DIVISION.
FILE SECTION.
FD  USER-FILE
    LABEL RECORDS ARE OMITTED.
01  USER-DATA.
    05  USER-NAME               PIC X(26).
    05  USER-CODE               PIC X(4).
FD  OUT-FILE
    LABEL RECORDS ARE OMITTED.
01  OUT-DATA                    PIC X(40).
WORKING-STORAGE SECTION.
01  END-OF-DATA-INDICATOR       PIC X      VALUE 'N'.
01  END-MESSAGE                 PIC X(16)
                    VALUE 'ALL ITEMS LISTED'.
01  OUT-FORMAT.
    05  FILLER                  PIC X(3)  VALUE SPACES.
    05  OUT-CODE                PIC X(4).
    05  FILLER                  PIC X(3)  VALUE SPACES.
    05  OUT-NAME                PIC X(26).
PROCEDURE DIVISION.
PREPARE-COMPLETE-LIST.
    OPEN INPUT USER-FILE
        OUTPUT OUT-FILE.
    PERFORM READ-USER-FILE.
    PERFORM PREPARE-LIST-LINES
        UNTIL END-OF-DATA-INDICATOR = 'Y'.
    DISPLAY END-MESSAGE.
    CLOSE USER-FILE OUT-FILE.
    STOP RUN.
PREPARE-LIST-LINES.
    MOVE USER-NAME TO OUT-NAME.
    MOVE USER-CODE TO OUT-CODE.
    WRITE OUT-DATA FROM OUT-FORMAT.
    PERFORM READ-USER-FILE.
READ-USER-FILE.
    READ USER-FILE
        AT END MOVE 'Y' TO END-OF-DATA-INDICATOR.
```

Environment Division Errors   Figure 9.2 shows the messages generated when the ASSIGN key word is misspelled. Since "ASSGN" is not a valid word, the compiler skips to the next clause. Then it issues another message, since it found no ASSIGN clause. Since USER-FILE wasn't completely defined, the OPEN and READ statements (on lines 31 and 44) do not recognize USER-FILE as a file name. All these messages disappear when the spelling of ASSIGN is corrected and the program recompiled.

Figure 9.2 Effect of Misspelled ASSIGN

Source code:

```
00005      FILE-CONTROL.
00006          SELECT USER-FILE
00007             ASSGN TO USER821.
```

Messages:

```
00007      ASSGN INVALID IN SELECT CLAUSE. SKIPPING TO NEXT CLAUSE.
00007      ASSIGN CLAUSE MISSING IN SELECT. CONTINUING.
00006      NO VALID OPEN FOR FILE. FILE IGNORED.
00031      SYNTAX REQUIRES FILE-NAME IN OPEN STATEMENT. FOUND USER-FILE.
              DELETING TILL LEGAL ELEMENT FOUND.
00044      SYNTAX REQUIRES ' FILE-NAME '. FOUND ' USER-FILE '.
              STATEMENT DISCARDED.
```

Figure 9.3 shows the effect of omitting the SELECT and ASSIGN clauses for a file. The messages here are similar to the ones in Figure 9.2. The FD entry is ignored, since USER-FILE wasn't selected. This invalidates the OPEN statement, causing OUT-FILE to be ignored also; thus, references to OUT-DATA are also invalid. Inserting the correct Environment Division entries for USER-FILE clears up all these messages.

Some compilers will let you omit either the INPUT-OUTPUT SECTION or FILE-CONTROL header and not consider it an error. You should include the headers, however, to help document the program and to make it transferable to other systems.

Figure 9.3 Effect of Omitting SELECT/ASSIGN

Source code:

```
00005      FILE-CONTROL.
00006          SELECT OUT-FILE
00007             ASSIGN TO PRINTER.
00008      DATA DIVISION.
00009      FILE SECTION.
00010      FD  USER-FILE
00011          LABEL RECORDS ARE OMITTED.
00012      01  USER-DATA.
00013          05  USER-NAME                 PIC X(26).
00014          05  USER-CODE                 PIC X(4).
00015      FD  OUT-FILE
00016          LABEL RECORDS ARE OMITTED.
00017      01  OUT-DATA                      PIC X(40).
```

Messages:

```
00011      FILE-NAME NOT DEFINED IN A SELECT. DESCRIPTION IGNORED.
00006      NO VALID OPEN FOR FILE. FILE IGNORED.
00028      ' USER-FILE ' NOT DEFINED. DELETING TILL LEGAL ELEMENT FOUND.
00028      SYNTAX REQUIRES FILE-NAME IN OPEN STATEMENT. FOUND USER-FILE.
              DELETING TILL LEGAL ELEMENT FOUND.
00028      OPEN STATEMENT INCOMPLETE. STATEMENT DISCARDED.
00038      SYNTAX REQUIRES ' RECORD-NAME '. FOUND ' OUT-DATA  .
              STATEMENT DISCARDED.
00041      ' USER-FILE ' NOT DEFINED. STATEMENT DISCARDED.
```

Figure 9.4 Effect of Omitting FD

Source code:

```
00025      PROCEDURE DIVISION.
00026      PREPARE-COMPLETE-LIST.
00027          OPEN INPUT USER-FILE
00028              OUTPUT OUT-FILE.
00029          PERFORM READ-USER-FILE.
00030          PERFORM PREPARE-LIST-LINES
00031              UNTIL END-OF-DATA-INDICATOR = 'Y'.
00032          DISPLAY END-MESSAGE.
00033          CLOSE USER-FILE OUT-FILE.
00034          STOP RUN.
00035      PREPARE-LIST-LINES.
00036          MOVE USER-NAME TO OUT-NAME.
00037          MOVE USER-CODE TO OUT-CODE.
00038          WRITE OUT-DATA FROM OUT-FORMAT.
```

Messages:

```
00027      ' OUT-FILE ' NOT DEFINED. DELETING TILL LEGAL ELEMENT FOUND.
00033      ' OUT-FILE ' NOT DEFINED. DELETING TILL LEGAL ELEMENT FOUND.
00038      ' OUT-DATA ' NOT DEFINED. STATEMENT DISCARDED.
```

Data Division Errors   Figure 9.4 shows the effect of omitting the entire FD entry for a file. Here the OPEN, CLOSE, and WRITE statements are invalid, since the file was not completely defined.

Figure 9.5 shows the effect of reversing the FD and 01 indicators for a file. Since the first entry isn't FD, this compiler assumes a Working-Storage Section is being defined. All the messages result from miscoding level indicators.

Some errors in the Data Division won't generate messages but may cause problems later. If you code LABEL RECORDS ARE STANDARD for a unit record file, the source program will compile, but the system will not be able to access the records correctly and a bomb will probably result. If you omit the LABEL clause, be sure you know what default will be used. It is better to include the correct LABEL clause for documentation.

Figure 9.5 Effect of Reversing FD and 01

Source code:

```
00010       DATA DIVISION.
00011       FILE SECTION.
00012       01   USER-FILE
00013            LABEL RECORDS ARE OMITTED.
00014       FD   USER-DATA.
00015            05   USER-NAME              PIC X(26).
00016            05   USER-CODE              PIC X(4).
00017       FD   OUT-FILE
00018            LABEL RECORDS ARE OMITTED.
00019       01   OUT-DATA                    PIC X(40).
00020       WORKING-STORAGE SECTION.
```

Messages:

```
00012       IMPROPER LEVEL NUMBER FOR FILE-SECTION.
00013       LABEL INVALID IN DATA DESCRIPTION. SKIPPING TO NEXT CLAUSE.
00013       RECORDS INVALID IN DATA DESCRIPTION. SKIPPING TO NEXT CLAUSE.
00013       IS -  ARE INVALID IN DATA DESCRIPTION. SKIPPING TO
                 NEXT CLAUSE.
00013       OMITTED INVALID IN DATA DESCRIPTION. SKIPPING TO NEXT CLAUSE.
00014       FD INVALID AS USED IN WORKING-STORAGE SECTION. SKIPPING TO
                 NEXT LEVEL, SECTION OR DIVISION.
00017       FD INVALID AS USED IN WORKING-STORAGE SECTION. SKIPPING TO
                 NEXT LEVEL, SECTION OR DIVISION.
00020       WORKING-STORAGE INVALID AS USED IN WORKING-STORAGE SECTION.
                 SKIPPING TO NEXT LEVEL, SECTION OR DIVISION.
00032       SYNTAX REQUIRES FILE-NAME IN OPEN STATEMENT. FOUND USER-FILE.
                 DELETING TILL LEGAL ELEMENT FOUND.
00032       ' OUT-FILE ' NOT DEFINED. DELETING TILL LEGAL ELEMENT FOUND.
00032       OPEN STATEMENT INCOMPLETE. STATEMENT DISCARDED.
00042       SYNTAX REQUIRES ' RECORD-NAME '. FOUND ' OUT-DATA '.
                 STATEMENT DISCARDED.
00045       SYNTAX REQUIRES ' FILE-NAME '. FOUND ' USER-FILE '.
                 STATEMENT DISCARDED.
```

Procedure Division Errors If a file is not OPENed with a valid mode (INPUT or OUTPUT for a unit record file), the file is not considered valid for the program. All references to the file or its record therefore generate errors. Figure 9.6 shows three sets of error messages.
Set A was generated by this statement:

```
OPEN INPUT USER-FILE
     OUTPUT OUT-DATA.
```

Since the record rather than the file was named for the output file, all references to the file-name and the record-name are invalid.

Set B shows the result of omitting the OPEN statement. A missing OPEN statement makes the READ, WRITE, and CLOSE statements invalid.

Set C shows the result of using this OPEN statement:

```
OPEN USER-FILE
     OUT-FILE.
```

Figure 9.6 Messages Resulting from OPEN errors

```
A:   00008   NO VALID OPEN FOR FILE.  FILE IGNORED.
     00030   SYNTAX REQUIRES FILE-NAME IN OPEN STATEMENT.
                 FOUND OUT-DATA. DELETING TILL LEGAL ELEMENT FOUND.
     00040   SYNTAX REQUIRES ' RECORD-NAME '.  FOUND OUT-DATA.
                 STATEMENT DISCARDED.

B:   00006   NO VALID OPEN FOR FILE.  FILE IGNORED.
     00008   NO VALID OPEN FOR FILE.  FILE IGNORED.
     00034   SYNTAX REQUIRES FILE-NAME IN CLOSE STATEMENT.
                 FOUND USER-FILE. DELETING TILL LEGAL ELEMENT FOUND.
     00034   SYNTAX REQUIRES FILE-NAME IN CLOSE STATEMENT.
                 FOUND OUT-FILE. DELETING TILL LEGAL ELEMENT FOUND.
     00034   CLOSE STATEMENT INCOMPLETE.  STATEMENT DISCARDED.
     00039   SYNTAX REQUIRES ' RECORD-NAME '.  FOUND ' OUT-FILE '.
                 STATEMENT DISCARDED.
     00042   SYNTAX REQUIRES ' FILE-NAME '.  FOUND ' USER-FILE '.
                 STATEMENT DISCARDED.

C:   00006   NO VALID OPEN FOR FILE.  FILE IGNORED.
     00008   NO VALID OPEN FOR FILE.  FILE IGNORED.
     00030   SYNTAX INCORRECT.  TREATED AS COMMENTS.
                 SKIPPING TO NEXT CLAUSE.
     00036   SYNTAX REQUIRES FILE-NAME IN CLOSE STATEMENT.
                 FOUND USER-FILE. DELETING TILL LEGAL ELEMENT FOUND.
     00036   SYNTAX REQUIRES FILE-NAME IN CLOSE STATEMENT.
                 FOUND OUT-FILE.  DELETING TILL LEGAL ELEMENT FOUND.
     00036   CLOSE STATEMENT INCOMPLETE.  STATEMENT DISCARDED.
     00041   SYNTAX REQUIRES ' RECORD-NAME '.  FOUND ' OUT-FILE '.
                 STATEMENT DISCARDED.
     00044   SYNTAX REQUIRES ' FILE-NAME '.  FOUND ' USER-FILE '.
                 STATEMENT DISCARDED.
```

Omitting the mode actually results in more messages than omitting the entire statement because the compiler must point out the incorrect syntax as well as rejecting other statements.

Figure 9.7 shows the effect of reading a record instead of a file. The READ statement is discarded.

Figure 9.7 Effect of Reading a Record

Source code:

```
00011       FILE SECTION.
00012       FD   USER-FILE
00013            LABEL RECORDS ARE OMITTED.
00014       01   USER-DATA.
00015            05   USER-NAME              PIC X(26).
00016            05   USER-CODE              PIC X(4).
00017       FD   OUT-FILE
               .
               .
               .

00043       READ USER-DATA
00044            AT END MOVE 'Y' TO END-OF-DATA-INDICATOR.
```

Messages:

```
00043       SYNTAX REQUIRES ' FILE-NAME '. FOUND ' USER-DATA '.
                 STATEMENT DISCARDED.
```

Figure 9.8 shows the effect of reading an output file. Here, too, the READ statement is discarded. The AT END clause generates a second message.

With most compilers, file-related errors in the Procedure Division usually generate fewer messages than those involved in defining files. Some compilers will generate messages if you define and open a file but neglect to include the appropriate I/O statement. Some compilers will let you omit CLOSE statements, while others produce messages for any missing statement.

PERFORM-Related Errors   The PERFORM statement can be a source of errors in your program. If the paragraph-name isn't spelled the same in both places, the PERFORM statement will generate messages. The message in Figure 9.9 refers to line 00013, where a paragraph-name is used in a PERFORM statement. Paragraph-names are defined where they are coded, beginning in area A. If you look at line 00017, you'll see that the name is not identical to that in line 00013. You could correct the error by changing either of the lines so that the paragraph-name definition and the reference are the same.

Errors in coding conditions also generate error messages at compilation time. You'll be able to correct these without much difficulty.

Analyzing Error Messages   When you receive a compilation listing, scan the error messages. If any file-related message refers to lines in the Environment or Data divisions check those lines for errors. If you find an error, chances are you've identified a problem that caused

Figure 9.8 Effect of Reading Output File

```
Source code:
00030          OPEN INPUT USER-FILE
00031               OUTPUT OUT-FILE.
                 .
                 .
                 .
00042     READ-USER-FILE.
00043     READ OUT-FILE
00044          AT END MOVE ' Y ' TO END-OF-DATA-INDICATOR.

Messages:
00043     ILLEGAL TO READ PRINT FILE OUT-FILE. STATEMENT DISCARDED.
00043     EXPECTING NEW STATEMENT. FOUND AT . DELETING TILL NEXT
               VERB OR PROCEDURE-NAME.
```

Figure 9.9 Compiler Listing Excerpts

Source code:

```
00013            PERFORM PREPARE-LIST-LINES
00014               UNTIL USER-NAME = SPACES.
        .
        .
        .
00017        PREPARE-LIST-LINE.
00018           WRITE LIST-LINE.
```

Message:

```
00013    PREPARE-LIST-LINES NOT DEFINED.  STATEMENT DISCARDED.
```

many error messages. Cross off the messages that you think resulted from that error. Then go on to deal with the other messages before recompiling.

Summary Compiling programs that use files is similar in process to compiling and testing file-free programs. During compilation, many messages may be generated by errors in defining files in the Environment and Data Divisions, since any reference to an undefined file is invalid. In most cases, reexamining the file definitions carefully will allow you to locate and correct the error. Problems in the Procedure Division are usually caused by invalid definitions in the earlier divisions or by syntax errors.

Comprehension Questions

1. True or false? Unit record input data is needed to compile a program that uses it. _____

2. True or false? A compilation error in the SELECT clause may generate more messages than an error in a WRITE statement. _____

3. True or false? Compilation messages related to files can be ignored until you are ready to test the program. _____

Answers

1. False   2. True   3. False

Application Questions

Each set of messages below is accompanied by the relevant source program lines. Specify how to correct the errors.

1. Source code:

```
00011              FILE SECTION.
00012         FD   EMPLOYEE-FILE.
00013              LABEL RECORDS ARE OMITTED.
00014         01   EMPLOYEE-DATA.
```

Messages:

```
00013  INVALID WORD LABEL . SKIPPING TO NEXT RECOGNIZABLE WORD.
```

2. Source code:

```
00006              SELECT EMPLOYEE-FILE
00007                  ASIGN TO SYS006.
  .
  .
  .
00047              OPEN INPUT EMPLOYEE-FILE
00048                  OUTPUT LISTING-FILE.
00049              PERFORM GET-EMPLOYEE-DATA.
00050              PERFORM PROCESS-DATA
00051                  UNTIL END-OF-EMPLOYEES = 'Y'.
00052              WRITE PRINT-RECORD FROM FOOTING-LINE.
00053              CLOSE EMPLOYEE-FILE LISTING-FILE.
  .
  .
  .
00070         GET-EMPLOYEE-DATA.
00071              READ EMPLOYEE-FILE
00072                  AT END MOVE 'Y' TO END-OF-EMPLOYEES.
```

Messages:

```
00007  ASIGN INVALID IN SELECT CLAUSE. SKIPPING TO
           NEXT CLAUSE.
00007  ASSIGN CLAUSE MISSING IN SELECT. CONTINUING.
00006  NO VALID OPEN FOR FILE. FILE IGNORED.
00047  SYNTAX REQUIRES FILE-NAME IN OPEN STATEMENT. FOUND
           EMPLOYEE-FILE. DELETING TILL LEGAL ELEMENT FOUND.
00053  SYNTAX REQUIRES FILE-NAME IN CLOSE STATEMENT. FOUND
           EMPLOYEE-FILE. DELETING TILL LEGAL ELEMENT FOUND.
00071  SYNTAX REQUIRES ' FILE-NAME '. FOUND ' EMPLOYEE-FILE '.
           STATEMENT DISCARDED.
```

3. Source code:

```
00006          SELECT EMPLOYEE-FILE
00007              ASSIGN TO SYS006.
00008          SELECT LISTING-FILE
00009              ASSIGN TO SYS008.
    .
    .
    .
00047          WRITE PRINT-RECORD FROM FOOTING-LINE.
00048          CLOSE EMPLOYEE-FILE LISTING-FILE.
    .
    .
    .
00052          WRITE PRINT-RECORD FROM HEADING-LINE.
00053          MOVE SPACES TO PRINT-RECORD.
00054          WRITE PRINT-RECORD.
    .
    .
    .
00062          WRITE PRINT-RECORD FROM OUT-LINE.
00063          MOVE SPACES TO PRINT-RECORD.
00064          WRITE PRINT-RECORD.
00065      GET-EMPLOYEE-DATA.
00066          READ EMPLOYEE-FILE
00067              TO END-OF-EMPLOYEES.
```

Messages:

```
00006  NO VALID OPEN FOR FILE. FILE IGNORED.
00008  NO VALID OPEN FOR FILE. FILE IGNORED.
00047  SYNTAX REQUIRES ' RECORD-NAME '. FOUND ' PRINT-RECORD '.
 STATEMENT DISCARDED.
00048  SYNTAX REQUIRES FILE-NAME IN CLOSE STATEMENT.
          FOUND EMPLOYEE-FILE. DELETING TILL LEGAL ELEMENT FOUND.
00048  SYNTAX REQUIRES FILE-NAME IN CLOSE STATEMENT.
          FOUND LISTING-FILE. DELETING TILL LEGAL ELEMENT FOUND.
00048  CLOSE STATEMENT INCOMPLETE.  STATEMENT DISCARDED.
00052  SYNTAX REQUIRES ' RECORD-NAME '.  FOUND ' PRINT-RECORD '.
          STATEMENT DISCARDED.
00054  SYNTAX REQUIRES ' RECORD-NAME '.  FOUND ' PRINT-RECORD '.
          STATEMENT DISCARDED.
00062  SYNTAX REQUIRES ' RECORD-NAME '.  FOUND ' PRINT-RECORD '.
          STATEMENT DISCARDED.
00064  SYNTAX REQUIRES ' RECORD-NAME '.  FOUND ' PRINT-RECORD '.
          STATEMENT DISCARDED.
00066  SYNTAX REQUIRES ' FILE-NAME '.  FOUND ' EMPLOYEE-FILE '.
          STATEMENT DISCARDED.
```

Answers

1. Remove period after FD EMPLOYEE-FILE.   **2.** Correct spelling of ASIGN.
3. Include OPEN statement for both files.

Testing Programs That Use Files

Introduction to Computer Programming covered many testing concepts. You learned to write a test plan and to consider various error possibilities. In this lesson, we'll apply those concepts to simple programs of the type you have learned to code and compile.

Objectives You'll be able to design test data and specify expected output for a simple program. You'll also find out how to test a program that uses unit record input and output.

Rationale You'll be concerned about testing for every program you write. The better your test plan, the more likely your program will perform correctly when it goes into volume testing and then into production.

When to Test

When you receive a clean compilation for a program, you are ready to test it. You prepare for testing by designing a test plan and preparing input files. Actually, this preparation is usually done at the program design stage. In this lesson, you'll see the steps by walking though a simple test plan.

The Test Plan The test plan begins with a controlled test; this includes sample input data along with a sketch of the expected output for a program. You determine the expected output in advance so that you'll be able to tell at a glance if the test was successful.

Your controlled test data should include bad input data as well as good. You'll start with only good data, however. The data should include all options handled by the program. For example, look at Figure 9.10. This program reads input records and lists data from all the records.

Figure 9.10 Simple Source Program

```
IDENTIFICATION DIVISION.
PROGRAM-ID.  COB2FILE.
ENVIRONMENT DIVISION.
INPUT-OUTPUT SECTION.
FILE-CONTROL.
    SELECT USER-DATA-FILE
        ASSIGN TO ...
    SELECT USER-LISTING
        ASSIGN TO ...
DATA DIVISION.
FILE SECTION.
FD  USER-DATA-FILE
    LABEL RECORDS ARE OMITTED.
01  USER-DATA.
    05  USER-NAME              PIC X(26).
    05  USER-CODE              PIC X(4).
FD  USER-LISTING
    LABEL RECORDS ARE OMITTED.
01  REPORT-LINE                PIC X(40).
WORKING-STORAGE SECTION.
01  END-OF-USER-DATA           PIC X         VALUE "N".
01  REPORT-HEADING.
    05  FILLER                 PIC X(5)       VALUE SPACES.
    05  FILLER                 PIC X(12)
                               VALUE "LIST OF USERS".
01  REPORT-DETAIL.
    05  FILLER                 PIC X(3)       VALUE SPACES.
    05  USER-CODE-OUT          PIC X(4).
    05  FILLER                 PIC XX         VALUE SPACES.
    05  USER-NAME-OUT          PIC X(26).
PROCEDURE DIVISION.
PREPARE-COMPLETE-LIST.
    OPEN INPUT USER-DATA-FILE
        OUTPUT USER-LISTING.
    WRITE REPORT-LINE FROM REPORT-HEADING.
    PERFORM GET-INPUT-DATA.
    PERFORM PREPARE-LIST-LINES
        UNTIL END-OF-USER-DATA = "Y".
    CLOSE USER-DATA-FILE  USER-LISTING.
    STOP RUN.
PREPARE-LIST-LINES.
    MOVE USER-CODE TO USER-CODE-OUT.
    MOVE USER-NAME TO USER-NAME-OUT.
    WRITE REPORT-LINE FROM REPORT-DETAIL.
    PERFORM GET-INPUT-DATA.
GET-INPUT-DATA.
    READ USER-DATA-FILE
        AT END MOVE "Y" TO END-OF-USER-DATA.
```

It can use very simple test data, such as this:

Input:

```
JUDI N. FERNANDEZ        1111
RUTH ASHLEY              2222
BARBARA TABLER           3333
HELEN HIEBERT            4444
```

Expected output:

```
LIST OF USERS
1111   JUDI N. FERNANDEZ
2222   RUTH ASHLEY
3333   BARBARA TABLER
4444   HELEN HIEBERT
```

Testing the Program   Logically, not much can go wrong with this program. In all likelihood it will run the first time. Since the data is defined with Xs, any input values are acceptable. If the input file is formatted correctly, it should be displayed as expected.

Now let's see what else might happen. Suppose your output looks like this:

```
LIST OF USERS
  11    JUDI N. FERNANDEZ
  22    RUTH ASHLEY
  33    BARBARA TABLER
  44    HELEN HIEBERT
```

Notice that the USER-CODE values aren't correct on output. Each begins with two spaces. This is caused here by wrong input. The USER-CODE value on input occupied columns 29 to 32 instead of 27 to 30.

Here's another example of unexpected output:

```
LIST OF USERS
1111    JUDI N. FERNANDEZ
2222    RUTH ASHLEY
3333    BARBARA TABLER
4444    HELEN HIEBERT
INTERRUPT message
```

Here the four data records are listed correctly, but the program was interrupted by something. Either it bombed, the system stopped it, or the system crashed. None of these is very likely in such a simple program.

Different systems have different ways of telling you the program was interrupted. Some systems will display a message such as DATA CHECK INTERRUPTION or PROGRAM CANCELED BY OPERATOR REQUEST. Some will display a "status" or "completion" code indicating an abnormal termination. Some systems will tell you what line was being executed and what went wrong. Some will display the address (in hexadecimal or octal or binary) of the instruction being executed at the time of the interruption. You'll have to deal with whatever information your system gives you. Most of the messages relating to bombs and system crashes are cryptic, at best, and don't tell you what really happened. After a while you'll get used to interpreting the more common ones, but at first you'll probably need to get help from colleagues and advisors.

When you get some output, as in the example above, you have a start toward finding out what caused the interruption. You know the system could read your input and produce at least some of the output. You can look at the data and the source program and see what might have happened.

For this program any input data would be good. Since it is defined with Xs, you won't have data type problems. Therefore, you do not need to test zero cases, negative cases, empty cases, and so forth. You should, however, make sure the program will not bomb if the input file is empty.

Once the program works correctly with controlled data, it's ready for live data. Your participation in the live tests depends on the size of the project and whether the program is online or batch. Live testing may also identify errors to be corrected. Here again, you'll have to look at what resulted and try to figure out the source of the errors. Toward the end of the testing phase, you'll probably also fine tune the program.

Executing a Program with Test Data

You already know how to submit a program for execution in your system. If the program uses unit record files, you have to tell the system where to find the input and where to put the output. You have to provide the input in the way the program expects. You'll probably prepare your test data using your system's editor. When you run the program, you may have to tell the system where the input unit record file is. How you do this depends on your compiler and computer system. Some systems use the ASSIGN clause to identify the file. Others use a special clause in the FD entry (VALUE OF FILE-ID IS "filename"). Others require special instructions in the operating system control language to identify the data. You'll have to check out the requirements of your system with your training manager or an experienced colleague before you prepare your first test run for submission.

Summary Your test plan should include a controlled test step and possibly a live test and fine tuning step. Test both correct and incorrect input data.

After each test run, examine the results and figure out what corrections to make to the program. If the program terminates prematurely, the system will provide some type of message explaining why, although it may not identify the program's real problem.

After you have corrected the source program, compile, link, and test it again.

Comprehension Questions

1. Once you have a clean compile and a set of test data, you are ready to:

   a. Recompile the program
   b. Test the program
   c. Specify the expected output

2. A program is supposed to list item names from each record. The test data should include:

   a. An assortment of item descriptions
   b. An assortment of item names
   c. An assortment of quantity values

3. Suppose you want to test the program shown in Figure 9.10. Which of the following shows a set of good test data?

```
a. 1234 GEORGE WASHINGTON
   2345 JOHN ADAMS
   3456 THOMAS JEFFERSON
   4567 JAMES MADISON
   5678 JAMES MONROE
   6789 JOHN QUINCY ADAMS
   ↑    ↗
   |    column 6
   |
   column 1
```

```
b. 1234 GEORGE WASHINGTON
   2345 JOHN ADAMS
   3456 THOMAS JEFFERSON
   4567 JAMES MADISON
   5678 JAMES MONROE
   6789 JOHN QUINCY ADAMS
   ↑    ↗
   |    column 10
   |
   column 4
```

```
c. GEORGE WASHINGTON        1234
   JOHN ADAMS               2345
   THOMAS JEFFERSON         3456
   JAMES MADISON            4567
   JAMES MONROE             5678
   JOHN QUINCY ADAMS        6789
   ↑                        ↗
   |                        column 26
   column 1
```

```
d. GEORGE WASHINGTON        1234
   JOHN ADAMS               2345
   THOMAS JEFFERSON         3456
   JAMES MADISON            4567
   JAMES MONROE             5678
   JOHN QUINCY ADAMS        6789
   ↑                        ↗
                            column 27
   column 1
```

Suppose you need to test the program in Figure 9.10. It is stored on disk as COB2FILE. Check with your training manager or a helpful colleague to answer the following questions.

4. What ASSIGN clauses are needed?

   a. USER-DATA-FILE _____

   b. USER-LISTING _____

5. What changes, if any, are needed in the FD entry for each file?

   a. USER-DATA-FILE _____

   b. USER-LISTING _____

6. How do you run the program and provide the test data?

   _____

   _____

   _____

   _____

7. How do you see your printout?

   _____

   _____

   _____

   _____

Answers

1. c   **2.** b (The assortment of records is needed so you can interpret the output. The test would work if each test record had the same data, but you wouldn't know which records were printed.)   **3.** d   **4.** This depends on your installation.
5. This depends on your installation.   **6.** This depends on your installation.
7. This depends on your installation.

Application Questions

Here is a copy of the program you coded at the end of Chapter 8.

```
IDENTIFICATION DIVISION.
PROGRAM-ID. CH8REV.
ENVIRONMENT DIVISION.
INPUT-OUTPUT SECTION.
FILE-CONTROL.
    SELECT CUSTOMER-FILE
        ASSIGN TO ....
    SELECT LIST-FILE
        ASSIGN TO ....
DATA DIVISION.
FILE SECTION.
FD  CUSTOMER-FILE
    LABEL RECORDS ARE OMITTED.
01  CUSTOMER-RECORD.
    05  FILLER                PIC X(7).
    05  CUSTOMER-NAME         PIC X(26).
    05  FILLER                PIC X(45).
FD  LIST-FILE
    LABEL RECORDS ARE OMITTED.
01  LIST-RECORD               PIC X(36).

WORKING-STORAGE SECTION.
01  END-OF-INPUT             PIC X       VALUE "N".
01  REPORT-TITLE.
    05  FILLER                PIC X(10)   VALUE SPACES.
    05  FILLER                PIC X(16)
                        VALUE "CUSTOMER LISTING".
    05  FILLER                PIC X(10)   VALUE SPACES.
01  REPORT-LINE.
    05  FILLER                PIC X(10)   VALUE SPACES.
    05  CUSTOMER-NAME-OUT     PIC X(26).
PROCEDURE DIVISION.
PRODUCE-LISTING.
    OPEN INPUT CUSTOMER-FILE
        OUTPUT LIST-FILE.
    PERFORM PRINT-HEADING.
    PERFORM READ-RECORD.
    PERFORM PRINT-LINE
        UNTIL END-OF-INPUT = "Y".
    CLOSE CUSTOMER-FILE LIST-FILE.
    STOP RUN.
PRINT-HEADING.
    WRITE LIST-RECORD FROM REPORT-TITLE.
    MOVE SPACES TO LIST-RECORD.
    WRITE LIST-RECORD.
PRINT-LINE.
    MOVE CUSTOMER-NAME TO CUSTOMER-NAME-OUT.
    WRITE LIST-RECORD FROM REPORT-LINE.
    MOVE SPACES TO LIST-RECORD.
    WRITE LIST-RECORD.
    PERFORM READ-RECORD.
READ-RECORD.
    READ CUSTOMER-FILE
        AT END MOVE "Y" TO END-OF-INPUT.
```

Continued

1. Prepare a set of input data for testing the program. Use at least a dozen records.

2. Sketch the expected output, based on your input data.

1. Any data with customer name in columns 7 through 33 can be used. Include other data on the card, like this:

```
123456RUTH ASHLEY            OTHER DATA
```

2. You should see your values double-spaced in this format:

```
CUSTOMER LISTING

RUTH ASHLEY

JUDI FERNANDEZ
```

Chapter Review Questions

1. Suppose you receive these messages from a compilation:

Source code:

```
00027      01  FOOTING-LINE.
00028          05  FILLER                PIC X(5)    VALUE SPACES.
00029          05  FILLER                PIC X(35)
00030                                    VALUE 'END OF EMPLOYEE DATA REPORT'.
00031
00032      PROCEDURE DIVISION.
00033      PREPARE-EMPLOYMENT-REPORT.
00034          PERFORM DO-HEADING.
00035          PERFORM GET-RECORD.
00036          PERFORM PROCESS-DATA
00037              UNTIL EMPLOYEE-NUMBER IS 999999999.
00038          WRITE OUT-LINE FROM FOOTING.
00039          STOP RUN.
```

Messages:

```
00036      RELATIONAL MISSING IN IF OR CONDITION STATEMENT.
               'EQUAL' ASSUMED.
00038      FOOTING    IS ILLEGALLY USED IN WRITE STATEMENT.
               DISCARDED.
00038      DISPLAY STATEMENT INCOMPLETE.  STATEMENT DISCARDED.
```

What two corrections would you make?

_____

_____

2. Suppose you test this program:

```
IDENTIFICATION DIVISION.
PROGRAM-ID.  COB1REP.
ENVIRONMENT DIVISION.
DATA DIVISION.
WORKING-STORAGE SECTION.
01  USER-DATA.
    05  USER-NAME              PIC X(4).
    05  USER-CODE              PIC X(26).
PROCEDURE DIVISION.
PREPARE-COMPLETE-LIST.
    PERFORM PREPARE-LIST-LINES
        UNTIL USER-NAME = SPACES.
    DISPLAY "ALL ITEMS LISTED".
    STOP RUN.
PREPARE-LIST-LINES.
    DISPLAY USER-CODE, "    ", USER-NAME.
    ACCEPT USER-DATA.
```

with these records:

```
JUDI N. FERNANDEZ        1111
RUTH ASHLEY              2222
BARBARA TABLER           3333
HELEN HIEBERT            4444
(blank record)
```

You are expecting this output:

```
1111     JUDI N. FERNANDEZ
2222     RUTH ASHLEY
3333     BARBARA TABLER
4444     HELEN HIEBERT
ALL ITEMS LISTED
```

Unfortunately, the output looks like this:

```
 N. FERNANDEZ            1111JUDI
 ASHLEY                  2222RUTH
ARA TABLER               3333BARB
N HIEBERT                4444HELE
ALL ITEMS LISTED
```

What went wrong?

_____

_____

_____

3. Now you run another version of the program. The Procedure Division looks like this:

```
PROCEDURE DIVISION.
PREPARE-COMPLETE-LIST.
    ACCEPT USER-DATA
    PERFORM PREPARE-LIST-LINES
        UNTIL USER-NAME = SPACES.
    DISPLAY "ALL ITEMS LISTED".
    STOP RUN.
PREPARE-LIST-LINES.
    DISPLAY USER-CODE, "    ", USER-NAME.
```

You test it using the same controlled data and get this output:

```
1111     JUDI N. FERNANDEZ
1111     JUDI N. FERNANDEZ
1111     JUDI N. FERNANDEZ
1111     JUDI N. FERNANDEZ
1111     JUDI N. FERNANDEZ
1111     JUDI N. FERNANDEZ
1111     JUDI N. FERNANDEZ
1111     JUDI N. FERNANDEZ
1111     JUDI N. FERNANDEZ
1111     JUDI N. FERNANDEZ
1111     JUDI N. FERNANDEZ
1111     JUDI N. FERNANDEZ
1111     JUDI N. FERNANDEZ
1111     JUDI N. FERNANDEZ
1111     JUDI N. FERN**PROGRAM CANCELED**
```

The last output line indicates that the program was canceled by someone (probably you). What went wrong?

_____

_____

_____

4. Suppose you have compiled another program and received several messages. What would you do to correct each of these?

a. **Source line:**   READ PART-REPORT

```
00101           ILLEGAL TO READ PRINT FILE PART-REPORT.
                STATEMENT DISCARDED
```

```
b. 00006   NO VALID OPEN FOR FILE.  FILE IGNORED.
   00049   SYNTAX REQUIRES FILE-NAME IN CLOSE STATEMENT.
   00168   SYNTAX REQUIRES FILE-NAME IN READ STATEMENT.
```

```
c. 00012   01  INVENTORY
   00013       LABEL RECORDS ARE OMITTED.
   00014   01  INVENTORY-INFORMATION.

   00012   IMPROPER LEVEL NUMBER FOR FILE-SECTION
   00013   LABEL INVALID IN DATA DESCRIPTION.
                       SKIPPING TO NEXT CLAUSE.
```

Answers

1. Change IS to = (or add EQUAL TO after IS) in the PERFORM UNTIL statement. Change FOOTING to FOOTING-LINE in the DISPLAY statement.   **2.** The input data doesn't match the record description. Probably the description is incorrect: USER-NAME should be X(26) and USER-CODE should be X(4).   **3.** The program is processing the first record over and over again (and would do so forever if not stopped externally) because it never accepts a second record. PREPARE-LIST-LINES should include a line to ACCEPT USER-DATA.   **4.** a. Change to read an input file-name b. Insert the appropriate OPEN statement c. Change first 01 to FD

Section Four Exercise

You completed a program that uses input and output unit record files at the end of Chapter 8 (see page 402). You specified test data and expected output for this program at the end of Lesson 9.2.

For this exercise, compile and test the program in your installation. You may want to verify the following before you begin:

- ASSIGN clause format

- FD entry

- How to provide the input file

- How to access the output file

Early steps in this exercise include:

- Enter source program into system

- Enter input data into unit record file

If you have problems getting a clean compile or making the program run, see your training manager or a helpful colleague. Once this program runs, you'll have a model for running all other programs in this and the following books.

Implementing Decision Structures in COBOL

Decision Structures

Virtually all COBOL programs include one or more decision structures, primarily IF statements. You can already code them using pseudocode. In this chapter you'll learn to translate these structures into COBOL in order to solve more involved problems in a COBOL Procedure Division.

This chapter consists of three lessons:

The Basic Decision Structure

Much programming involves making decisions. The logic of a decision structure (IF-ELSE-ENDIF) can be translated into COBOL fairly easily.

Objectives   By the end of this lesson, you'll be able to code basic decision structures in COBOL using the IF statement. You'll also be able to use IF statements in COBOL programs.

Rationale   Most programs include many decisions. Decision structures are used to validate input data, identify error conditions, select the type of processing to perform on a record, perhaps even to terminate the program. You will code many COBOL IF statements in every program you write.

Decision Structure Logic

Figure 10.1 diagrams the logic of a decision structure.
   The first step in a decision structure is testing of the condition. If the condition is true, one block of code (routine A) is executed. If the condition is false, a different block of code (routine B) is executed. Then the decision structure is completed and the next statement in sequence is executed.

Figure 10.1 Decision Structure Logic

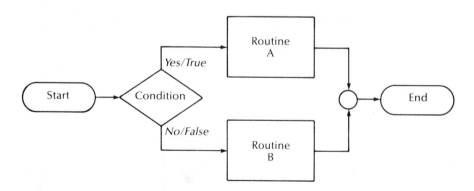

Here's an example of the logic in pseudocode:

```
IF   name is blank
THEN
     display message
ELSE
     process name (3.2)
ENDIF
```

In this example, one statement (display message) is executed if the condition is true. If the condition is false, the process name routine is executed. Then, in either case, control will continue with the statement following ENDIF.

Here's how that pseudocode translates to COBOL:

```
IF USER-NAME = SPACES
    DISPLAY NO-NAME-MESSAGE
ELSE
    PERFORM PROCESS-NAME.
```

Notice that COBOL does not include the words THEN and ENDIF. Some compilers recognize them, but we aren't covering them here since they aren't standard. The IF statement is terminated with a period, which is an important part of the IF logic. It symbolizes the ENDIF of pseudocode.

IF Statement

The COBOL IF statement is used to establish a decision structure. Figure 10.2 shows the format of this statement. Any valid condition can be used, just as in PERFORM...UNTIL statements. We'll continue using relation conditions in this book.

The IF statement must be coded entirely within area B. We'll use indentation to portray the meaning of the statement. However, the compiler ignores the indentation.

Examine the format carefully. Some compilers don't recognize the word THEN, so most programmers omit it.

For each path (true or false) you can specify statements to be executed, or you can bypass the path. The first example shows how two paths can be included. If the values of CURRENT-YEAR and YEAR-HIRED are the same, a line is displayed. If the two values aren't the same, paragraph HANDLE-OLD-HIRES is executed.

You use the words NEXT SENTENCE to indicate that no action should be taken for a path. If the condition produces that path, con-

Figure 10.2 IF Statement Format

Format:

```
IF   condition
[THEN]
     { NEXT SENTENCE }
     { statement...  }
[ELSE
     { NEXT SENTENCE } ].
     { statement...  }
```

Examples:

```
IF CURRENT-YEAR = YEAR-HIRED
     DISPLAY EMPLOYEE-NAME, HIRE-MESSAGE
ELSE
     PERFORM HANDLE-OLD-HIRES.

IF USER-NAME = AUTHORS-NAME
     NEXT SENTENCE
ELSE
     PERFORM VERIFY-NAME.

IF AGE = LAST-AGE-FLAG
     PERFORM END-OF-AGES.
```

Notes:

1. Any valid condition can be used.
2. Use NEXT SENTENCE to identify empty THEN or ELSE path.
3. You can omit ELSE NEXT SENTENCE.
4. Use a period to end the scope of the IF.
5. If the condition is true, the THEN path, if any, is taken.
6. If the condition is false, the ELSE path, if any, is taken.

trol will skip to the statement following the period that terminates the IF. The period has the logical effect of ENDIF. The second example shows how you indicate a blank true path. If you use a blank false path (or ELSE action), you can code "ELSE NEXT SENTENCE" or omit it as in the third example. Unnested IFs generally omit ELSE NEXT SENTENCE.

You'll want to pay attention to programming style and recall logic guidelines when you code decision structures. For example, the second example in the figure could be coded this way:

```
IF USER-NAME NOT = AUTHORS-NAME
     PERFORM VERIFY-NAME.
```

This will be clearer to readers. Try to put the most common or most desirable path as the true path. When these guidelines conflict or become confusing, consider the reader and write statements that are meaningful as well as correct and easy to understand.

Examples The statements below will all display the message "FIRST NAME WAS BLANK" if the value of FIRST-NAME is blank.

This statement omits ELSE NEXT SENTENCE:

```
IF FIRST-NAME = SPACES
    DISPLAY NAME-BLANK-MESSAGE.
```

This statement includes ELSE NEXT SENTENCE:

```
IF FIRST-NAME = SPACES
    DISPLAY NAME-BLANK-MESSAGE
ELSE
    NEXT SENTENCE.
```

The following statement specifies the condition negatively. It has the same effect as the earlier ones (but it's harder to read).

```
IF FIRST-NAME NOT = SPACES
    NEXT SENTENCE
ELSE
    DISPLAY NAME-BLANK-MESSAGE.
```

Suppose you need the field OUT-NAME filled with blanks when PART-NUMBER = PART-LIMIT. When the condition is false, OUT-NAME should hold the PART-NAME. Here's how you'd code that:

```
IF PART-NUMBER = PART-LIMIT
    MOVE SPACES TO OUT-NAME
ELSE
    MOVE PART-NAME TO OUT-NAME.
```

Here are some pseudocode and corresponding COBOL decision structures:

```
IF   balance is positive      IF TEMP-BALANCE > ZERO
     flag = Y                      MOVE "Y" TO BALANCE-FLAG
ELSE                          ELSE
     flag = N                      MOVE "N" TO BALANCE-FLAG.
ENDIF

IF   subject is female        IF SUBJECT-SEX = FEMALE-CODE
     base = 50                     MOVE LOWER-AMOUNT TO SCORE-BASE.
ELSE                          ELSE
     base = 70                     MOVE HIGHER-AMOUNT TO SCORE-BASE.
ENDIF

base = 70                     MOVE HIGHER-AMOUNT TO SCORE-BASE.
IF   subject is female        IF SUBJECT-SEX = FEMALE-CODE
     base = 50                     MOVE LOWER-AMOUNT TO SCORE-BASE.
ELSE
ENDIF
```

Notice that a period is used to terminate the IF sentence in all cases. The true path is ended by the appearance of ELSE or a period. The ELSE path is ended by the period at the end of the IF statement.

Decision Structures in Programs

Figure 10.3 shows a complete Procedure Division that incorporates a decision structure. Notice that the value of EMPLOYEE-CODE determines whether a record is written to the output file.

What would happen if the period after the WRITE statement were omitted? The COBOL compiler (which ignores indentation) would assume that PERFORM GET-ONE-RECORD is part of the true path. A new record would be read only if EMPLOYEE-CODE = NEW-EMPLOYEE. The first employee record without the NEW-EMPLOYEE code would cause an endless loop to be created. EMPLOYEE-CODE in that record would be repeatedly compared to NEW-EMPLOYEE.

Figure 10.4 shows another complete Procedure Division. If only a few parts are on hand, a special message is moved to a message field. Otherwise, the message field is cleared to get rid of any special message left over in memory from the previous loop. (If this field were not cleared, *every* output record after the first one that had too few parts on hand would say LOW QUANTITY IN STOCK.) The WRITE statement is executed for any value of PART-ON-HAND.

What would happen if you accidentally included a period before ELSE? You'd get an error message from the compiler. The COBOL compiler knows that no statement begins with ELSE.

Figure 10.5 shows a variation of the program in Figure 10.4. Now the program prepares a list of only certain records. The DISPLAY statement is executed only if the value of PART-ON-HAND is greater than MINIMUM-ON-HAND. If MINIMUM-ON-HAND = 100 and the records contain these values:

```
2070SCREWDRIVERS,FLAT 6"      030
2071SCREWDRIVERS,FLAT 8"      127
3132HAMMER,CLAW,2#            099
6020SAW,RIP                  100
7010SANDPAPER,FINE           682
```

only the second and the last records will be listed. None of the others are greater than MINIMUM-ON-HAND.

In this example the IF statement includes a series of statements. Notice that the period follows the last one.

Figure 10.3 Sample Coding

```
PROCEDURE DIVISION.
LIST-SELECTED-RECORDS.
    OPEN INPUT EMPLOYEE-FILE
         OUTPUT EMPLOYEE-LIST.
    PERFORM GET-ONE-RECORD.
    PERFORM LIST-CODED-RECORDS
        UNTIL END-OF-EMPLOYEES = "Y".
    CLOSE EMPLOYEE-FILE EMPLOYEE-LIST.
    STOP RUN.
LIST-CODED-RECORDS.
    IF EMPLOYEE-CODE = NEW-EMPLOYEE
        WRITE EMPLOYEE-LIST-RECORD FROM EMPLOYEE-DATA.
    PERFORM GET-ONE-RECORD.
GET-ONE-RECORD.
    READ EMPLOYEE-FILE
        AT END MOVE "Y" TO END-OF-EMPLOYEES.
```

Figure 10.4 IF Statement in Context

```
PROCEDURE DIVISION.
PREPARE-DATA-LIST.
    OPEN INPUT PART-FILE OUTPUT PART-LIST.
    WRITE LIST-LINE FROM LIST-HEADING.
    PERFORM READ-RECORD.
    PERFORM LIST-SELECTED-RECORDS
        UNTIL END-OF-PART-FILE = "Y".
    CLOSE PART-FILE PART-LIST.
    STOP RUN.
LIST-SELECTED-RECORDS.
    IF PART-ON-HAND LESS THAN LOW-LIMIT
        MOVE LOW-QUANTITY TO OUT-MESSAGE
    ELSE
        MOVE SPACES TO OUT-MESSAGE.
    MOVE PART-NAME TO OUT-PART-NAME.
    MOVE PART-NUMBER TO OUT-PART-NUMBER.
    WRITE LIST-LINE FROM LIST-DETAIL.
    PERFORM READ-RECORD.
READ-RECORD.
    READ PART-FILE
        AT END MOVE "Y" TO END-OF-PART-FILE.
```

Figure 10.5 IF Statement in Context, Modified Program

```
PROCEDURE DIVISION.
PREPARE-DATA-LIST.
    OPEN INPUT PART-FILE OUTPUT PART-LIST.
    WRITE LIST-LINE FROM LIST-HEADING.
    PERFORM READ-RECORD.
    PERFORM LIST-SELECTED-RECORDS
        UNTIL END-OF-PART-FILE = "Y".
    CLOSE PART-FILE PART-LIST.
    STOP RUN.
LIST-SELECTED-RECORDS.
    IF PART-ON-HAND GREATER THAN MINIMUM-ON-HAND
        MOVE PART-NAME TO OUT-PART-NAME
        MOVE PART-NUMBER TO OUT-PART-NUMBER
        WRITE LIST-LINE FROM LIST-DETAIL.
    PERFORM READ-RECORD.
READ-RECORD.
    READ PART-FILE
        AT END MOVE "Y" TO END-OF-PART-FILE.
```

Summary of IF Statement Decision structures in COBOL are coded using the IF statement. You have seen how control is affected by use of the IF statement.

Nested IFs

The examples you've seen so far have used imperative statements in IF sentences. You can include DISPLAY, ACCEPT, MOVE, or basic PERFORM statements in the true or false path. You can also include OPEN, CLOSE, and WRITE statements, or a series of such statements, in either path. As you've seen, you can include statements to be executed **in line**; that is, the statements are coded directly in the IF statement instead of being PERFORMed. Here's another example:

```
IF USER-NAME = CONSTANT-NAME
    DISPLAY WELCOME-MESSAGE
    MOVE USER-CODE TO OUT-CODE
    DISPLAY OUT-LINE.
```

This could also be coded as:

```
IF USER-NAME = CONSTANT-NAME
    PERFORM DO-MESSAGES.
.
.
.
DO-MESSAGES.
DISPLAY WELCOME-MESSAGE.
MOVE USER-CODE TO OUT-CODE.
DISPLAY OUT-LINE.
    .
    .
    .
```

Notice that when the statements are coded as part of an IF statement, you use a period only after the last one. Remember that the entire IF statement will be terminated after the first period.

Now suppose DO-MESSAGES looks like this:

```
DO-MESSAGES.
    IF CURRENT-MONTH = 12
        DISPLAY CHRISTMAS-MESSAGE.
    ELSE
        DISPLAY WELCOME-MESSAGE.
```

In effect, one IF is nested within another. Here's how that could be coded in line:

```
IF USER-NAME = CONSTANT-NAME
    IF CURRENT-MONTH = 12
        DISPLAY CHRISTMAS-MESSAGE
    ELSE
        DISPLAY WELCOME-MESSAGE.
```

Notice the period at the very end. This terminates the IF statement.

The COBOL compiler pairs each ELSE it encounters with the most recent unpaired IF, so the ELSE in the example above will be applied to the CURRENT-MONTH condition. The indentation has no effect on the compiler; it just makes the logic easier to see.

You are already familiar with the logic of a decision structure. Remember that whenever the logic gets very complex, you should go back and simplify the design. Any nested IF can be replaced with PERFORMed paragraphs that contain the inner IFs. Many complicated nested IFs should be simplified this way.

The IF sentence in Figure 10.6 includes an IF nested in each path. Each item under consideration has an ITEM-NUMBER, a value called VALUE-OF-ITEM, and an ITEM-CODE.

The outer IF tests VALUE-OF-ITEM. If it's less than the maximum value, one routine is executed; if not, the other is. Notice that the entire sentence could be represented like this:

```
IF condition
    PERFORM HANDLE-TRUE
ELSE
    PERFORM HANDLE-FALSE.
```

If the value is less than the maximum value, the ITEM-NUMBER and a LOW-VALUE-MESSAGE are displayed. For these "low value" items, the ITEM-CODE is also tested. If this is equal to the special-case code, the program performs a special-case routine; otherwise it continues. The ELSE NEXT SENTENCE is required here. If it were omitted, the next ELSE would be paired with IF ITEM-CODE = SPECIAL-CASE-CODE instead of with the outer IF.

Figure 10.6 Nested IF Example

```
IF VALUE-OF-ITEM < MAXIMUM-VALUE
    DISPLAY ITEM-NUMBER LOW-VALUE-MESSAGE
    IF ITEM-CODE = SPECIAL-CASE-CODE
        PERFORM SPECIAL-CASE
    ELSE
        NEXT SENTENCE
ELSE
    IF VALUE-OF-ITEM > MAXIMUM-VALUE
        DISPLAY ITEM-NUMBER HIGH-VALUE-MESSAGE
    ELSE
        DISPLAY ITEM-NUMBER ON-TARGET-MESSAGE.
```

Now let's look at the outer ELSE. Control will reach here only if VALUE-OF-ITEM is **not** less than MAXIMUM-VALUE. The program will display different messages for exactly MAXIMUM-VALUE and for greater than MAXIMUM-VALUE, following the instructions in the inner IF.

Nesting Guidelines   The example in Figure 10.6 is probably too complex. It should be simplified so a reader can understand it without too much effort.

One way to simplify it is by PERFORMing the inner IF in the true path to get rid of ELSE NEXT SENTENCE.

```
IF VALUE-OF-ITEM < MAXIMUM-VALUE
    DISPLAY ITEM-NUMBER LOW-VALUE-MESSAGE
    PERFORM CHECK-ITEM-CODE
ELSE
    IF VALUE-OF-ITEM > MAXIMUM-VALUE
        DISPLAY ITEM-NUMBER HIGH-VALUE-MESSAGE
    ELSE
        DISPLAY ITEM-NUMBER ON-TARGET-MESSAGE.
```

Another way is to turn the logic around so that the empty path is last:

```
IF VALUE-OF-ITEM > MAXIMUM-VALUE
    DISPLAY ITEM-NUMBER HIGH-VALUE-MESSAGE
ELSE
    IF VALUE-OF-ITEM = MAXIMUM-VALUE
        DISPLAY ITEM-NUMBER ON-TARGET-MESSAGE
    ELSE
        DISPLAY ITEM-NUMBER LOW-VALUE-MESSAGE
        IF ITEM-CODE = SPECIAL-CASE-CODE
            PERFORM SPECIAL-CASE.
```

Use nested IFs only when they make the logic clear. Try not to nest more than two or three levels deep, even though COBOL can handle many more levels. As long as a casual reading of the nested IF structure makes the meaning clear, the structure is probably appropriate. If the reader must puzzle over the structure to figure out what it is doing, it needs to be simplified. You'll learn another technique for handling multiple decisions in the next lesson.

Summary   In this lesson you've learned to code and use the IF statement to handle a decision structure in COBOL. You can handle a simple IF with two paths or with either path bypassed. You have also learned to code a nested IF to handle more complex logic.

Comprehension Questions

1. Which elements of the pseudocode decision structure are **not** included in a COBOL decision structure?

_____

2. Which of the IF statements below is/are a valid translation of the pseudocode?

```
IF  hours > 0
THEN
     flag = Y
ELSE
     report invalid data
     flag = N
ENDIF
```

a. IF HOURS-WORKED GREATER THAN ZERO
       MOVE "Y" TO HOURS-FLAG
   ELSE
       PERFORM REPORT-INVALID-DATA
       MOVE "N" TO HOURS-FLAG.

b. IF HOURS-WORKED GREATER THAN ZERO
       MOVE "Y" TO HOURS-FLAG.
   ELSE
       PERFORM REPORT-INVALID-DATA
       MOVE "N" TO HOURS-FLAG.

c. IF HOURS-WORKED GREATER THAN ZERO
       MOVE "Y" TO HOURS-FLAG
   ELSE
       PERFORM REPORT-INVALID-DATA.
       MOVE "N" TO HOURS-FLAG.

3. A program is to execute paragraph SAVE-THE-WHALES if ANIMAL-CODE indicates WHALES and RESCUE-SEALS if ANIMAL-CODE indicates SEALS.
   Which of the following accomplishes this?

a. IF ANIMAL-CODE = WHALES
       PERFORM SAVE-THE-WHALES
   ELSE
       PERFORM RESCUE-SEALS.

b. IF ANIMAL-CODE = WHALES
       PERFORM SAVE-THE-WHALES.
   IF ANIMAL-CODE = SEALS
       PERFORM RESCUE-SEALS.

c. IF ANIMAL-CODE = WHALES
       PERFORM SAVE-THE-WHALES
       IF ANIMAL-CODE = SEALS
           PERFORM RESCUE-SEALS.

d. IF ANIMAL-CODE = WHALES
       PERFORM SAVE-THE-WHALES
   ELSE
       IF ANIMAL-CODE = SEALS
           PERFORM RESCUE-SEALS.

4. Examine this code:

```
IF TRANSACTION-CODE > MASTER-CODE
    PERFORM READ-MASTER
ELSE
    IF TRANSACTION-CODE = MASTER-CODE
        PERFORM PROCESS-CHANGES
    ELSE
        PERFORM MISSING-MASTER.
PERFORM BUILD-AUDIT.
```

a. What paragraphs will be executed for these values:

A. TRANSACTION-CODE = 683   MASTER-CODE = 683

_____

B. TRANSACTION-CODE = 726   MASTER-CODE = 772

_____

C. TRANSACTION-CODE = 726   MASTER-CODE = 714

_____

b. For which set(s) of values above will paragraph BUILD-AUDIT be

executed? _____

c. Suppose the period following MISSING-MASTER were omitted. Now for which set(s) of values above will BUILD-AUDIT be executed?

Application Questions

1. Write a COBOL decision structure to test the value of IN-VALUE. If it does not equal QUORUM, execute paragraph PROCESS-VALUE.

2. Translate each pseudocode structure below into COBOL. Create valid data- and paragraph-names.

   a. ```
   IF   name is blank
   THEN
         summarize data
   ELSE
         process employee
   ENDIF
   ```

   b. ```
   IF item code > first code wanted
   THEN
         move name to display field
         display line
   ELSE
   ENDIF
   ```

3. Write a COBOL decision structure that will test the value of AGE. If AGE is greater than 40, place the value "MATURE" in OUT-MESSAGE. If not, place the value "YOUNG" in OUT-MESSAGE. In either case, place the value of STUDENT-NAME in OUT-NAME, then send LIST-RECORD to the output file LIST-STUDENTS. You may use the following items:

   ```
   05   CUTOFF-AGE          PIC 99     VALUE 40.
   05   MATURE-MESSAGE      PIC X(6)   VALUE "MATURE".
   05   YOUNG-MESSAGE       PIC X(5)   VALUE "YOUNG".
   ```

4. Suppose you want to display the ITEM-NUMBER for all items in a list. You also want to display the IN-STOCK-MESSAGE for every item that has more than three ON-HAND, VERY-FEW-MESSAGE for 1 to 3 ON-HAND, and OUT-OF-STOCK-MESSAGE if the value of ON-HAND is zero. In all cases you want to read another ITEM-RECORD from ITEM-FILE after each record is processed. Write the COBOL code to accomplish this. You may use the following item:

```
05  ENOUGH-ITEMS          PIC 9     VALUE 3.
```

Answers

```
1. IF IN-VALUE NOT = QUORUM     or   IF IN-VALUE = QUORUM
      PERFORM PROCESS-VALUE.              NEXT SENTENCE
                                    ELSE
                                         PERFORM PROCESS-VALUE.

2. a. IF EMPLOYEE-NAME = SPACES
         PERFORM SUMMARIZE-DATA
      ELSE
         PERFORM PROCESS-EMPLOYEE.

   b. IF ITEM-CODE > FIRST-CODE-WANTED
         MOVE ITEM-NAME TO DISPLAY-NAME
         DISPLAY LINE-CONTAINING-NAME.

3. IF AGE > CUTOFF-AGE
      MOVE MATURE-MESSAGE TO OUT-MESSAGE
   ELSE
      MOVE YOUNG-MESSAGE TO OUT-MESSAGE.
   MOVE STUDENT-NAME TO OUT-NAME.
   WRITE LIST-RECORD.

4. One way to handle this is:

   IF ON-HAND > ENOUGH-ITEMS
      DISPLAY ITEM-NUMBER, IN-STOCK-MESSAGE
   ELSE
       IF ON-HAND > ZERO
           DISPLAY ITEM-NUMBER, VERY-FEW-MESSAGE
       ELSE
           DISPLAY ITEM-NUMBER, OUT-OF-STOCK-MESSAGE.
   PERFORM READ-ITEM-RECORD.
```

Decision Structure Variation: Case Structure

The standard COBOL decision structure is coded using the IF statement. Each IF creates two paths. You can use nested IFs to generate multiple paths, but that can get messy.

The case structure allows control to follow any of several branches, based on the value of a field. COBOL does not have a CASE statement, but you'll learn to create a case structure using COBOL statements in this lesson.

Objectives   When you have finished this lesson, you'll be able to code a case structure in COBOL.

Rationale   Many decisions in a COBOL program are based on a value. Rather than coding an extremely nested IF to handle five or ten different situations, you can use a case structure to allow one of several different blocks of code to be executed depending on the value of a field.

Case Structure Logic

A case structure is used when a decision structure has three or more paths. Figure 10.7 shows the pseudocode format for a case structure.

In COBOL you need one paragraph for the initiating statement and another one for each case to be handled. Figure 10.8 diagrams the relationships between paragraphs in a case structure. Notice that there is one paragraph at the beginning and one at the end. To execute such a case structure in COBOL, you could code PERFORM CASE-A-ENTER THRU CASE-A-EXIT.

Figure 10.7 Pseudocode Format

```
CASE:    name

CASE1:   condition #1
            instructions
CASE2:   condition #2
            instructions
  .
  .
  .
CASEn:   condition #n
            instructions
ENDCASE
```

Figure 10.8 COBOL Case Structure Module

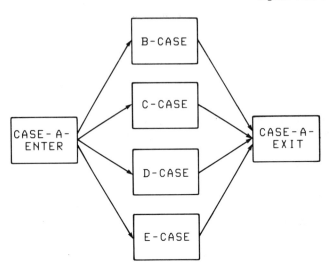

Coding a COBOL Case Structure

You need to know a few more statements before you can code a case structure in COBOL.

The EXIT Statement When you use PERFORM...THRU in a COBOL program, a series of paragraphs is executed. You can use other PERFORMs and PERFORM...THRUs within the range of the outer PERFORM, but the ranges cannot overlap. It is often useful to have a special exit paragraph as the last paragraph in the range of a PERFORM...THRU. Some installations require the specification of an exit paragraph whenever the THRU option is used.

The format of the EXIT statement is shown in Figure 10.9. EXIT must be the only statement in a paragraph. A paragraph that contains

Figure 10.9 The EXIT Statement Format

Format:
```
EXIT.
```

Examples:
```
EXIT-PARAGRAPH.
    EXIT.
```

Notes:
1. EXIT must be the only statement in the paragraph.
2. EXIT is used to give a name to a point in the program.

only an EXIT statement provides a single exit point for the whole case structure module.

Using the Basic GO TO Statement The basic GO TO statement transfers control unconditionally to the paragraph it names. Once control is transferred, execution continues from the transfer point. There is no automatic return.

Figure 10.10 shows the format of the basic GO TO statement. Programmers who write structured programs usually avoid using it. GO TO is needed, however, in a COBOL case structure. Use GO TO very carefully; it confuses the logic. Every basic GO TO statement used in this course transfers control to an exit paragraph.

The Expanded GO TO Statement Another format of the GO TO statement selects a paragraph for execution based on the value of a field. You can use this format as the first statement in a case structure. Figure 10.11 shows the format. You can name as many paragraphs as you have cases. Control is transferred based on the value of the data-name; if data-name = 1, control is transferred to the first paragraph; if data-name = 6, control is transferred to the sixth paragraph; and so forth. Notice that this particular structure depends on a numeric value between 1 and n being in the field identified by data-name.

The first example in the figure uses BALANCE-FLAG. At some point *before* this statement is executed, BALANCE-FLAG received the value 1 for a negative balance, 2 for a positive balance, and 3 for a zero balance. When the statement is executed, control will be transferred to the appropriate paragraph. You don't have to use CASE1, CASE2, etc., as prefixes for your paragraph-names, but if you do, the structure is much easier to read and follow.

Paragraph-names can be repeated in the list. For example, you may

Figure 10.10 The Basic GO TO Statement Format

Format:
```
GO TO paragraph-name
```

Example:
```
GO TO EXIT-PARAGRAPH.
```

Notes:
1. Control is transferred to the named paragraph.
2. No return, such as with PERFORM, occurs.
3. Use with a great deal of caution.

Figure 10.11 GO TO...DEPENDING ON Statement Format

Format:

```
GO TO {paragraph-name}...

    DEPENDING ON data-name.
```

Examples:

```
GO TO CASE1-CREDIT-BALANCE
        CASE2-MONEY-BALANCE
        CASE3-ZERO-BALANCE
     DEPENDING ON BALANCE-FLAG.

GO TO CASE1-CHANGE-VITAL-DATA
        CASE2-CHANGE-TRIVIAL-DATA
        CASE3-ADD-RECORD
        CASE4-DELETE-RECORD
     DEPENDING ON TRANSACTION-REQUEST.
```

Notes:

1. Data-name must be defined as a numeric integer variable (PIC 9, PIC 99, etc.).
2. If data-name = 1, control is transferred to first paragraph; if data-name = 2, control is transferred to second paragraph; and so on.
3. If data-name value is 0 or greater than the number of paragraph-names, control falls through to next statement.
4. All transfers are done as in basic GO TO rather than as in basic PERFORM.
5. Your compiler may limit the number of paragraph-names.

want the same processing for two or more codes. You would have to code the paragraph-name for each appropriate value. If you never have codes 1 and 6, but do have others up to 9, you still must include paragraph-names for values 1 and 6. You could include a dummy DISPLAY statement in paragraphs that won't be used.

Layout of the Case Structure   Figure 10.12 shows how a COBOL case structure is laid out. The invoking PERFORM...THRU occurs at the place in the program where the structure should be executed. Control is transferred to the first-named paragraph. Then the GO TO...DEPENDING ON statement is executed.

If the value of the data-name is less than 1 or larger than the number of paragraphs listed (3 in this example), control falls through to the next statement after the GO TO ... DEPENDING ON statement. This may print an error message or whatever is appropriate. A basic GO TO statement must be used to bypass the other paragraphs and skip to the exit paragraph. Without this GO TO statement, control would fall through to the first case.

If the value of the data-name matches the number in one of the paragraph-names, control is transferred to that paragraph. The statements in the paragraph are executed. Each of the specific routines ends with a GO TO statement to reach the exit paragraph.

Figure 10.12 Case Structure Layout

```
PERFORM CASE-HANDLE-BALANCE
    THRU CASE-HANDLE-BALANCE-EXIT.
    .
    .
    .
CASE-HANDLE-BALANCE.
    GO TO CASE1-CREDIT-BALANCE
          CASE2-MONEY-BALANCE
          CASE3-ZERO-BALANCE
        DEPENDING ON BALANCE-FLAG.
    statement(s)
    GO TO CASE-HANDLE-BALANCE-EXIT.
CASE1-CREDIT-BALANCE.
    statement(s)
    GO TO CASE-HANDLE-BALANCE-EXIT.
CASE2-MONEY-BALANCE.
    statement(s)
    GO TO CASE-HANDLE-BALANCE-EXIT.
CASE3-ZERO-BALANCE.
    statement(s)
    GO TO CASE-HANDLE-BALANCE-EXIT.
CASE-HANDLE-BALANCE-EXIT.
    EXIT.
```

Notice that the entire case structure has one entrance (CASE-HANDLE-BALANCE) and one exit (CASE-HANDLE-BALANCE-EXIT). Other paragraphs (outside the structure) can be included and PERFORMED from specific routines, but GO TO should be used only to reach the exit paragraph.

Avoiding GO TO Statements   Some installations prefer to code case structures using nested IFs. For example, the code in Figure 10.12 could be replaced with this nested IF:

```
IF BALANCE-FLAG = 1
    PERFORM CASE1-CREDIT-BALANCE
ELSE
    IF BALANCE-FLAG = 2
        PERFORM CASE2-MONEY-BALANCE
    ELSE
        IF BALANCE-FLAG = 3
            PERFORM CASE3-ZERO-BALANCE
        ELSE
            PERFORM BALANCE-FLAG-INVALID.
```

Separate paragraphs handle the functions, then control returns to the main routine.

Coping with Limitations   One limitation of the case structure is that it requires an integer value in the DEPENDING ON field. If your application uses other types of codes, you could convert them to numbers in the program and then do a standard case structure, or you could use a nested IF to accomplish the case structure. For example, suppose your input data includes an ANIMAL-CODE of W, S, C, or O (for Whale, Seal, Condor, or Other). You could define working-storage constants and change each code value to a number from 1 to 4 and do a standard case structure, like this:

```
IF ANIMAL-CODE = WHALE
    MOVE 1 TO CASE-CODE
ELSE
    IF ANIMAL-CODE = SEAL
        MOVE 2 TO CASE-CODE
    ELSE
        IF ANIMAL-CODE = CONDOR
            MOVE 3 TO CASE-CODE
        ELSE
            IF ANIMAL-CODE = OTHER-CASE
                MOVE 4 TO CASE-CODE
            ELSE
                MOVE 9 TO CASE-CODE.
GO TO CASE1-SAVE-THE-WHALES
    CASE2-RESCUE-SEALS
    CASE3-CAGE-THE-CONDORS
    CASE4-RESTOCK-SPECIES
DEPENDING ON CASE-CODE.
```

Alternatively, you could code a neat, clear nested IF like this:

```
IF ANIMAL-CODE = WHALE
    PERFORM SAVE-THE-WHALES
ELSE
    IF ANIMAL-CODE = SEAL
        PERFORM RESCUE-SEA S
    ELSE
        IF ANIMAL-CODE = CONDOR
            PERFORM CAGE-THE-CONDORS
        ELSE
            IF ANIMAL-CODE = OTHER-CODE
                PERFORM RESTOCK-SPECIES
            ELSE
                PERFORM NONSTANDARD-CODE.
```

Summary   You have seen how the standard case structure is coded using COBOL statements. The case structure, while it runs very efficiently, has some limitations from the programmer's point of view. The main one is that it can handle only a numeric code ranging from one to the number of cases. Although other codes can be converted to numbers, it may be just as clear to code a nested IF to handle small nonnumeric cases.

Comprehension Questions

1. What statement is generally used in the last paragraph executed by a PERFORM...THRU statement?

---

2. What statement is used to transfer control unconditionally to another paragraph?

---

3. Examine this statement:

```
GO TO CASE1-SAVE-THE-WHALES
       CASE2-RESCUE-SEALS
       CASE3-CAGE-THE-CONDORS
       CASE4-RESTOCK-SPECIES
    DEPENDING ON ANIMAL-INDICATOR.
```

a. Where will control go if the value of ANIMAL-INDICATOR is 2?

---

b. Where will control go if the value of ANIMAL-INDICATOR is 0?

---

c. Where will control go if the value of ANIMAL-INDICATOR is 6?

---

d. How many paragraphs (minimum) would be in the case structure?

---

4. Suppose a program must execute different paragraphs based on the letter value (A to G) in a field. How can this be accomplished?

a. Use a standard case structure.
b. Convert letter codes A to G to 1 to 7, then use a standard case structure.
c. Use a nested IF.

Continued

5. Refer to Figure 10.12. This structure is invoked by PERFORM CASE-A-ENTER THRU CASE-A-EXIT and controlled by the value of CASE-CODE.

a. Write the first statement in CASE-A-ENTER.

b. Write the last statement in C-CASE.

c. Write the last paragraph in the structure.

Answers

1. EXIT   **2.** GO TO   **3.** a. Paragraph CASE2-RESCUE-SEALS b. Statement following DEPENDING ON c. Statement following DEPENDING ON d. 6 (entry, exit, and four cases)   **4.** b, c

5. a. GO TO B-CASE
```
             C-CASE
             D-CASE
             E-CASE
         DEPENDING ON CASE-CODE.
```

b. GO TO CASE-A-EXIT.

c. CASE-A-EXIT.
```
       EXIT.
```

Application Questions

Assume you want to display a different message giving the ITEM-NAME and the meaning of the ITEM-CODE for each value of ITEM-CODE. Here is the pseudocode for the case structure:

```
CASE:    handle codes

CASE1:   item code = perishables
             handle perishables (6.1.1)
CASE2:   item code = canned goods
             handle canned goods (6.1.2)
CASE3:   item code = bagged goods
             handle bagged goods (6.1.3)
CASE4:   item code = frozen food
             handle frozen food (6.1.4)
CASE5:   item code = vacuum-packed food
             handle vacuum-packed food (6.1.5)
CASE6:   item code = loose goods
             handle loose goods (6.1.6)
CASE7:   other
             handle invalid code (6.1.7)
ENDCASE
```

You will code a case structure using GO TO statements in questions 1 through 5.

1. Code the first paragraph in the case structure. Create reasonable paragraph-names.

2. Code the paragraphs for the first two cases. PERFORM any detail code.

3. Code the paragraph for the last valid case (ITEM-CODE = LOOSE-GOODS).

4. Code the last paragraph in the case structure.

5. Write a statement to execute the case structure if the value of ITEM-ON-HAND is greater than 1000 (OVERSTOCKED-LIMIT).

6. Now code the entire structure as a nested IF, using PERFORM statements to execute specific paragraphs.

Answers

```
1.   CASE-HANDLE-CODE.
         GO TO CASE1-PERISHABLE
               CASE2-CANNED
               CASE3-BAGGED
               CASE4-FROZEN
               CASE5-VACUUM-PACKED
               CASE6-LOOSE
             DEPENDING ON ITEM-CODE.
         PERFORM HANDLE-INVALID-CODE.
         GO TO CASE-HANDLE-CODE-EXIT.
```

You could use different paragraph-names. Be sure the names are consistent in your following answers.

```
2.   CASE1-PERISHABLE.
         PERFORM HANDLE-PERISHABLES.
         GO TO CASE-HANDLE-CODE-EXIT.
     CASE2-CANNED.
         PERFORM HANDLE-CANNED-GOODS.
         GO TO CASE-HANDLE-CODE-EXIT.
```

```
3.   CASE6-LOOSE.
         PERFORM HANDLE-LOOSE-GOODS.
         GO TO CASE-HANDLE-CODE-EXIT.
```

You could omit the GO TO statement here, since the next paragraph is the exit.

```
4.   CASE-HANDLE-CODE-EXIT.
         EXIT.
```

```
5.   IF ITEM-ON-HAND > OVERSTOCKED-LIMIT
         PERFORM CASE-HANDLE-CODE THRU CASE-HANDLE-CODE-EXIT.
```

6. Here's one solution:

```
         IF ITEM-ON-HAND > OVERSTOCKED-LIMIT
             PERFORM CASE-HANDLE-CODE.
     . . .

     CASE-HANDLE-CODE.
         IF ITEM-CODE = PERISHABLE-CODE
             PERFORM HANDLE-PERISHABLES
         ELSE
             IF ITEM-CODE = CANNED-CODE
                 PEFORM HANDLE-CANNED-GOODS
             ELSE
                 IF ITEM-CODE = BAGGED-CODE
                     PERFORM HANDLE-BAGGED-GOODS
                 ELSE
                     IF ITEM-CODE = FROZEN-CODE
                         PERFORM HANDLE-FROZEN-FOOD
                     ELSE
                         IF ITEM-CODE = VACUUM-PACKED-CODE
                             PERFORM HANDLE-VACUUM-PACKED-FOOD
                         ELSE
                             IF ITEM-CODE = LOOSE-CODE
                                 PERFORM HANDLE-LOOSE-GOODS
                             ELSE
                                 PERFORM HANDLE-INVALID-CODE.
```

(This solution assumes you defined constants in working storage like this:
05 PERISHABLE-CODE PIC 9 VALUE.)

Summary Program Walkthrough

Now that you can code the major control structures using COBOL statements, it's time to see how everything fits together in a COBOL program. In this lesson we'll walk through a complete program that uses many of the COBOL features you've learned about in this book.

Objective You will be able to write complete programs using the major COBOL control structures.

Rationale As a programmer, you won't be coding isolated statements. You need to consider the surrounding statements and the overall structure of a program. In this lesson you'll see how the control structures interact in a program. You'll also see how unit record files are used in programs.

Problem Statement

Suppose you work for a medium-sized company. You have a unit record file containing records about each employee in the format shown in Figure 10.13.
  The valid categories are these:

1 executive
2 managerial
3 clerical
4 shop
5 road

Your job is to print out a specially formatted list, including only employees who worked some hours. The line will be formatted differently for each category of employee.

Figure 10.13 Input Record Format

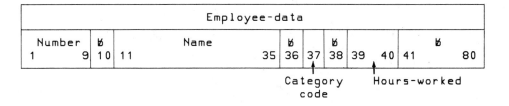

Figure 10.14 shows the hierarchical structure of the problem.

Figure 10.14 Sample Problem Hierarchy

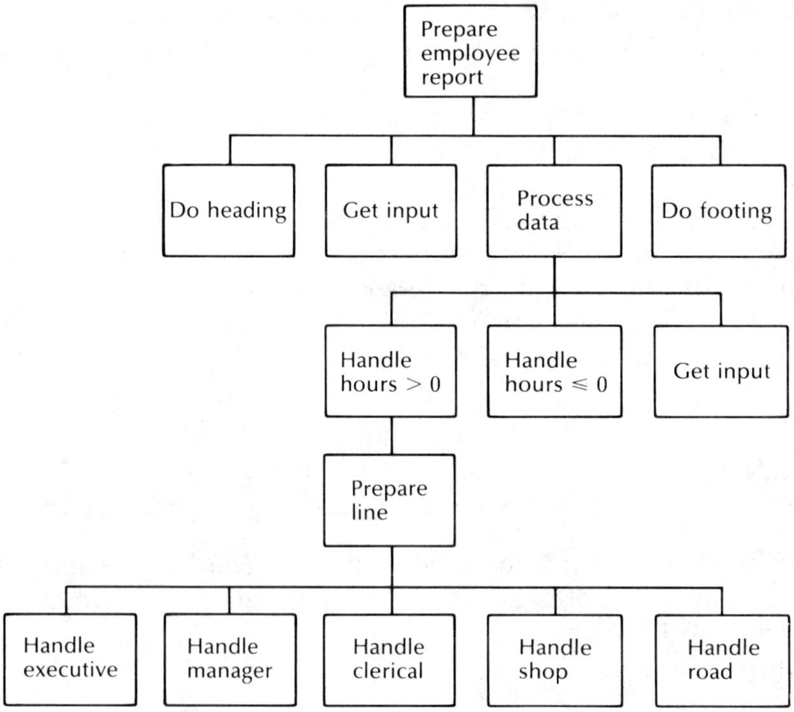

Figure 10.15 shows a pseudocode design. You can tell that the program will require a PERFORM...UNTIL, an IF, and a case structure. Feel free to refer back to the hierarchy and pseudocode at any time during the rest of this lesson.

Figure 10.15 Sample Problem Pseudocode

```
0 - Prepare employee report
        do heading
        get input data
        DO UNTIL no more data
            process data (1)
        ENDO
        do footing
        STOP
1 - Process data
        IF  hours > 0
        THEN
            handle employee (1.1)
        ELSE
        ENDIF
        get input data
1.1 - Handle employee
        set up name
        prepare line (1.1.1)
        print line
1.1.1 - Prepare line
        CASE:    handle category
        CASE1:   executive
                    handle executive
        CASE2:   manager
                    handle manager
        CASE3:   clerical
                    handle clerical
        CASE4:   shop
                    handle shop
        CASE5:   road
                    handle road
        CASE6:   invalid category
                    handle error
        ENDCASE
```

The COBOL Program

The program to solve this problem is shown in Figures 10.16, 10.17, and 10.18. Figure 10.16 shows the first three divisions, while Figures 10.17 and 10.18 show the Procedure Division.

Let's examine the first three divisions first. You can see that no optional paragraphs are used in the Identification or Environment Divisions.

Data Division Entries   The files and the associated I/O areas are defined in the Environment Division and the File Section of the Data Division.

The Working-Storage Section includes several records. The end-of-file flag is defined here, of course, as are constants and record formats for output lines.

The MESSAGES are all used within the case structure. DATE-FIELD is used to store the date as received from the system. HEADING-LINE is used for the report heading; it includes the formatted date. FOOTING-LINE will appear as the last line of the report.

OUT-LINE formats the detail line. It includes the name and hours from the input data. The OUT-CATEGORY field will contain the meaning of the category code. Notice that we've inserted one character between the output fields and initialized it with a space. This spacing will help make the resulting report easier to read.

All the data items defined in the Data Division are used in the Procedure Division. As you saw in Figures 10.14 and 10.15, the Procedure Division contains a case structure in addition to other coding. We'll examine the basic Procedure Division first.

Figure 10.16 Sample Program Part 1

```
IDENTIFICATION DIVISION.
PROGRAM-ID. COB1SUMM.
ENVIRONMENT DIVISION.
INPUT-OUTPUT SECTION.
FILE-CONTROL.
    SELECT EMPLOYEE-FILE
        ASSIGN TO ...
    SELECT LISTING-FILE
        ASSIGN TO ...
DATA DIVISION.
FILE SECTION.
FD  EMPLOYEE-FILE
    LABEL RECORDS ARE OMITTED.
01  EMPLOYEE-DATA.
    05  EMPLOYEE-NUMBER    PIC 9(9).
    05  FILLER             PIC X.
    05  EMPLOYEE-NAME      PIC X(25).
    05  FILLER             PIC X.
    05  EMPLOYEE-CATEGORY  PIC 9.
    05  FILLER             PIC X.
    05  EMPLOYEE-HOURS     PIC 99.
FD  LISTING-FILE
    LABEL RECORDS ARE OMITTED.
01  LISTING-LINE           PIC X(50).
WORKING-STORAGE SECTION.
1   EMPLOYEE-EOF-SWITCH    PIC X          VALUE "N".
01  MESSAGES.
    05  CATEGORY-SMALL     PIC X(18)
                           VALUE "CATEGORY 0 INVALID".
    05  CATEGORY-LARGE     PIC X(18)
                           VALUE "CATEGORY TOO LARGE".
    05  CATEGORY-NAMES.
        10  EXECUTIVE      PIC X(9)       VALUE "EXECUTIVE".
        10  MANAGER        PIC X(7)       VALUE "MANAGER".
        10  CLERICAL       PIC X(8)       VALUE "CLERICAL".
        10  SHOP           PIC X(4)       VALUE "SHOP".
        10  ROAD           PIC X(4)       VALUE "ROAD".
01  DATE-FIELD.
    05  THIS-YEAR          PIC XX.
    05  THIS-MONTH         PIC XX.
    05  THIS-DAY           PIC XX.
01  HEADING-LINE.
    05  FILLER             PIC X(5)       VALUE SPACES.
    05  FILLER             PIC X(24)
                           VALUE "EMPLOYEE DATA AS OF ".
    05  HEADING-DATE.
        10  HEADING-MONTH  PIC XX.
        10  FILLER         PIC X          VALUE "/".
        10  HEADING-DAY    PIC XX.
        10  FILLER         PIC X          VALUE "/".
        10  HEADING-YEAR   PIC XX.
01  OUT-LINE.
    05  FILLER             PIC X          VALUE SPACE.
    05  OUT-NAME           PIC X(25).
    05  FILLER             PIC X          VALUE SPACES.
    05  OUT-HOURS          PIC XX.
    05  FILLER             PIC X          VALUE SPACES.
    05  OUT-CATEGORY       PIC X(20).
01  FOOTING-LINE.
    05  FILLER             PIC X(5)       VALUE SPACES.
    05  FILLER             PIC X(35)
                           VALUE "END OF EMPLOYEE DATA REPORT".
```

Procedure Division Coding Figure 10.17 shows the Procedure Division entries for the entire program, with the exception of the case structure.

The main control paragraph opens the file, then executes a basic PERFORM statement. Paragraph DO-HEADING accepts and formats the current date and then displays HEADING-LINE, followed by a blank line. In IBM systems you could use MOVE CURRENT-DATE TO HEADING-DATE instead of ACCEPT DATE-FIELD FROM DATE as you see here. Since CURRENT-DATE includes slashes, you wouldn't need DATE-FIELD or the subdivisions of HEADING-DATE.

Reading Input After DO-HEADING returns control to the main paragraph, the program PERFORMS the READ routine to access the first record. Notice that the READ statement names the file. The AT END clause sets the end-of-file indicator.

Figure 10.17 Sample Program Part 2

```
PROCEDURE DIVISION.
PREPARE-EMPLOYEE-REPORT.
    OPEN INPUT EMPLOYEE-FILE
        OUTPUT LISTING-FILE.
    PERFORM DO-HEADING.
    PERFORM GET-A-RECORD.
    PERFORM PROCESS-DATA
        UNTIL EMPLOYEE-EOF-SWITCH = "Y".
    WRITE LISTING-LINE FROM FOOTING-LINE.
    CLOSE EMPLOYEE-FILE LISTING-FILE.
    STOP RUN.
DO-HEADING.
    ACCEPT DATE-FIELD FROM DATE.
    MOVE THIS-MONTH TO HEADING-MONTH.
    MOVE THIS-DAY TO HEADING-DAY.
    MOVE THIS-YEAR TO HEADING-YEAR.
    WRITE LISTING-LINE FROM HEADING-LINE.
    PERFORM SKIP-A-LINE.
PROCESS-DATA.
    IF EMPLOYEE-HOURS GREATER THAN 0
        PERFORM HANDLE-EMPLOYEE.
    PERFORM GET-A-RECORD.
HANDLE-EMPLOYEE.
    MOVE EMPLOYEE-NAME TO OUT-NAME.
    PERFORM CASE-PREPARE-LINE THRU CASE-PREPARE-LINE-EXIT.
    WRITE LISTING-LINE FROM OUT-LINE.
    PERFORM SKIP-A-LINE.
GET-A-RECORD.
    READ EMPLOYEE-FILE
        AT END MOVE "Y" TO EMPLOYEE-EOF-SWITCH.
SKIP-A-LINE.
    MOVE SPACES TO LISTING-LINE.
    WRITE LISTING-LINE.
```

Processing Records Now that it has some input data, the program must process it. The PERFORM...UNTIL statement sets up the major processing loop. EMPLOYEE-EOF-SWITCH is set to "Y" after the last record has been read.

In the PROCESS-DATA routine, the value of EMPLOYEE-HOURS is tested. If it is zero or less, meaning that employee didn't work during the time period, the employee is bypassed. All other employees require further processing in the HANDLE-EMPLOYEE paragraph.

We could have included ELSE NEXT SENTENCE in the program coding, but the logic is clearer without it.

HANDLE-EMPLOYEE is executed for every employee who worked any time at all. The function of this routine is to format and print a line of output. The first statement moves the name field from the input record to the detail output record. The other data varies depending on the EMPLOYEE-CATEGORY. The case structure sets up the OUT-HOURS and OUT-CATEGORY fields. We'll look at the case structure after we finish this part of the Procedure Division. After OUT-LINE is completely set up, the HANDLE-EMPLOYEE paragraph writes the detail data line, as well as a blank line to double space the output.

At the end of HANDLE-EMPLOYEE, control returns to the statement following the PERFORM that invoked it from the PROCESS-DATA paragraph. Here another record is read by PERFORMing GET-A-RECORD.

Ending the Loop All of this has been under the control of the PERFORM UNTIL statement in the main paragraph. Suppose the last record has already been read. The next READ will cause the AT END clause to be activated. This makes the condition true, so PROCESS-DATA isn't executed again. Control falls through to print a footing line, close the files, and end the program. If you omit STOP RUN, control will fall through to the next instruction—DO-HEADING in Figure 10.17.

Case Structure Coding Now let's consider the case structure invoked with the statement PERFORM CASE-PREPARE-LINE THRU CASE-PREPARE-LINE-EXIT. Figure 10.18 shows the COBOL coding for this structure. You might want to refer back to the pseudocode in Figure 10.15 for comparison.

Figure 10.18 Sample Program Part 3

```
CASE-PREPARE-LINE.
    GO TO CASE1-HANDLE-EXECUTIVES
          CASE2-HANDLE-MANAGERS
          CASE3-HANDLE-CLERICAL-STAFF
          CASE4-HANDLE-SHOP-FOLKS
          CASE5-HANDLE-ROAD-CREWS
       DEPENDING ON EMPLOYEE-CATEGORY.
    IF EMPLOYEE-CATEGORY = ZERO
        MOVE CATEGORY-SMALL TO OUT-CATEGORY
    ELSE
        MOVE CATEGORY-LARGE TO OUT-CATEGORY.
    MOVE SPACES TO OUT-HOURS.
    GO TO CASE-PREPARE-LINE-EXIT.
CASE1-HANDLE-EXECUTIVES.
    MOVE EXECUTIVE TO OUT-CATEGORY.
    MOVE SPACES TO OUT-HOURS.
    GO TO CASE-PREPARE-LINE-EXIT.
CASE2-HANDLE-MANAGERS.
    MOVE MANAGER TO OUT-CATEGORY.
    MOVE EMPLOYEE-HOURS TO OUT-HOURS.
    GO TO CASE-PREPARE-LINE-EXIT.
CASE3-HANDLE-CLERICAL-STAFF.
    MOVE CLERICAL TO OUT-CATEGORY.
    MOVE EMPLOYEE-HOURS TO OUT-HOURS.
    GO TO CASE-PREPARE-LINE-EXIT.
CASE4-HANDLE-SHOP-FOLKS.
    MOVE SHOP TO OUT-CATEGORY.
    MOVE EMPLOYEE-HOURS TO OUT-HOURS.
    GO TO CASE-PREPARE-LINE-EXIT.
CASE5-HANDLE-ROAD-CREWS.
    MOVE ROAD TO OUT-CATEGORY.
    MOVE EMPLOYEE-HOURS TO OUT-HOURS.
    GO TO CASE-PREPARE-LINE-EXIT.
CASE-PREPARE-LINE-EXIT.
    EXIT.
```

Case Control   The CASE-PREPARE-LINE paragraph selects the specific paragraph to receive control for each of the five valid values of EMPLOYEE-CATEGORY. If the value is anything besides 1, 2, 3, 4, or 5, control will fall through, so we've included special code here to handle these invalid cases. The program uses an IF statement to put special messages in the OUT-CATEGORY field if the value is 0 or larger than 5. The name from the input data with an invalid category will be printed to help readers identify the data that was in error.

Cases   Each case moves the appropriate value to the OUT-CATEGORY field and either blanks out or sets up the OUT-HOURS field. We aren't divulging the number of hours worked in the case of executives. Each case paragraph ends with GO TO CASE-PREPARE-LINE-EXIT.

Case End   The last paragraph in the case structure contains only the EXIT statement. This provides a common, single exit point for the structure.

Figure 10.19 Sample Program Variation

```
HANDLE-EMPLOYEE.
    MOVE EMPLOYEE-NAME TO OUT-NAME.
    IF EMPLOYEE-CATEGORY = 1
        MOVE EXECUTIVE TO OUT-CATEGORY
        MOVE SPACES TO OUT-HOURS
      ELSE
        IF EMPLOYEE-CATEGORY = 2
            MOVE MANAGER TO OUT-CATEGORY
            MOVE EMPLOYEE-HOURS TO OUT-HOURS
          ELSE
            IF EMPLOYEE-CATEGORY = 3
                MOVE CLERICAL TO OUT-CATEGORY
                MOVE EMPLOYEE-HOURS TO OUT-HOURS
              ELSE
                IF EMPLOYEE-CATEGORY = 4
                    MOVE SHOP TO OUT-CATEGORY
                    MOVE EMPLOYEE-HOURS TO OUT-HOURS
                  ELSE
                    IF EMPLOYEE-CATEGORY = 5
                        MOVE ROAD TO OUT-CATEGORY
                        MOVE EMPLOYEE-HOURS TO OUT-HOURS
                      ELSE
                        IF EMPLOYEE-CATEGORY < 1
                            MOVE CATEGORY-SMALL TO OUT-CATEGORY
                            MOVE SPACES TO OUT-HOURS
                          ELSE
                            MOVE CATEGORY-LARGE TO OUT-CATEGORY
                            MOVE SPACES TO OUT-HOURS.
    WRITE LISTING-LINE FROM OUT-LINE.
    PERFORM SKIP-A-LINE.
```

Case Structure Variation   Alternatively, the case structure can be coded as a nested IF, as shown in Figure 10.19.

The figure shows paragraph HANDLE-EMPLOYEE (from Figure 10.17) recoded to include the effects of the coding in Figure 10.18. Here we coded a nested IF with the statements to be executed in line. If you compare the nested IF in Figure 10.19 to the case structure in Figure 10.18, you will see that the effect of both is the same for any possible value of EMPLOYEE-CATEGORY.

Summary   As we walked through the summary program in detail, you saw how the control structures determined execution of various statements in the program. The program included examples of all the major structures discussed in this book. By now you should be able to code complete programs using the major control structures.

Comprehension Questions

Refer back to Figures 10.16, 10.17, and 10.18 as needed to determine what will be displayed by the program as a result of these sets of input data. Make sure you walk through each instruction in the program. Follow the program exactly. Make no assumptions. The ability to walk through a program is vital to successful programming.

1. `111111111 DAVID SIMONSON          3 20`

---

2. `222222222 CORISANDE ELLISON        1 48`

---

3. `333333333 PAUL CHARLES ASHLEY       0 12`

---

4. `444444444 JUDI N. FERNANDEZ         8 56`

---

5. `999999999 RUTH ASHLEY               5 38`

Answers

```
1. DAVID SIMONSON           20 CLERICAL
2. CORISANDE ELLISON           EXECUTIVE
3. PAUL CHARLES ASHLEY         CATEGORY 0 INVALID
4. JUDI N. FERNANDEZ           CATEGORY TOO LARGE
5. RUTH ASHLEY             38 ROAD
```

Application Questions

For this exercise you'll write a complete Procedure Division of a program. The first three divisions and the pseudocode are shown below:

```
IDENTIFICATION DIVISION.
PROGRAM-ID. C1CH10.
ENVIRONMENT DIVISION.
INPUT-OUTPUT SECTION.
FILE-CONTROL.
     SELECT USER-FILE
         ASSIGN TO ...
     SELECT USER-LIST
         ASSIGN TO ...
DATA DIVISION.
FILE SECTION.
FD  USER-FILE
    LABEL RECORDS ARE OMITTED.
01  USER-DATA.
    05  USER-CODE           PIC X(4).
    05  FILLER              PIC X.
    05  USER-STATE          PIC XX.
    05  FILLER              PIC X.
    05  USER-NAME           PIC X(20).
FD  USER-LIST
    LABEL RECORDS ARE OMITTED.
01  LIST-LINE               PIC X(30).
WORKING-STORAGE SECTION.
01  END-OF-DATA             PIC X        VALUE "N".
01  EXTRA-CONSTANTS.
    05  OUT-SPACE           PIC X        VALUE SPACE.
    05  DESIRED-STATE       PIC XX       VALUE "CA".
    05  CODE-MARKER         PIC X(4)     VALUE ALL "*".
    05  SELECTION-CUTOFF    PIC 9(4)     VALUE 5000.
01  HEADING-LINE.
    05  TOP-LINE            PIC X(30)
                           VALUE "  REPORT OF HIGH CODE USERS".
01  COLUMN-HEADS            PIC X(30)
                           VALUE "   CODE      NAME".
01  OUT-LINE.
    05  FILLER              PIC X(4)     VALUE SPACES.
    05  OUT-CODE            PIC X(4).
    05  FILLER              PIC X        VALUE SPACE.
    05  OUT-NAME            PIC X(20).

  0 - Prepare employee report
          do headings
          get user data
          DO UNTIL no more input data
              process data (1)
          ENDO
          STOP
  1 - Process data
          IF user code > 5000
          THEN
              list record (1)
          ELSE
          ENDIF
          get user data
1.1 - List record
          IF state = CA
          THEN
              out code = user code
          ELSE
              out code = ****
          ENDIF
          out name = user name
          print output record
```

1. Write the main paragraph of the Procedure Division first. Call a separate paragraph to print the headings.

2. Two heading lines are set up in the Working-Storage Section. Use a blank line following each as you write the heading paragraph.

3. Write the paragraph to get a record of input data.

4. Processing the data involves two steps. First you must select records with user codes greater than 5000. Write this paragraph. Use a PERFORM statement to execute a further paragraph (LIST-RECORD) for all selected records.

5. In the final paragraph you need to set the user code for display, depending on the state indicated; build the rest of the line; and print it. Write this paragraph to complete the program.

Answers

You have written all the components of a complete Procedure Division. Your code should be very similar to this. Check your coding carefully.

```
1. PROCEDURE DIVISION.
   PREPARE-EMPLOYEE-REPORT.
       OPEN INPUT USER-FILE
           OUTPUT USER-LIST.
       PERFORM DO-HEADINGS.
       PERFORM GET-USER-DATA.
       PERFORM PROCESS-DATA
           UNTIL END-OF-DATA = "Y".
       CLOSE USER-FILE USER-LIST.
       STOP RUN.
2. DO-HEADINGS.
       WRITE LIST-LINE FROM HEADING-LINE.
       WRITE LIST-LINE FROM OUT-SPACE.
       WRITE LIST-LINE FROM COLUMN-HEADS.
       WRITE LIST-LINE FROM OUT-SPACE.
3. GET-USER-DATA.
       READ USER-FILE
           AT END MOVE "Y" TO END-OF-DATA.
4. PROCESS-DATA.
       IF USER-CODE > SELECTION-CUTOFF
           PERFORM LIST-RECORD.
       PERFORM GET-USER-DATA.
5. LIST-RECORD.
       IF USER-STATE = DESIRED-STATE
           MOVE USER-CODE TO OUT-CODE
       ELSE
           MOVE CODE-MARKER TO OUT-CODE.
       MOVE USER-NAME TO OUT-NAME.
       WRITE LIST-LINE FROM OUT-LINE.
```

Chapter Review Questions

As a chapter review you will write a complete COBOL program that will access records from a file and prepare a listing of selected data from selected records.

1. First write the first division.

2. Write the second division as required by your installation to read records from a unit record file (INVENTORY) and print a report (LISTING-FILE) on the main printer.

3. The input area will be laid out like this:

Inventory information				
Part number	Part name	Part description	On hand (digits)	On order (digits)
1 5	6 20	21 50	51 53	54 56

The output area will require a single 40-character field. Code the first section of the third division, including the required division and section headers as well as the file and record description entries.

You might want to check your answers to the first three questions before you go on to question 4.

4. The report produced should have this format:

```
Heading:            INVENTORY DATA REPORT
Blank line
Data lines      part number    part name    on hand
                part number    part name    on hand

Blank line
Last line:          END OF LISTING
```

Code the second section of the Data Division to include an end-of-file flag as well as record descriptions for the three report lines. Use enough spacing to separate the fields to be printed. Center the heading and footing (approximately) before and after the detail lines. Leave room to add items to this division as you code the Procedure Division.

You might want to check your answer to this question before going on to question 5.

5. The program will print data from all input records that have more than 48 items on order.
   Create a pseudocode design for the program.

You might want to check your answer to this question before going on to question 6.

6. Code the Procedure Division for the program. Define any additional
items you need and add them to the Working-Storage section.

Answers

```
1. IDENTIFICATION DIVISION.
   PROGRAM-ID. COB10R.
2. ENVIRONMENT DIVISION.
   INPUT-OUTPUT SECTION.
   FILE-CONTROL.
        SELECT USER-FILE
            ASSIGN TO ...
        SELECT USER-LIST
            ASSIGN TO ...
3. DATA DIVISION.
   FILE SECTION.
   FD  USER-FILE
       LABEL RECORDS ARE OMITTED.
   01  INVENTORY-INFORMATION.
       05  PART-NUMBER         PIC X(5).
       05  PART-NAME           PIC X(15).
       05  PART-DESCRIPTION    PIC X(30).
       05  PART-ON-HAND        PIC 9(3).
       05  PART-ON-ORDER       PIC 9(3).
   FD  LISTING-FILE
       LABEL RECORDS ARE OMITTED.
   01  LIST-LINE               PIC X(80).
4. WORKING-STORAGE SECTION.
   01  END-OF-DATA             PIC X            VALUE "N".
   01  REPORT-HEADING.
       05  FILLER              PIC X(10)        VALUE SPACES.
       05  FILLER              PIC X(21)
                               VALUE "INVENTORY DATA REPORT".
   01  REPORT-LINE.
       05  FILLER              PIC X(3)         VALUE SPACES.
       05  PART-NUMBER-OUT     PIC X(5).
       05  FILLER              PIC X            VALUE SPACES.
       05  PART-NAME-OUT       PIC X(15).
       05  FILLER              PIC X(6)         VALUE SPACES.
       05  PART-ON-HAND-OUT    PIC X(3).
   01  REPORT-ENDING.
       05  FILLER              PIC X(15)        VALUE SPACES.
       05  FILLER              PIC X(14)
                               VALUE "END OF LISTING".
5. 0 - Prepare inventory report
       prepare files
       write heading
       read inventory record
       DO UNTIL no more records
            process data (1)
       ENDO
       write footing
       end
   1 - Process data
       IF  on order > 48
       THEN
            prepare a line (1.1)
       ELSE
       ENDIF
       read inventory record
   1.1 - Prepare a line
        move fields to report line
        write line
   01  REPORT-SPACE            PIC X            VALUE SPACE.
   01  SELECTION-CUTOFF        PIC 99           VALUE 48.
```

```
6. PROCEDURE DIVISION.
   PREPARE-INVENTORY-REPORT.
       OPEN INPUT INVENTORY
           OUTPUT LISTING-FILE.
       WRITE LIST-LINE FROM REPORT-HEADING.
       WRITE LIST-LINE FROM REPORT-SPACE.
       PERFORM READ-INVENTORY-RECORD.
       PERFORM PROCESS-DATA
           UNTIL END-OF-DATA = "Y".
       WRITE LIST-LINE FROM REPORT-ENDING.
       CLOSE INVENTORY LISTING-FILE.
       STOP RUN.
   PROCESS-DATA.
       IF PART-ON-ORDER > SELECTION-CUTOFF
           PERFORM PREPARE-A-LINE.
       PERFORM READ-INVENTORY-RECORD.

   PREPARE-A-LINE.
       MOVE PART-NUMBER TO PART-NUMBER-OUT.
       MOVE PART-NAME TO PART-NAME-OUT.
       MOVE PART-ON-HAND TO PART-ON-HAND-OUT.
       WRITE LIST-LINE FROM REPORT-LINE.

   READ-INVENTORY-RECORD.
       READ INVENTORY
           AT END MOVE "Y" TO END-OF-DATA.
```

You could have coded the statements in PREPARE-A-LINE in line as part of the IF statement.

Section Five Exercise

Now compile and test your program. Here are some considerations:

- Enter the source program into your system
- Prepare an input unit record file:
  - use the correct record format
  - use test data to test all branches

```
PART-ON-ORDER > 48
PART-ON-ORDER = 48
PART-ON-ORDER < 48
```

- You should be able to use the same compilation procedure as before.
- You should be able to use the same run procedure as before. Just be sure to reference the correct input file.

Solution Discussion

When your program compiles and runs, examine the output carefully. Were the correct records listed? Is the report readable? If you have serious problems, compare your coding to the Chapter 10 Review solution. If you still have problems, consult with your training manager or a helpful programmer.

Course Summary   Now you have finished this first COBOL book. You can write a basic program involving unit record files. The remaining books in this course will teach you how to write much more complex, sophisticated programs. But you have the basics now.

Throughout this book, we have stressed programming practices that will produce good, effective, maintainable programs. If you follow these practices, you will be very valuable to your organizaton. Let's summarize them:

1. Make your source code as clear as possible for future readers.
   a. Assign meaningful, unique, and pronounceable names.
   b. For data-names, use prefixes or suffixes to indicate where the reader can find the item definition in the Data Division.
   c. For procedure-names in longer programs, use a numerical prefix to indicate how the paragraph fits into the overall hierarchy.
   d. Assemble working storage items into meaningful records.
   e. Use optional words to make statements as readable as possible.
   f. Put one clause per line.
   g. Use indentation freely to indicate the structure of the program.

2. Keep literals out of the Procedure Division; define them as constants in the Data Division and use the data-names in the Procedure Division. Exception: short values that will never require maintenance, such as flag values "Y" and "N".

3. Avoid tricky code; take the long way around if it's the clearer path.

4. Code comments freely to document your program for future readers. But don't lean on comments to clarify muddy, illogical code.

5. Don't skimp on testing. The more thoroughly you test, the better your program will be when other people begin to test and use it.

COBOL Coding Form

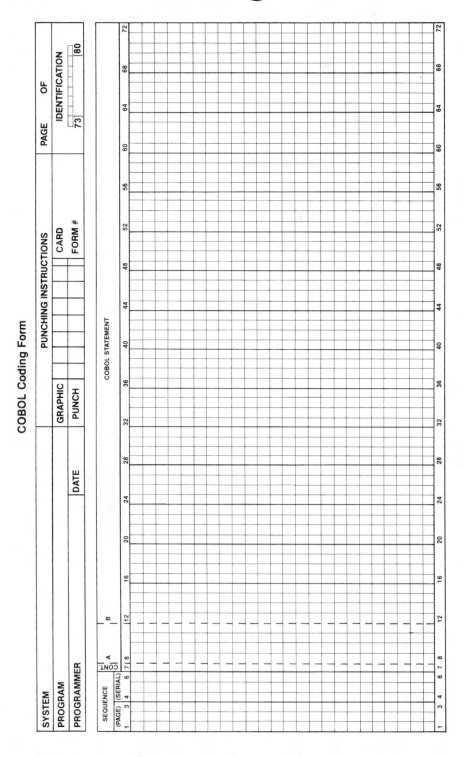

COBOL Reserved Words

ACCEPT	DEBUG-SIZE	HEADING	PADDING	SPACE
ACCESS	DEBUG-START	HIGH-VALUE	PAGE	SPACES
ADD	DEBUG-SUB	HIGH-VALUES	PAGE-COUNTER	SPECIAL-NAMES
ADVANCING	DEBUG-SUB-ITEM		PERFORM	STANDARD
AFTER	DEBUG-SUB-N	I-O	PF	STANDARD-1
ALL	DEBUG-SUB-NUM	I-O-CONTROL	PH	STANDARD-2
ALPHABET	DEBUGGING	IDENTIFICATION	PIC	START
ALPHABETIC	DECIMAL-POINT	IF	PICTURE	STATUS
ALPHABETIC-LOWER	DECLARATIVES	IN	PLUS	STOP
ALPHABETIC-UPPER	DELETE	INDEX	POINTER	STRING
ALPHANUMERIC	DELIMITED	INDEXED	POSITION	SUB-QUEUE-1
ALPHANUMERIC-	DELIMITER	INDICATE	POSITIVE	SUB-QUEUE-2
EDITED	DEPENDING	INITIAL	PRINTING	SUB-QUEUE-3
ALSO	DESCENDING	INITIALIZE	PROCEDURE	SUBTRACT
ALTERNATE	DESTINATION	INITIATE	PROCEDURES	SUM
AND	DETAIL	INPUT	PROGRAM	SUPPRESS
ANY	DISABLE	INPUT-OUTPUT	PROGRAM-ID	SYMBOLIC
ARE	DISPLAY	INSPECT	PURGE	SYNC
AREA	DIVIDE	INSTALLATION		SYNCHRONIZED
AREAS	DIVISION	INTO	QUEUE	
ASCENDING	DOWN	INVALID	QUOTE	TABLE
ASSIGN	DUPLICATES	IS	QUOTES	TALLYING
AT	DYNAMIC			TAPE
AUTHOR		JUST	RANDOM	TERMINAL
	EGI	JUSTIFIED	RD	TERMINATE
BEFORE	ELSE		READ	TEST
BLANK	EMI	KEY	RECEIVE	TEXT
BLOCK	ENABLE		RECORD	THAN
BOTTOM	END	LABEL	RECORDS	THEN
BY	END-ADD	LAST	REDEFINES	THROUGH
	END-CALL	LEADING	REEL	THRU
CALL	END-COMPUTE	LEFT	REFERENCE	TIME
CANCEL	END-DELETE	LENGTH	REFERENCE-MODIFIER	TIMES
CD	END-DIVIDE	LESS	REFERENCES	TO
CF	END-EVALUATE	LIMIT	RELATIVE	TOP
CH	END-IF	LIMITS	RELEASE	TRAILING
CHARACTER	END-MULTIPLY	LINAGE	REMAINDER	TRUE
CHARACTERS	END-OF-PAGE	LINAGE-COUNTER	REMOVAL	TYPE
CLOSE	END-PERFORM	LINE	RENAMES	
CODE	END-READ	LINE-COUNTER	REPLACE	UNIT
CODE-SET	END-RECEIVE	LINES	REPLACING	UNSTRING
COLLATING	END-RETURN	LINKAGE	REPORT	UNTIL
COLUMN	END-REWRITE	LOCK	REPORTING	UP
COMMA	END-SEARCH	LOW-VALUE	REPORTS	UPON
COMMON	END-START	LOW-VALUES	RESERVE	USAGE
COMMUNICATION	END-STRING		RESET	USE
COMP	END-SUBTRACT	MERGE	RETURN	USING
COMPUTATIONAL	END-UNSTRING	MESSAGE	REWIND	
COMPUTE	END-WRITE	MODE	REWRITE	VALUE
CONFIGURATION	ENVIRONMENT	MOVE	RF	VALUES
CONTAINS	EOP	MULTIPLE	RH	VARYING
CONTENT	EQUAL	MULTIPLY	RIGHT	
CONTINUE	ERROR		ROUNDED	WHEN
CONTROL	ESI	NATIVE	RUN	WITH
CONTROLS	EVALUATE	NEGATIVE		WORKING-STORAGE
CONVERSION	EXCEPTION	NEXT	SAME	WRITE
CONVERTING	EXIT	NO	SD	
COPY	EXTEND	NOT	SEARCH	ZERO
CORR	EXTERNAL	NUMBER	SECTION	ZEROES
CORRESPONDING		NUMERIC	SECURITY	ZEROS
COUNT	FALSE	NUMERIC-EDITED	SEGMENT	
CURRENCY	FD		SEGMENT-LIMIT	+
	FILE	OBJECT-COMPUTER	SELECT	−
DATA	FILE-CONTROL	OCCURS	SEND	*
DATE	FILLER	OF	SENTENCE	/
DATE-COMPILED	FINAL	OFF	SEPARATE	**
DATE-WRITTEN	FIRST	OMITTED	SEQUENCE	
DAY	FOOTING	ON	SEQUENTIAL	>
DAY-OF-WEEK	FOR	OPEN	SET	<
DE	FROM	OPTIONAL	SIGN	=
DEBUG-CONTENTS		OR	SIZE	
DEBUG-ITEM	GENERATE	ORDER	SORT	
DEBUG-LENGTH	GIVING	ORGANIZATION	SORT-MERGE	
DEBUG-NAME	GLOBAL	OTHER	SOURCE	
DEBUG-NUMERIC-	GO	OUTPUT	SOURCE-COMPUTER	
CONTENTS	GREATER	OVERFLOW		
	GROUP			

Index

A
ACCEPT . . . FROM, 131
ACCEPT statement, 95–97, 128
ALL, 107
A margin, 24, 32
ANS COBOL, 5
A picture character, *See* Picture character
Area A, 24, 31, 51, 61, 71, 72, 74, 88
Area B, 24, 31, 51, 62, 71, 74, 88, 94
ASCII sequence, 244
ASSIGN, 32, 210
Asterisk (*), 23
AT END, 232
AUTHOR, 53

B
Blank lines, 33, 54
Blocking, 202
B margin, 24, 32
Bomb, 191, 285
Braces, 41
Brackets, 40
Buffer, 203, 215
Byte, 69, 72

C
Card-image file, 21, 202
Carriage-control byte, 251
Case structure, 311
CLOSE, 229
CODASYL, 4
Coding form, 22
Coding rules, 31–32
Column, 7, 23
Comment, 23, 53, 54, 61
Comment-entry, 52, 62
Compilation, 147, 174, 183, 202, 272
Compile-link-and-go, 158
Compiler, 157
Compiler listing, 149, 174
Condition, 298
Conditional statement, 87
Configuration Section, 60, 61
CONSOLE, 128
Constant, 104
Continuation, 24, 33, 34
Cross-reference listings, 178
CURRENT-DATE, 134

D
Data Division, 14, 32, 66–76, 215
  area A, 67, 74
  division header, 67, 74
  section name, 74
Data definition, 183

Data-name, 40, 67, 68, 71, 178
Data record, 67
DATE, 132
DATE-COMPILED, 53
DATE-WRITTEN, 53
DAY, 133
Decision structure, 298
Default, 41
Desk check, 146
Detail line, 253
Display data format, 69
DISPLAY, 93–95, 128
DISPLAY . . . UPON, 130
Division-name, 31

E
EBCDIC sequence, 244
Edit problems, 7
Elementary item, 72, 123
Ellipsis (. . .), 41
Environment Division, 13, 14, 32, 60–62, 209
  division header, 61
  area A, 61
Error message, 157, 175, 183
  file, 272
  Procedure Division, 184
Errors
  fatal, 149
  high-level, 149
  low-level, 149
Executable program, 158
EXIT, 312–13

F
Fatal error, 149
FD, 31, 32, 216
Figurative constant, 106
FILE-CONTROL, 32, 209
File label, 215
File-name, 207
File Section, 66, 216
FILLER, 74
Format notation, 38–43
FROM, 234

G
Garbage, 108
GOBACK, 97
GO TO, 313
GO TO . . . DEPENDING ON, 313–14
Group item, 72
Group move, 123

H
Hand-coded material, 26
High-level error, 149
HIGH-VALUE, 107
Hyphen (-), 24

I
ICCF, 164
Identification Division, 13, 32, 50–54
  area A, 32, 51
  area B, 32
  division header, 32, 51
  paragraph-names, 32
  PROGRAM-ID, 32
Imperative statement, 87
IF, 299
Indentation, 33, 88, 219
Independent data items, 67, 70–71
Indicators
  asterisk (*), 23
  hyphen (-), 24
  slash (/), 23
Initial value, 108
INPUT, 229
Input-Output Section, 209
Input-Output Section header, 32
INSTALLATION paragraph, 53
INTO option, 232
I/O area, 216

J–K–L
Julian date, 133
LABEL clause, 216
Level 49, 71, 72
Level numbers, 31, 32, 71, 72, 74, 219
Level, 77, 71, 72, 74, 218
Level 01, 31, 32, 71, 72, 74, 217
Linker, 150, 158
Literals, 40, 94, 105
Logical name, 207
Lowercase letters, 24
Lowercase words, 39
Low-level errors, 149
LOW-VALUE, 107

M
Memory map, 176
Mnemonic-name, 129
MOVE, 117
MVS, 165–66

N
Naming rules, 67–68
Nested IF, 304–06
NEXT SENTENCE, 299
9 picture character, *See* Picture character
Nonnumeric data, 118
Nonnumeric literal, 40, 105
Nonnumeric MOVE, 118
Numeric data, 96, 119

Numeric literals, 40, 106
Numeric MOVE, 119

O
OBJECT-COMPUTER, 61
Object program, 149, 157
OPEN, 228
ORGANIZATION, 211
OUTPUT, 229

P
Padding, 108, 118
Paragraph-name, 31, 40, 67, 86, 88, 178
Paragraph number, 86
PDP/11, 167
PERFORM statement, 239
PERFORM . . . THRU, 312
PERFORM . . . UNTIL, 241
Permitted MOVEs, 122–123
Physical name, 207
Picture character
    A 69, 96
    9 69, 96
    X 69, 96
PICTURE, 69, 70, 72
Printer file, 202
Print record, 72
Problem
    edit, 7
    report, 7
    summary, 7
    update, 7
Procedure Division, 14, 32, 74, 86–87
    area A, 33
    area B, 33
    clauses, 86
    division header, 32
    indentation, 33
    paragraph-names, 32
    paragraphs, 86–87
    section header, 32
    statements, 87
Procedure-name, 40
PROGRAM-ID, 32, 51
Program-name, 51, 67

Q–R
QUOTE, 107
READ statement, 230
Receiving field, 118
Record description, 217, 218
Record-name, 72
Relational operator, 242
Relation condition, 234

REMARKS paragraph, 53
Repetition structure, 241
Report problems, 7
Reserved words, 68

S
Section header, 32, 67
Section-name, 31
SECURITY, 54
SELECT, 32, 210
Sending field, 118
Sentence, 87
Sequence numbers, 22
Sequence structures, 85, 93
SEQUENTIAL, 211
"77", See Level 77
Slash (/), 23
SOURCE-COMPUTER, 61
Source listing, 174
SPACE, 106–07
Special registers, 131
SPECIAL-NAMES paragraph, 129
SPF, 165
STOP RUN statement, 97
Structured COBOL, 6, 34
Summary problems, 7
Syntax, 19
Syntax check, 157
Syntax errors, 147
System-name, 211

T
Testing, 158, 283
Test plan, 190, 283
TIME, 133–34
TIME-OF-DAY, 134
Truncation, 118

U
Unit record file, 202
Update problems, 7
Uppercase words, 39

V
VALUE, 108, 218
Variable, 104
VSE, 164

W
Walkthrough, 147
Words, 39–40
    data-name, 40
    literal, 40
    lowercase word, 39
    procedure-name, 40
    uppercase word, 39

working-storage data, 66
Working-Storage Section, 66
WRITE, 234

X–Y–Z
X picture character, See Picture character
ZERO, 107
"01," See Level 01